LIFE AMONG THE WOLVERINES

LIFE AMONG THE WOLVERINES

AN INSIDE VIEW
OF U OF M SPORTS

Tom Hemingway
with Bill Haney

DIAMOND COMMUNICATIONS, INC.
SOUTH BEND, INDIANA
1985

LIFE AMONG THE WOLVERINES

Manufactured in the United States of America

DIAMOND COMMUNICATIONS, INC.
P.O. BOX 88
SOUTH BEND, INDIANA 46624
(219) 287-5008

Library of Congress Cataloging-in-Publication Data

Hemingway, Tom, 1933–
    Life among the Wolverines.

    1. University of Michigan — Athletics — History.
I. Haney, Bill, 1936–   . II. Title.
GV691.U56H46 1985   796'.07'1177435   85-25315
ISBN   0-912083-13-1

To My Mom

Contents

They Played Basketball Here?

I had arrived at Yost Ice Arena a few minutes early that day in 1983 for my scheduled interview with hockey coach, John Giordano. Pushing open the side entrance door, I thought of the times I had been waved through that gate by Charlie, the gatekeeper, during the golden days of Cazzie Russell.

"Think we gotta chance?" Charlie would ask, with a wide smile and wink.

"Yeah," was my standard reply, "if we get lucky we might be able to stay with 'em."

A Michigan loss at Yost in those days was about as common as an empty seat.

Plunking myself down in the first row, I sat staring out at the ice, something I still found hard to accept at Yost. Eight thousand empty seats stared back in the soundless expanse.

"Silence and emptiness," I mused. "There sure wasn't a whole lot of that around back then."

Twisting around, I glanced at the ancient pressbox where Les Etter tried to find places for all who insisted on being on hand for Michigan's basketball renaissance. My gaze wandered to the right where now only steel girders, erected in 1920, jutted out from the crown of the building. At one time, an enclosed wooden platform hung from those girders. It was that platform, in 1963, that I inched onto to broadcast my first Wolverine basketball game. Some five hundred games later, I could still feel that thrill.

"Damn," I muttered, "why did they have to tear our booth down? It certainly wasn't hurting anything up there."

"Excuse me," a soft voice said.

Standing only a few feet away was a very pretty young lady bundled up against the January cold.

"Excuse me," she repeated, "I'm trying to find the ticket window. My boyfriend sent me over to get some tickets for Friday's game."

"Lucky fellow," I smiled, "do you like hockey?"

"Yeah, but basketball is really my game."

Then she spotted my tape recorder.

"Are you a reporter?"

"Well, that's close enough," I replied, going on to explain who I was and what I was doing sitting in a deserted Yost Arena.

"Oh," she exclaimed, "We listen to you all the time, we love the way you carve up those refs."

I decided I had better work on toning down the comments about the contents of some officials' skulls.

"We've got season tickets to Crisler," she continued. "We go to about all the games. Tim McCormick's my favorite, he's really cute."

"Yeah," I agreed, "He's good looking, all right. Too bad you weren't around when C.J. Kupec was playing. He may have been the handsomest of them all."

"Oh well," she laughed, "my boyfriend would probably have been jealous anyway. How many years have you been broadcasting the games?"

"Far, far too many," I sighed. "Chances are you were hardly born when I did my first one."

"Really?" she asked.

"Really." I answered. "See that space up there between those two girders?" I said, motioning towards the press box. "Well, twenty years ago I broadcast my first game from there."

"You mean hockey?" she questioned, looking a bit confused.

"No, basketball."

"You mean they played basketball here?" she gasped. After a long pause, I replied, "They sure did."

"No kidding? I thought it was always an ice rink. Well, that just shows you what I know about Michigan sports history."

She thanked me for the directions and started towards the doors. Stopping, she looked back.

"Hey, you know something?" she ventured.

"You ought to write a book about your experiences. I'll bet there are a lot of people that don't remember that far back."

"A book?" I chuckled, "I have trouble writing a three-line opening for my broadcasts."

At that moment, Giordano passed my new friend on her way out and strode over to me.

"Sorry I'm late," he offered, "but it looked like you had some nice company."

"Absolutely," I smiled, "but I think her boyfriend is a defensive tackle for Bo."

"Shoot," said John, "I thought she might be a hockey fan."

"Oh, she is," I told him, "but her real sport is basketball. I was telling her about when Yost was a basketball court."

"You mean they used to play basketball here?"

Reaching for the tape recorder, I decided maybe a book wasn't such a bad idea after all. At least I knew of two readers who might be interested.

ONE

Bo, Bennie, Bob, and A Bunch More

I n December, 1968, I was moonlighting at Channel 4 in Detroit when it was still known as WWJ-TV. Just prior to my early evening show, the bell on the Associated Press wire machine started jangling.

"WJBK-TV Sports Director Van Patrick reports that he has learned Glenn 'Bo' Schembechler will be named as Michigan football coach replacing Bump Elliott. Schembechler has spent the last six years as coach at Miami of Ohio where his teams have compiled a 40-17-3 record. The 38-year-old Schembechler is a former player and assistant of Ohio State coach Woody Hayes."

I turned to Larry Adderley and said, "Who?"

A day later, Bo was ushered into the VIP lounge at Crisler Arena. A mob of journalists and broadcasters had gathered to assess this pleasant-looking fellow who had become the fourteenth man to coach U-M football. One of the first questions concerned the way he pronounced his name.

"It's SCHEM-bechler," says Bo. "No, wait a minute, it's Schem-BECH-ler, I think. Now, let me see . . . ah, hell, pronounce it anyway you want."

For the rest of the morning he had us all eating out of his hand.

Now, there's no doubt about it, there was a great adjustment for those of us who had lived around Bump for years to get used to this intense mover of mountains who hit Ann Arbor running and slowed down only for heart attacks. In one of his luncheon sessions with the media, Bo summed it up this way:

"When I arrived in town I felt I was wasting my time if I spent one minute away from the practice field, or studying film, or talking with my players and coaches. It took me a long time to realize that I could get out and talk with the fans or the press without jeopardizing my preparations for next week's game."

Actually, he has always treated the press and media with a tantalizing mixture of respect, humor, philosophy, and cussedness. I never have found him to be anything but a delight to be around but on the other hand I've never ripped him in a column either.

Bo's skirmishes with the media or press are almost as legendary as the coach himself. He has been flayed unmercifully for his predilection for the run versus the pass. I can understand this. It's more fun to describe a 75-yard bomb for a touchdown than a 15-play drive over the same distance. I was once accosted by a Michigan fan who demanded to know why I didn't tell it like it was during the football broadcasts.

"Like last Saturday's game. How come you didn't get on Bo for not throwing more?"

"But they won by 14 points."

"Yeah, but if they'd just passed more they could have won by 28!"

And that seems to be the crux of the matter. During the nine-year period when the "Pass, Bo, Pass" movement really got rolling, Bo's team won 88 games while losing 12. Of course, eight of those losses came on the final game of the season, including four in the Rose Bowl. Thus grew the feeling that Bo couldn't beat the West Coast teams, that the Michigan stodgy offense couldn't contain the high-powered and versatile attacks of USC, Washington and UCLA. I've often wondered how firing the football all over Pasadena aids a defense in stopping the other guy from doing the same? And since the running of Lytle, Bell, Davis, Leach and others got U-M the 88 wins in the first place, it seems unlikely that they would fare better as receivers in the bowls. But Bo's record is his best defense. And when he marches into the Hall of Fame someday along with Woody, Bear and the rest, the inscription on his plaque will probably read: *"Bo, why didn't you pass more?"*

During my early years, I spent three years as a member of the Strategic Air Command. Our squadron commander was a rough, tough old bird known as Hard-Ass Harry. God help the poor unfortunate soul who screwed up a mission. He would be in the major's office shortly after his aircraft touched down where he would be relieved of most of his hide. In the summer of 1958, SAC was placed on a 24-hour alert after another Mideast crisis. We all filed into the briefing room to get our strike orders for targets easily guessed. Major Harry strolled out to the rostrum and calmly told us what the situation was.

I glanced around the room and realized that there wasn't a guy sitting there that wasn't tickled to death to have that damned SOB at the controls. I suspect Bo commands the same type of feelings from his players.

Bo's first quarterback at Michigan, Don Moorhead, had an early taste of the Schembechler temper. Don, like the entire 1969 squad, had trouble adjusting from the low-keyed Bump Elliott to the volatile Bo. During a passing drill, wrapping up a pre-season practice, Don was having trouble hitting his receivers. The more Bo yelled, the more Don pressed. Several throws came up yards short of the mark. Finally Bo could stand it no more.

"Moorhead, you throw one more ball into the ground and I'm going to kick your butt all the way back to South Haven."

Don gulped, took the snap and made sure he didn't throw it short—he unloaded one a mile over Billy Harris's head. Bo headed toward Moorhead in full gallop. Don beat a full retreat to the locker room with Bo in full pursuit. But by the time they got there, Bo was too winded to carry the matter any further. Moorhead stayed clear of his coach and was relieved when Bo promptly forgot the whole thing.

According to Rick Leach, quickly blowing up then forgetting it was characteristic of Bo. He could rip you to shreds one minute and pass it all off the next. But Bo is not always effusive about his quarterbacks on the field either. Tom Slade recalls that during the all-winning 1971 season, a Wolverine ball carrier fumbled into the end zone where Slade fell on it for a touchdown. Trotting over to the sidelines, Slade waited for a word of commendation from his coach. Bo stared at his sophomore star for a minute and then grinned, "Slade, you lucky SOB."

But pity the outsider who takes a shot at one of Bo's boys. One writer's ears rang for weeks after he suggested in print that Michigan could not win with Steve Smith at quarterback. I'm not sure he has changed his mind but he at least got the other side of the picture in detail from Bo.

"Rip me all you want," Bo says, "but leave my players alone."

In 1982, following a Michigan win over Minnesota, Wolverine linebacker Mike Boren expounded on the upcoming meeting with Illinois in Champaign. Boren made it clear that the Blue didn't care very much for the Illini and felt that U-M would be at a rather high level of intensity by game time Saturday. Nothing unusual there, and nothing more than many Wolverine players had said the previous year, but at the media luncheon on Monday, Bo wasted little time in making clear he didn't feel it was a typical comment at all; he blistered the offending writers, especially Lynn Henning of the *Detroit News* who had done the interview. Lynn, an accurate and honest reporter, tried to offer a response to Bo's accusation that Lynn had placed words in Boren's mouth. Bo cut him off brusquely as he snapped, "Yes, you did and I don't want to hear any more about it."

That ended that.

(I should point out that within a week, Bo was treating Henning no differently than the rest of us.)

Bo has often been described as having taken over a failing program and breathing new life into it. It would be more accurate to say Bo inherited a good program and turned it into a consistently great one. The year prior to Bo's arrival, Bump had taken an 8-1 team into Columbus on the final day of the season with a first-game loss to California the only blot on the record. Four years earlier Bump had gone into Columbus under similiar circumstances and emerged with a 10-0 win and the conference title. Three mediocre seasons followed but now Michigan was back for a repeat opportunity. But the 1968 squad was one of Woody's greatest, one that would give him his second national championship. Michigan played the Bucks even for a half but then were snowed under 50-14.

No, Bo wasn't left with an empty cupboard when he opened the doors for that first spring practice in 1969. One of those on hand was captain Jim Mandich who rates behind only Ron Kramer on the U-M all-time listing of tight ends. Following the season, Jim visited our station for a special taping session and reflected back on those tortuous weeks of spring practice under Bo.

"It really took a long time for some of us to understand Bo after living with Bump for three years. I had a lot of heated discussions with him but I finally came to see that he just wanted to win as badly as the rest of us."

Mandich had some monumental bouts with defensive back Barry Pierson during that spring and fall. Members of that squad still chuckle about those confrontations whenever they meet.

"I'd go downfield and make a catch and this little son-of-a-gun would clobber me," Jim says. "I'd get up swinging and Bo would come racing out, jawing at me all the way."

Later that season Pierson would intercept three passes against Ohio State to gain instant immortality with Michigan fans. Apparently his matches with Mandich paid off.

I think it's a well-known fact that you never appreciate someone fully until you realize that person may no longer be there. And that was the situation facing us early in

1970. I had made my first trip to the Rose Bowl that year and had just settled into my seat in the pressbox when fellow broadcaster Ray Lane came by.

"Hey, listen, I just heard from a *Michigan Daily* reporter that Bo is sick and not with the team. Have you heard anything?"

I hadn't but soon the announcement came over the press box P.A. that Bo had been taken to the hospital for tests and would not be with the team. Stunned disbelief is probably too mild a term to use for the reaction of those who had been around Bo for that year.

"Bo sick?" we thought. "That's impossible! He wouldn't stand for it."

We watched as the team gathered around assistant coach Jim Young who relayed the word on Bo. Mandich and many of the others would have tears in their eyes as they took the field against Southern Cal. I don't remember any outward emotions in the press box but it is a measure of Bo's popularity that we all felt as though a member of our family had gone down. And that, mind you, was before we learned the severity of the heart attack which wasn't revealed until the next day. And while there was no doubt in Bo's mind that he would be back to lead the Wolverines that fall, for the rest of us there was nervous anticipation.

When Bo showed up at the stadium on that hot August morning for press day we all were a little curious to see how the long recuperation had affected him. Our first problem was accepting the fact that this trim individual was really Glenn E. Schembechler. That first year, Bo had allowed himself to balloon to 220 pounds and we all assumed this was his normal silhouette. But it was a Bump Elliott look-alike that showed up in T-shirt and

shorts much to the amazement of us all. This was about
the only change though, as he kidded, jabbed, lectured,
instructed and then dismissed the media.

The 1970 season also proved that he hadn't lost his
coaching savvy either. He soon began his incredible five-
year stretch of not losing more than one game a year. This
included the 1972-73-74 teams of Dennis Franklin who
rolled up a 30-2-1 mark *without one trip to a bowl!* Bo
has always maintained that these might have been his
greatest teams. But two losses to Ohio State—one by three
points and another by two—plus a 10-10 tie kept Michigan from a legitimate shot at a national crown. This, however, was during the period when the conference was still
living by its antiquated set of rules which prohibited a
Big Ten team from showing its wares anywhere but the
Rose Bowl.

Actually, the 1973 team that gained the tie with OSU
should have been in Pasadena but was nudged in a vote
of the athletic directors by a 5-4 margin favoring the
Buckeyes with Burt Smith voting for his own Spartans.
Their rationale was that the shoulder injury suffered by
Franklin in the Buckeye game would diminish Michigan's
chances against USC. It was hogwash then and still is as
a completely healed Dennis Franklin watched the game
at his home in Massillon.

It was also during that period that I thought I had gone
two-for-two in coaching doghouses.

One Friday, Michigan's charter to Minneapolis was
scheduled to leave Metro airport at 10:00 A.M. which
meant that the fringe personnel had better be there by
9:30. Bo is a great believer in punctuality. I was riding to
the airport with my color man at the time, Dave McKay,
in a car that among other things lacked windshield wipers.

A typical autumn rain was pelting down as we inched onto I-94. We had to make a number of stops to squeegee off the windshield, so it was 10:05 by the time we rolled into the charter parking lot. Surprised to see the aircraft still parked on the apron, we scooped up our equipment and scrambled aboard. Unfortunately, the boarding was through the front door with the only remaining pair of seats in the rear which meant a stroll down the aisle past Bo. We heard a chorus of catcalls from our friends in the media who made doubly sure that Bo noticed our entrance. I didn't dare look Bo in the eye. As we sat down, I suggested to Dave that maybe if we simply avoided Bo for a few years he might forget.

"Yeah, and he might go 1-10 some year too," was his reply.

After a 34-7 romp over the Gophers we reboarded the plane for the return trip home. I had taken the first available seat. Minutes later the team paraded on board and who moves into the next seat but the man himself. I tried to vanish into the seat while waiting for the blast. But Bo quickly lost himself in studying the play-by-play sheet and statistics; I kept a very low profile. Shortly after takeoff, dinner was served and while we were eating, Bo glanced over at me.

"How ya doing, Hemingway?"

Oh, oh, here it comes, I thought.

"You still doing the Pistons?" he asked. "Man, I don't known how you stand it. 'Pass over the middle, now to the left, back to the right.' It must get to be pretty old."

I agreed with him that it was a struggle at times and for the rest of the flight we talked basketball. For somebody not that interested in the game, he sure knew a lot about it. I don't know to this day if he simply forgot about the tardy arrival or if he figured that anybody broadcasting the Pistons wasn't that responsible for his actions.

Bill Cusamano, assistant sports information director through Bo's early years, recalls trying to convince Bo that basketball featured some of the very ingredients that he stressed on the gridiron. But Bo remained skeptical over any game that frequently saw more than 200 points scored. Finally Cooze got him to watch the NBA's championship playoffs featuring Bill's beloved Knicks. Following the Knicks' win over the Lakers, Bo arrived in Cusamano's office the next morning and admitted, "Hey, your team's not too bad."

Surprised at the unexpected praise, Bill replied, "That's what I've been trying to tell you, coach."

"Yeah, but do you know why they're good? Because they play defense," Bo declared.

They sure did and defense is something that never escapes Bo's notice.

Forty-five years before Bo arrived in Ann Arbor, a big handsome Dutchman from Muskegon moved onto the U-M campus with about the same impact. Those who watched Bennie Oosterbaan in action claim that no other Michigan athlete before or after has ever duplicated his feats. Not Harmon, not Kipke, not Kramer or Leach or Carter or Chappius.

In 1979, the Michigan Alumni Association celebrated the 100th year of Wolverine football by inviting all living All-Americans who had worn the Maize and Blue to a reunion on the weekend of the Indiana game. (The Wangler-to-Carter miracle, remember?)

A total of 26 U-M All-Americans showed up at the Friday night smoker. Master of Ceremonies Bob Forman wisely decided not to attempt a recount of all the accomplishments of each hero as he read off the list to generous applause. Each player was identified only by name, year and position. At the end of his list he paused and said, "Ladies and gentlemen, I must break precedent here. If there is an All-American among All-Americans, then this man is it. Mr. Bennie Oosterbaan."

The other U-M greats leaped to their feet as one and participated in a standing ovation of over two minutes. Bennie sat stunned that these fellow members of Michigan's most elite crew could consider him worthy of such acclaim.

During my visits with Bennie in the all-too-brief period prior to his retirement, I always had to remind myself that I was talking with possibly Michigan's greatest athlete. To hear him tell it, he was a guy who wandered into Ann Arbor, then was lucky enough to be surrounded by talented teammates who pushed him into unwarranted national fame. In fact, not knowing of his exploits personally, it was not until I listened to the old timers and dug out newspaper articles of those days that I fully realized his greatness.

I once asked him about the days of the Zuppke-Yost duels between Illinois and Michigan, starting with the famed '24 game that saw Red Grange score five touchdowns in a 39-14 rout.

"Well, of course, I was a freshman that season," Bennie began, "so I wasn't involved in that game. But the next year we went to Champaign again and the papers were playing it up as the game of the year. We boarded the train in Ann Arbor and when we got to Niles somebody came on board with a sports page that had a headline that said, 'OOSTERBAAN MEETS GRANGE.' Well,

I felt that was pretty unfair since here I was just a 19-year-old kid who had nothing to show for my efforts so far. How was I supposed to do something about stopping the great Red Grange?"

In the first three games of the season, Bennie had led Michigan to victories of 39-0, 63-0 and 21-0 with offensive and defensive performances that left the fans gasping. But not Bennie.

"So by the time we got to Champaign," continued Bennie, "I was so nervous I could hardly walk. Well, we played the game and thank heavens I didn't embarrass myself. Our defense shut them down and we won 3-0. As our old coach said afterwards, 'Grange didn't gain enough ground to bury him in . . . standing on his head.' It sure was a relief to not make too many mistakes and the next day the papers were very kind to me."

The papers were kind all right as Bennie's defense had just about destroyed Grange and the Illinois attack, limiting the "Wheaton Iceman" to just 36 yards. The *Detroit Times* would proclaim:

"Grange spent most of the afternoon staring at the Illinois sky with the young Michigan sophomore end Oosterbaan on top of him."

When the season was complete, Bennie would become the first sophomore in University annals to gain All-American honors. Only Anthony Carter has duplicated that feat in 60 years.

Sitting in with us often in Bennie's office during those years was Wally Weber who would join with his old teammate in bringing back the wild stories of the Yost era. The only problem was that I really never knew when the stories were genuine or Wally's imagination.

One of my favorite Weber-Bennie tales involves Fritz

Crisler and the bugler. It seems that Fritz would wind up his pre-game pep talks by telling his team, "And boys, if all else fails, don't worry because we've got the bugler in the stands."

This mystified me but Wally explained that during their tenure on Fritz' staff, Crisler had convinced his team that the opponents wouldn't get away with any trick plays because a Michigan student had been stationed in the stands to sound the warning on a trumpet. Wally swore that some players spent half the afternoon trying to spot the musician. This sounded pretty far-fetched to me but other players from that era swore it was true.

I once brought up the point to Wally that on the 1925 line, of which he was part, there were four All-Americans, Bennie at end, Tom Edwards at tackle, guard Harry Hawkins and Bob Brown at center.

"Yes," Wally replied, "true, but it must be kept in mind that in that time span we were without numerical listings on our jerseys. So much of my endeavor was incorrectly credited to my teammates."

Incidentally that team placed a fifth All-American on the national squad that year, quarterback Bennie Friedman who joined Oosterbaan in the National Football Foundation Hall of Fame in later years. You wonder how they managed to lose to Northwestern, their only defeat of the year.

Upon retiring from coaching, Bennie moved into the broadcasting booth to do the color on WWJ radio with Don Kremer. Bennie had a hard time being critical of anyone whether it be friend or foe. Don remembers the time Michigan was playing Army with the Cadets driving up the field at will. The Black Knights climaxed the series with a well-executed pass play that drew some rather caustic comments from both the crowd and Don. But not Bennie, who gently reminded Don and the listeners, "Yes, Don, but remember, they are *our* Army."

If Bennie was the nicest gentleman at Michigan, Bob Ufer was certainly the most unique. My first exposure to Ufe was when I was still at WKZO in Kalamazoo. At that time the station picked up his broadcasts. Oddly, my first impression of Bob was one of admiration for his ability to stay with the ball. I say oddly because later in his career he would be kidded by many for not letting the facts impede his play-by-play. I don't know about that since I never heard him after I arrived in Ann Arbor. But during the two years I did listen, I was in awe of his up-to-date rapid-fire style.

One Ufer game in particular I remember, not for the game itself but rather for his half-time interview with Fritz Crisler. Bob introduced Fritz by saying, "We are now going to call in athletic director Fritz Crisler whom we understand will shortly be named as the new commissioner not of the National Football League but of the new American Football League which will begin operations this fall."

There was a long, pregnant pause while Ufe chuckled in the background before Fritz announced, "Bob, you've been sitting out in the sun at these games too long—it's fried your brain."

I always meant to ask Bob if he was just putting Fritz on or whether he really had been given some inside information which didn't pan out. In any case, Pete Rozelle was shortly named as the successor to Bert Bell and Joe Foss became the first president of the AFL. But what if Fritz *had* become AFL chief? He would certainly never have let the new league submit to that stupid and humiliating merger after the AFL had brought the NFL to its knees. Under Fritz, the AFL probably would have come out as the stronger of the two leagues.

I suppose to many people Bob and I were adversaries since we both broadcast Michigan football over statewide networks. But that was never the case. First of all, I realized shortly after hitting Ann Arbor that no one was going to compete with Bob Ufer. He *was* Michigan football as far as thousands of Wolverine fans were concerned and nothing I was going to do could change that. Secondly, Bob was one of the first to make me feel at home in Ann Arbor and no one was more supportive over the years. He always included me in Quarterback Club functions and I spent many pleasant hours on the road listening to Bob rehash his early days at the microphone and the memorable moments from those years.

His fantastic recall amazed me. He could recount with astonishing accuracy drives that occurred 15 years before. He would stand before a crowd and regale them with his play-by-play of a long-forgotten game and by the time he was through they would be on their feet shouting. Of course, many times Bob would be, too, but this just added to his charisma. Following the 1972 game in Columbus when it appeared that Harry Banks had scored on that tremendous goal line stand by Ohio, I met Bob coming out of his booth.

"The same thing happened in 1954," screamed Bob, "when Danny Cline went over but the officials refused to allow it. He scored that day when we should have won the game and Banks scored today. This was a Michigan victory, not a loss!"

It took Bob a long time to get over that one.

Bob's enthusiasm was something I continued to marvel at even in his final days. He drew some criticism because of that unbridled fervor on the air but he never tried to be anything but Bob Ufer. Well, make that all but once. When Michigan went to the Orange Bowl to meet Oklahoma in 1976, NBC Radio selected Bob as one of the two announcers on the crew. During the weeks preceding the game, Bob was counseled by everybody that he should tone down his play-by-play a bit to accommodate the network. So he decided that to please the powers that be, he would attempt to gear his broadcasting to a more refined level. He later told me what had happened.

"I wrote about three or four openings until the network types agreed on one but when I read it over it just didn't sound like me," said Bob. "So after about two minutes of action, I forgot all about the new image. I went back to doing it the old way."

That was more than good enough for most Michigan fans.

Bob worried about the brickbats that would come his way over his frenzied calling of a game. Soon after he was named as WJR's new announcer, I saw him at the Michigan picture-day session. I was doing Detroit Piston games on WJR at the time.

"Congratulations," I told him. "Now that we're fellow staff members I expect to be treated to lunch."

"Great, we'll stick the station for the tab," he laughed. Then growing serious, he looked away as he said, "You know, when they first contacted me I told them that they had better be prepared for an onslaught of letters and calls after I did my first game. I seem to bring out the worst in fans."

Very soon a couple of writers got on him as he predicted they would. Prior to the Michigan State game we sat in Bob's booth which Joe Falls had decorated green and white.

"I know I'm too loud and get too carried away sometimes," he admitted, "but can't they understand that's just because I care so much about Michigan?"

Lost sometimes in the focus on his excitement was the fact that Bob was probably more prepared than any announcer I have ever seen. His notes, taped to his booth counter and hung on the walls, were legendary. Even Bob couldn't rely on memory all the time but when he quoted a statistic you knew it was accurate.

Bob Ufer will be remembered for many things. His sincerity, his devotion to Michigan, his gift of vocabulary, his lack of pretense, and his sensitivity. But the thing I will remember the most was simply that he was my friend.

About a block from WUOM runs the short street of Hamilton. Since there are few parking spaces available on the narrow, little-used thoroughfare, it was one of the least likely spots to park but always the first I checked out. The reason was simple, Ernie Vick might be outside tending his yard.

I never missed an opportunity to stop and listen to another Ernie Vick tale of the Wolverines of the early '20s or the Gashouse Gang of baseball lore. Ernie was a storehouse of information on both football and baseball and his memory remained sharp into his 80s. He had preceded even Bennie and Wally onto the Ann Arbor scene, coming over from Toledo in 1918 to join the football squad. He brought impressive credentials as a great fullback from his days with Scott High School. But it was as a center that Ernie wrote his name into the Michigan All-American rolls and later gained a berth in the Helms Foundation Hall of Fame. Ernie loved to tell the story about his introduction to the "Old Man"—Fielding Yost.

"Now see," Ernie would say, "we were still at war in '18 so when I got down to Ferry Field that fall I was given a suit even though I was just a freshman because everyone was eligible. After a couple of weeks the coach called me over and said, 'Young man, we have a pretty good fullback and you're kind of on the thin side so how about giving it a try at center?' Well, after watching Frank Steketee I knew I was outclassed at fullback anyway so I told him, 'Sure, I can play center.' And I did."

Then Ernie would pause and smile, "I went on to become an All-American at center weighing 181. Steketee was named All-American too. You know what he weighed? 182 pounds."

Ernie was amazed at the size of modern players. The biggest man on that 1918 line was tackle Gus Goetz who weighed a whopping 185 pounds. But that doesn't mean that Ernie was overawed by today's game versus his era.

"People these days get excited over the guys throwing the football 50 times a game but fans back in my day got pretty thrilled about watching guys like Grange, Nagurski, and the rest sailing up the field with the ball under their arm."

Ernie always felt that Grange was the greatest runner of all time but he called Chick Harley the best of his own day. Vick remembered facing Harley and the Ohio State powerhouse at old Ferry Field one afternoon.

"I'm playing linebacker and here comes Harley busting through the line. I go to put a shoulder into him and he puts a stiff arm out that buries my chin about six inches in the ground. I never even slowed him up and the last I saw of him was his cleats going up the field."

Not too many ball carriers buried Ernie. Incidentally, because of Ernie, Yost altered his defense which at the time was called the diamond. This employed the seven men on the offensive line at the same position on defense, with the fullback utilized as the lone linebacker and the two halfbacks and quarterback as the safeties. Ernie convinced Yost that because of his quickness he would be better employed as a linebacker in protecting against the sweeps and passing plays. It worked and Yost stuck with it.

Ernie often reminded me that playing center back in that period was different than today. He often shook his head in amazement watching punters scooping the ball off the turf or going high to field a snap from center.

"We had to be accurate with every snap or we would throw off the entire timing of a play," recalled Ernie. "I think centers today could probably be just as good but they just don't get the practice snapping deep anymore."

Apparently Ernie had few peers in this department as Yost once said of him, "Ernie is the most accurate passer who ever put the ball in play. Under pressure he was dependable at all times. Anybody can stand up when the sun shines, but it takes a real player to stand up during the storm."

In addition to his football feats, Ernie also spent some years with baseball's St. Louis Cardinals in the mid '20s — the famed Gashouse Gang.

Something that Ernie never failed to marvel at was the care given to the modern athlete in both football and baseball.

"It wasn't that they didn't care back in my day," he

explained, "but just that they weren't equipped. If we had a player hurt he was expected to keep playing unless he couldn't walk or move. Our trainer would tape him up as best he could but with the small squads we couldn't afford to be hurt."

The same thing held true with the Cardinals, according to Vick.

"A sore arm was treated with strong linament or a rubdown. Nobody even mentioned sprains, cuts, or muscle pulls. If a pitcher complained of not being able to throw, the chances were that somebody else would be in his place the next day."

Ernie felt deeply about his exclusion from the Helms Football Hall of Fame in his later years. He watched in vain for his name to be included among the newest inductees as the balloting was announced. Each time he was baffled why his name was never called. It finally was— only Ernie wasn't around to enjoy it. Every time I walk down Hamilton I enjoy it in his place.

As Ernie suggested, sports medicine has come a long way since the 1920s and Michigan was fortunate enough to have a fellow at the helm who was always about 20 years ahead of his time, Jim Hunt. Jim had already been head trainer of Michigan teams for 15 years when I arrived. He came to Ann Arbor from Minnesota to replace Ray Roberts. Having had first-hand knowledge of the size and brute strength of Clayton Tonnemaker and Leo Nommelini, Jim was concerned when the Gophers came to Michigan with their unbeaten powerhouse during his first year in Ann Arbor.

"I remembered how big those fellas were," Jim told me.

"I knew we didn't have anybody close to their size on our line. The paper didn't give us any kind of a chance but our boys just went out and did a magnificent job and it turned out I didn't have to be worried after all."

Between Jim and his right-hand man, Lennie Paddock, I probably learned more about the human body than I would have in ten anatomy courses. I also heard more terrible jokes from Lennie than I would have in ten Joe Miller joke books. He was a gem.

Jim often had come up with an ingenious device for protecting Michigan athletes long before the sporting goods manufacturer marketed the same item on a mass scale. Jim never stopped investigating, experimenting, and reading.

When the football rules committee decided that face masks should be a mandatory item to protect the face and mouth areas, Fritz Crisler was adamantly opposed, "The mask will simply be a convenient handle for tacklers and will cause injuries to the neck and spinal column in much greater severity than those they are trying to avoid."

Jim agreed and went to work. Before long he had come up with a cushioned insert that would fit snugly at the rear of the helmet to absorb any sudden snap of the head caused by an upward blow to the mask. It wasn't foolproof, no equipment is, but it was soon incorporated into all helmets by the manufacturers. The spinal cord injuries that Fritz had feared were kept to a minimum.

Something else that had always bothered Jim was the problem involving fluid intakes for football players. Ever since the game was introduced, coaches had counseled their players not to drink water during workouts. It was one of those things that everyone took for granted but Jim simply felt it wasn't true.

"I knew from my study of osmosis that great quantities of water taken during exertion would cause sickness. But I also knew that the salt lost by the body had to be replaced and tablets weren't the answer. So by figuring the ratio of salt to water in the body, I came up with a formula of one teaspoon salt to one gallon of water and started supplying this in practice. The players didn't need that much to satisfy their thirst and the effect was noticeable almost immediately."

Jim remembered Bennie Oosterbaan remarking, "You know it seems that the team is accomplishing in 2½ hours of practice what it used to take 3 and 3½ to do. I don't really understand why."

Of course a few years later an enterprising soul came up with the same idea with one exception. He flavored it with limeaid and came up with GATORADE. We know the result. The only thing Jim hadn't considered was the tastebuds.

The highly intricate strength and rehabilitating machines that are now common in every football weight room were not yet in vogue in Jim's early regime. This didn't faze the little guy as he simply created his own devices using the now-familiar concepts of isometrics. I really couldn't tell you how close they came to providing the same results as today's highly crafted apparatus but knowing Jim I would guess pretty darn close.

In this day of mammoth squads and training staffs, I'm sure the relationship between player and trainer can't be the same as in Jim's era when he, Lennie, and Mike Willie were the whole staff. Jim used to describe himself as part father, part mother, part doctor, part psychiatrist, and part dutch uncle. Players would tell him things that they never would think of divulging to Fritz or Bump or Bennie. Did this create a problem for Jim?

"No, not really," he told me. "We were all interested in one thing. The welfare of the boy and his part in the success of the team. Thus all of us, the coaches, the doctor, and the trainer, worked with the player toward that common goal."

That doesn't mean Jim told the coaches everything. He used to chuckle about Ted Cachey who played in the '50s. Ted was slim and afraid the coaches would think him too small if he put down his real poundage. So he would tack on about 20 pounds to the weight chart while the amused trainer looked the other way.

"He always avoided taking showers when the coaches were around though," Jim laughed.

Jim's most famous moment came in the days prior to the 1948 Rose Bowl; it was one he still looks back on with a shudder. The team was going through its last heavy-hitting session when suddenly their great All-American tailback Bob Chappius pulled up lame and limped towards the sidelines. Jim raced halfway out to meet him.

"What's wrong, Chap?"

"It feels like someone slashed my thigh with a knife," was Chappius' answer.

Jim quickly found the break in the muscle and went to work.

"It was obvious it wasn't like a football injury at all but more like a track sprinter would experience," said Jim. "We walked back to the clubhouse and Chap started to lay down. But I told him he had to stay sitting with his legs over the table."

For the next hour and a half Jim got him to slowly extend his leg although it was extremely painful. Jim continued the treatment over the next two days while the press had a field day guessing whether Michigan's key to Crisler's intricate single-wing offense would face USC.

He played, all right. With Jim looking on with crossed fingers, Chappius set a Rose Bowl record with 279 yards in total offense to lead the Wolverines to a 49-0 rout of the Trojans. The following day Jim got almost as much ink as Bob.

Another Michigan All-American, Dick Rifenburg, probably put it best when summing up Jim Hunt as "the kind of guy who knew so well that it wasn't always the hurts that needed tending. I was always a nervous, emotional young man the night before a game and Jim was aware of this. Nothing escaped his notice. So every Friday night he made it a point to visit me and give me a massage that relaxed every muscle in my body. I can't imagine how he found enough hours in the day to tend his flock. Every member of the squad came in for that kind of attention."

Apparently the Helms Foundation agreed with Dick because just prior to his retirement, Jim was ushered into the Hall of Fame, a highly coveted honor for anyone but especially for a trainer. But of course, Jim was a whole lot more than just a trainer.

In 1967 Michigan celebrated its 150th birthday with a year-long celebration that included a 26-week series by our station entitled, "The Cornflower and the Maize." Two of the programs were devoted to athletics. We tried to locate some of the earliest Wolverine stars and were amazed at the willingness of some of these former greats to come back to Ann Arbor and participate.

One man in particular stunned us with his sharp, detailed remembrances — Stanford Wells. Keep in mind that Wells gained All-American honors at U-M when Bennie

Oosterbaan was all of four years old! And yet he could recall in vivid detail his arrival in Ann Arbor in 1906, the trip to old Waterman Gym where in those days the players picked out their equipment from a huge pile on the floor, the practice sessions under the immortal Yost and the canniness of the 'Old Man' in diagnosing opponents. His favorite story involved the great rivalry with Penn, at that time the power of the East.

"Coach Yost would spend hours trying to get a jump on the other fellow. This year we were scheduled to play the University of Pennsylvania who nobody could beat. Well, Yost decided that the week before the Penn game he would go and take a look for himself since we had a Saturday off. As far as I know no other coach ever thought about going to scout the other team but Yost wasn't just any other coach.

"So he goes and watches Penn roll over Navy and we all figure he'll come back and tell us we're in for a donnybrook. But here he comes on Monday with his pad and after we all gather down at Ferry Field he starts his rundown. 'Boys, they're a good team but we'll beat 'em because I know just what they're going to do on every play.'

"We all looked at each other like the Old Man was touched but he went on to tell us exactly what he had learned. If the right halfback lined up in one spot it meant they would do this. If he lined up over here it meant something else. By the time he got through we were bowled over that he could know that much about their team. But, you know, he was right about everything and when Saturday came we stopped them cold. Those fellas couldn't believe that we could do that to them."

Wells would also point out that Yost was one of the first to be a stickler for condition. He insisted that the players walk from Waterman, where they dressed, to the practice field and back.

"It was all uphill coming back but by the end of the season we were still going strong in the third and fourth quarters when the other team started to droop."

Wells also told us that the Michigan-Chicago rivalry of his era was every bit as intense as the current Ohio State-Michigan war.

"Yost and Stagg didn't like each other very much and they were always trying to get a leg up on the other. Before I got to Ann Arbor, Chicago had their great quarterback Walter Eckersall who some say was the best ever. Well, he never did that well against Michigan and I found out from the fellows who were on those teams the reason. Yost discovered that Eckie couldn't run as well to his right as he could his left. Well, of course, the Old Man would always put an extra tackler on the left side every time Chicago had the ball. I guess he never even told the writers until after Chicago left the Big Ten. Don't know why, guess he didn't want to tip off Stagg in case he wanted to do it again."

Stanford Wells — another great gentleman of Michigan's illustrious past.

TWO

A Bumpy Start

I t was a typically dull summer sports day that August afternoon in 1962 when the sports phone jangled in the WKZO newsroom. I outwaited Larry Osterman, who slowly unwound himself from his chair and punched the blinking button.

"If it's NBC, I accept," I said. But I visualized another caller asking if the city league softball games were still on after an early afternoon thunderstorm.

Larry arrived on the scene in Kalamazoo three years earlier—one month before I did—so he became sports director and I settled for a combination news-sports reporter position. I didn't mind the variety of the job but was eager to move into sports on a full-time basis.

"It's for you," Larry said. "Find out if they can use two announcers."

"Okay, but this time I'll be number one and you'll be *my* backup," I said.

"Tom Hemingway?" the voice on the phone said. "This is Ed Burrows. I'm station manager here at WUOM in Ann Arbor. Would you be interested in talking to us about our sports director's job?"

I glanced at Larry wondering if this was another of his elaborate practical jokes.

I turned back to the phone, "Well, Ed, that might be interesting. Can you tell me a little more about it?"

"I can, but I thought you might drive over here, discuss it, and have a look around. But I can tell you this—it would involve broadcasting Michigan football, basketball, hockey, and baseball. Along with some news and sportscasts. And a couple of features that you would be responsible for."

Michigan football? Me? A kid from a town of two hundred broadcasting the University of Michigan Wolverines of Tom Harmon, Fritz Crisler, Bob Chappius, and the whole god-like crew that I grew up worshipping. It took a while to answer.

"Is tomorrow too soon?" Nothing like playing hard to get.

So the following day, as soon as I had signed off my talk show, I headed east. I had been in Ann Arbor only twice before that hot August afternoon. Once as a lad of about eight I accompanied my grandfather to the state highway offices north of the city where he worked as a supervisor. The other trip was ten years later when I drove a neighbor's household goods to an apartment near the hospital.

So it was with some apprehension that I approached the city. The anxiety quickly increased as I failed to negotiate the State-Liberty island complex and found myself out at the Forest Hill Cemetery on Geddes heading directly away from the old Administration Building. Ed Burrows had given me his telephone number in case of trouble, but I wasn't about to admit that his potential sports director couldn't even find a five-story building in the middle of campus. After blankly staring at the rows of tombstones and hoping this wasn't an omen, I turned around and headed back to what I hoped was central campus.

Ed was patiently waiting as I panted into the station lobby after hurrying up five flights of stairs. In my rush not to be any later I never even noticed the elevator. Since this was 1962, well before the fitness craze, Ed was a little quizzical as he shook my shaky and sweating hand. However, he warmly led me into his office and told me about the station, the city, and the University. And he went over the station personnel as though they were already my co-workers. I had been prepared to plead my case eloquently but suddenly I realized that I was apparently the only candidate for the job.

"What's your current salary?" Ed asked.

"One hundred and twenty dollars a week." Remember, I worked for John Fetzer who didn't become a millionaire by squandering his money on his employees.

"Well, I think we can pay you $6,500 a year."

I knew that wasn't a whole lot more than I was making in Kalamazoo but we were talking the Michigan Wolverines not Kalamazoo softball.

"You'll broadcast Michigan sports, do some news and one 15-minute sportscast. And Bill Stegath, whom you are replacing, will be doing the football games this season since we promised him one final year before you take over."

That sounded good to me. I had decided on the trip over that along with moving a family, selling a house and finding new quarters, it would be hectic to also move into the football booth at the same time. And I was apprehensive about my ability to step into the Big Ten football scene. Maybe a year to think about it would calm my nerves.

As I threaded my way back onto I-94, I clicked on the

radio and tried to visualize what it would be like to do a broadcast of U-M football. (I never thought then about basketball although that would be my main association to many people.)

My memories drifted back to my days as a boy in Wacousta, a tiny town about ten miles from Lansing. I remembered camping by the radio on Saturdays listening to Michigan demolish another foe.

I remembered Ty Tyson, the legendary Tiger announcer, who doubled as a color man on the U-M game broadcasts. Years later I would walk into the radio-TV press box at Tiger Stadium and there, by himself, was Ty. He told me about the early years of broadcasting football at Michigan Stadium, during the late '20s before the players wore numerals so the only identification play-by-play men had was by position. On one particular day, Michigan met a strong Navy team with a fine left halfback named Roy Swafford. During the first half, Michigan's defense was shredded time and again by the running of the Middie halfback. By halftime, Ty had pretty well deified the young man. He was in the midst of his between-half remarks when handed a telegram by his engineer. It read: "Roy Swafford in hospital with broken leg. Appreciate publicity anyhow." Signed, Mr. and Mrs. Swafford.

Ty didn't find out who the phantom Navy back was until the game was over.

I remembered the great afternoon in 1949 when Michigan knocked off the Gophers of Tonnemaker and Nomellini, then ranked number one in the nation. That was the game that found Jim Hunt fearing for the lives of his Wolverines. I remembered the great upset of Bennie's Wolverines over California in the 1951 Rose Bowl. Yerges, Bump and Pete Elliott, Wistert, Pregulman, Chappius, White, Weise, Koceski, Ortmann . . . I could still remember those names.

"Good Lord," I thought, "What am I getting into?" My emotions fluctuated between euphoria and panic, so to take my mind off U-M for awhile I turned up Ernie Harwell's description of Whitey Ford's complete domination of the Tigers. I was a charter member of the Yankee Haters Marching and Chowder Society, but I listened to the feeble efforts of the Detroit hitters against the future Hall of Famer. By the time the fifth inning rolled around the Yankees were up 8-0 and I was thinking Michigan again.

Then it occurred to me that WUOM was an FM station —in 1962 FM stood for Frequently Maligned. FM receivers held only about 30 percent of the sales market and were just starting to become popular in an AM-FM combo. Most FM stations were regarded by the public as specialty entertainment, of interest only to a small, select audience. Did I want to go to a station where the listeners could be counted on a three-digit calculator? In three years at WKZO I had established some strong ties. I felt I had gained some listener respect, now did I want to start over in a place where I knew absolutely no one?

"Wait a minute, I didn't know anybody in Kalamazoo either when I arrived there," I reminded myself. And since that was my first job with a commercial station, that was much more of a jolt than this would be. I had worked for the Michigan State University station, WKAR, both as a student and graduate. I had been extremely lucky in landing a job as the number two sports man when only a sophomore. WKAR's long time sports director Bob Shackleton was the most popular broadcaster in the area and it took a year before I gathered up enough nerve to talk to him about a possible job. I had nervously poked my head into his office and stammered that I was the Tom Hemingway who had called for an appointment. He unwound his 6-4 frame from his chair and swallowed up my hand in his bear paw.

Since I had only worked a couple of weeks as staff announcer at WKAR at the time, I couldn't understand how he had obtained so much background on me. I found out later that station manager Larry Frymire had told him about this kid who babbled constantly about sports and seemed to know something about the subject. Since I had cut my teeth on *The Sporting News* and *Sport* magazine some of it was bound to sink in.

"I'm looking for a second man to help me in the sports department here. Would you be interested?"

"Sure, but don't you want an audition or something?"

"Nah, we don't need that. If you want the job, it's yours."

And that was the start. When the University TV channel went on the air Bob simply turned over the nightly TV sportscast to me and let me handle it without interference. He worked me into doing color on hockey and would even fake a case of laryngitis to allow me to get my feet wet with play-by-play. We would also broadcast minor sports—swimming, track, even gymnastics. Try describing an uneven parallel bar routine on radio sometime.

It was during that time that I experienced one of the most embarrassing moments in my career. We were doing a swimming meet between U-M and MSU during the era of Matt Mann's great teams in Ann Arbor. The Wolverines had a returning NCAA champion in the 100-yard backstroke while MSU offered the son of Spartan coach Charlie McCafferey, a heavy underdog. Neither Bob or I knew either swimmer from Johnny Weismuller so we simply went by the lane assignments on the starter sheets.

After two laps we appeared to be sitting in on an upset of major proportions—young McCafferey opened a five-length lead over the NCAA champ and was seemingly getting stronger. Bob's enthusiasm mounted as he described the final lap to our audience.

"And here comes Jimmy McCafferey, swimming his heart out as he nears the finish line, on the verge of turning in one of the greatest upsets in swimming history. The crowd is stunned as here he comes. And it's all over. MCCAFFEREY HAS DONE IT!!"

Not to be outdone, I quickly jumped in with some lavish prose of my own. Something like:

"With tears in her eyes, here comes Mrs. McCafferey out of the stands to share in this joyous moment. What motherly emotions must be surging through her mind right now as she races to the side of the pool to comgratulate her son who has just set the world of swimming on its ear with this fantastic performance . . ."

And on and on and on.

Soon we almost had ourselves in tears reflecting on this monumental accomplishment which surely would rank among the great moments in Michigan State history. I was momentarily non-plussed to watch Mrs. McCafferey embrace not her son but the defeated champion from Michigan but decided this was just a great show of sportsmanship on her part. I paused with Bob to listen to the public address announcement of the official final placements.

"Here are the results of the 100-yard backstroke. Finishing first in a new pool, meet and Big Ten record time of :52.85 is the defending NCAA champion from Michigan, Matt Ayers. Finishing second in the time of :54.72 is Jimmy McCafferey of Michigan State. Finishing third in the time of . . ."

I looked at Bob. He stared at me in horror. The swimmers had shifted lanes from the official sheet and no one had bothered to tell us. I waited for Bob to say something. He motioned to my mike. I shook my head and pointed back to him. He leaned over and whispered, "We've got to tell them what happened." I nodded in agreement and waited again for him to speak. He responded by turning his mike off and mine up while he took off his headset.

"Well, nothing like having your career end before it starts," I thought to myself.

"Ladies and gentlemen," I began, "we have a slight correction to make."

Recalling this incident as I made my exit from the freeway into Kalamazoo made me wonder how my background with MSU would be received in Ann Arbor. It hadn't seemed to make any difference to Ed Burrows — but he wasn't part of the Michigan family that I would be dealing with at Ferry Field. The animosity between the two schools had grown steadily since the Spartans officially entered the Big Ten football wars in 1953, a year that found them winning the championship. Since that time they had finished ahead of Michigan six times in football, a fact that Spartans fans were eager to point out. I was sure my Red Cedar Days wouldn't exactly be a plus on State Street.

"Okay, I've dealt with the negatives, how about the positives?"

First of all, regardless of how small the Ann Arbor audience was, I would finally get a chance to be a station's number one sports man. Since Larry and I were only in our twenties it did seem likely that I could be number two at WKZO for a long time. I knew Larry had his heart set on becoming a member of the Tiger broadcast crew and being a sports director for John Fetzer's key station didn't hurt that chance. (And eventually that's exactly what happened, as Larry became a Tiger broadcaster and didn't leave WKZO until the late '70s.) And how did I know if I would ever get a shot at doing Big Ten sports again? Also, Ann Arbor was only 50 miles from Detroit — it could lead to a possible connection there. (It did, but certainly not in the way I had imagined.)

Pluses, minuses, but the bottom line was still, MICHIGAN.

Moments later when Larry met me in the station's parking lot I had made up my mind.

"Larry, I'm heading for Ann Arbor."

Despite the fact that my official starting date with WUOM was September 17th, the football season was still two weeks off. Back in 1962 Michigan played only nine games, with seven in the conference. So, early that first week, Bill Stegath took me for an initial meeting with the staff. We arrived at the practice field, which at that time was directly behind Yost Fieldhouse. Although practice was already underway, Bump Elliott spotted us and quickly came over.

"Bump, this is Tom Hemingway. He'll be taking over for me and I hope you give him the same cooperation you gave me."

"Better, I hope," Bump grinned as he shook my hand.

"It's really a pleasure to meet you," I stuttered as I realized I was shaking the hand of the man whom I had idolized during his days in a Michigan uniform. I wondered how many other youngsters on the playgrounds of the state had pretended to be number 18. Fritz Crisler had called him the greatest right halfback he ever saw or coached. He was much smaller than I had expected, no more than 5-10 and as trim as a marathon runner. After a few more minutes of conversation he excused himself and returned to his chores.

"Gosh, I didn't realize he was that young, Bill!"

"Well, he's 37, Tom, but you're right, he doesn't look 30."

"Is he always that friendly?" I asked.

"Oh, yeah, in fact he is maybe too nice for his own good sometimes."

It was a comment I was to hear time and time again before Bump retired to the administrators' ranks. I never really knew whether it had merit. He certainly wasn't the screamer and intimidator in the style of a Bo or Woody. But he won a Big Ten title in the snakepit of Columbus and finished second another season to the number-one-rated Buckeyes.

Yet, there were those who felt he couldn't be a great coach simply because he was an exceedingly gracious and friendly gentleman. Before the season was over that graciousness would be put to its severest test and I became someone that Bump wished would have stayed in Kalamazoo.

Bill and I watched the team square off for live scrimmage sessions. There were a number of other spectators on hand since Bump had an open door policy when it came to practice. He did tighten up a bit when the season got underway but seldom closed drills to the media. This didn't seem at all unusual to me since at Western Michigan and Kalamazoo College we were always permitted to wander at will among the players. In looking back, however, it seems incredible that we were given that much latitude by Bump.

We wandered up and down the sidelines. Each assistant
coach followed Bump's lead and came over to shake hands
and chat briefly. I remembered Hank Fonde from his days
as a backfield teammate of Bump's on the great 1947
squad and was equally amazed at how small this likeable
Tennessean was. He had an easy-going manner which
combined with a wide smile and a residue of a southern
drawl always made him a pleasure to be around.

Another fellow whose name I quickly recognized was
Don Dufek, hero of the 1951 Rose Bowl game when he
scored both Michigan touchdowns. Unlike Bump and
Hank, he looked the part with his muscular build and
rolling gait. It wasn't hard to picture him slashing through
the enemy lines. His contributions didn't end with his
playing and coaching days — two of his sons, Donnie and
Bill, starred at Michigan and a third, Joey, was a star at
Yale. Even a daughter Anne got into the act by marrying
a coach on Bo's staff. No question about the football genes
in that family.

Don would later move into the athletic director job at
Kent State before returning to Ann Arbor to become a
highly successful businessman. He and Hank were always
accessible and were a tremendous help in those early days
to a young, struggling sportscaster. Jack Fouts was another extremely likeable individual and the most soft-
spoken of the crew. Within a couple of years he would
leave to return to his alma mater, Ohio Wesleyan, as
coach and athletic director.

Completing Bump's staff were the towering pair of Bob
Hollway and Jocko Nelson. Hollway was an Ann Arbor
native who after becoming one of the city's greatest athletes went on to star on the 1947-48 Michigan dynamite

teams. He eventually went to the pro coaching ranks as head man with St. Louis before returning to Bud Grant's staff in Minnesota where he has remained.

And that was the staff. Amazing as it seems now there were only five and since Dufek worked exclusively with the freshman, there were really only four. Fonde had charge of the backfield, Nelson the ends, Fouts coached the interior line and Hollway the line and defense. The *entire* defense. Of course, this was still in the era of limited substitution so in coaching the defense you worked with the same people you coached on offense. Nowadays, U-M has a staff of eleven not counting graduate assistants.

Since it was getting late in the day and my program would be coming up in about an hour, I mentioned to Bill that we probably should be getting back to the station. We started to make our way to the parking lot when a burly figure wearing a ten-gallon hat loomed in our path.

"Hi, taxpayer," his voice boomed out. "Need any information? I've got numbers, weights, heights, and salaries."

I had just met Wally Weber. Even with the luxury of over 20 years of knowing him, Wally still defies description. Many were the afternoons I would sneak down to Bennie Oosterbaan's office to listen to Wally and Bennie regale each other with stories of the days of Yost and Ferry Field. He was Falstaff reborn.

"Where you from, Hemingway?"

"Kalamazoo," Bill said quickly, glancing at me.

"Ah yes, Kalamazoo," Wally broke in sounding like W.C. Fields. "Know it well."

After we left Wally, I turned to Bill.

"Why did you tell him I was from Kalamazoo? I was only there three years."

"I think it's better we don't mention your Michigan State background right away. I think it's going to be a problem even if Ed doesn't."

I was starting to feel like an infiltrator in enemy ranks. It was a feeling I never was to erase completely although I have never been given any problems because of my Spartan days. I'm sure I was never accepted by some simply because I wasn't a Michigan graduate but that's only normal. No, any problems I had that first year had nothing to do with my college diploma. My problems that season were of my own making, especially with Bump.

Included in my duties at WUOM that first fall was the taping of a program called, "Wolverine Sports Report." It was a 10-minute weekly feature originated by the station's first sports director, Bill Flemming. It required going down to the athletic department each week and interviewing a coach. That didn't seem like too formidable a task when I first discussed it with Burrows and Stegath. Bill set up the first interview and offered to go along in case I had some problems with our ancient and bulky reel-to-reel tape recorder.

"Okay, Bill," I said, "sounds good, who's the guest?"

"Fritz Crisler."

I stared at Bill.

"Fritz Crisler?" I gulped.

"Yeah, we always do the first show with Fritz."

I tried to think of some rational reason we should break precedent. Was my old job at WKZO still open? How could I summon the courage to talk with *the* Fritz Crisler? He might as well have set up an interview with Mohammed or Buddha.

As we turned into the athletic building and proceeded down to Fritz Crisler's office, I thought to myself, "Next to Fielding H. Yost, this man is probably the most imposing name in Michigan football history. No wonder I'm nervous." His secretary motioned to us through the opened door to come in and quickly announced to the man that we were there.

"Come on in, I'll be with you in a moment," came the stentorian tones from the other side of the door. And there behind the desk was the man who did more to shape college football in its march to national prominence than any other individual. I thought then, as I have many times since, that if stage or screen had ever captured Fritz' interest he would have made one of the great leading men of our day. Tall, regal, elegant, distinguished, always dressed impeccably and always surrounded by the aura of dignity and class. To the day of his death I called him Mr. Crisler; it just never entered my mind to call him anything else.

He grinned that great smile of his and immediately put me at ease by welcoming me aboard. We sat down and spun off the interview with no difficulty. Of course it was almost impossible to do a bad interview with Fritz because of his mastery of the language. No matter how awful the questions might be, he would craft a meaningful answer.

As our chats progressed over the years however, I overcame that initial uneasy feeling with Fritz although the respect never diminished. He was ever the gracious host and spellbinding conversationalist. Once during a taping session I mentioned a visit to a pair of Civil War battlefields that summer. That sparked a full half-hour of discussion about the war with Fritz displaying a professor's knowledge of the subject.

"You know," he told me, "I found that being a student of military campaigns was a definite aid to me as a coach. I always knew Bernie Bierman would concentrate his forces on your strength, so sometimes by employing a quick thrust away from your own main base you could surprise him. Now, Ray Eliot tended to be just the opposite—he would try to hammer at your weak points. Yes, it paid to know your opponents' combat tendencies."

These days 12-man coaching staffs use miles and miles of film to track down these same tendencies that Fritz spotted while studying the campaigns of Robert E. Lee.

He also gave me some of the best advice I ever received. At the time I was working part-time as sportscaster for Channel 4 in Detroit and wondered out loud to Fritz if I shouldn't take the bigger salary of television.

"I remember Bill Flemming coming to me," Fritz said, "when he had been here a couple of years. He asked me if he should take this job in Detroit. It offered pretty good money but it meant he would have to give up broadcasting Michigan football which he loved. I told him that if he stayed in Ann Arbor a bit longer he would get offers double this one with much stronger security attached. He did and look what happened. Never give up a strong base for a quick buck. You'll always lose in the end."

One of my fondest memories of Fritz came one evening years later at the home of Bob Ufer. We had just finished roasting Bob at the old Roma Hall—Tom Harmon, Ron Kramer, Rob Lytle, and Bo Schembechler joining in the fun along with many others.

Following the dinner, Bob asked me if I would like to attend a small gathering at his home. Ufe, Harmon, Lytle—everyone had their favorite stories. Then Fritz recalled the 1940 game in California where the heavily soused fan came out of the stands in an attempt to tackle Harmon.

"I was afraid Tom wouldn't see him," Fritz remembered.

"I saw him, coach," Harmon replied, "and I sure as hell wasn't going to let some drunken salesman bring me down."

Fritz chuckled along with the rest of us at the thought of some beery, out-of-shape Walter Mitty trying to tackle one of football's greatest ball carriers.

Just prior to his retirement, Fritz met with me for about an hour as we taped a special show for later broadcast. We still have it in our file and I often take it out to refresh my memory about this dynamic gentleman. Here are some excerpts:

On Recruiting:

"It used to be that the young man recruited the school. Now it's the other way around. I really wonder which is best."

On Winning:

"I've never understood those who criticize winning. What should we play for — second place, fourth, sixth? I always hope that I am a gracious loser and have always instructed my team to be the same. But I also have the determination that the next time we meet, by God, I will be the victor."

On Tom Harmon:

"The greatest attributes of Tom were his power and balance. You see, Tom was a great high school hurdler back in Gary. Now, a lot of great sprinters come out of high school as highly touted football players but you can knock them down with a strong breeze. However, a hurdler needs strength plus speed and that is exactly what Tom had."

On Michigan:

"Tradition is something you can't bottle. You can't buy it at the corner store. But it is there to sustain you when you need it most. I've called upon it time and time again and so have countless other Michigan athletes and coaches. There is nothing like it. I hope it never dies."

Don't worry Fritz, it won't.

In August of 1962, Bump Elliot was to need every bit of tradition he could muster. He had lost some key personnel from the 1961 squad which registered a 6-3 record, Bump's best to that time. It also ranked as the best U-M mark overall since Bennie Oosterbaan was 7-2 in 1956.

Unfortunately for Bump, most of the media overlooked the player losses from that team and focused on the record instead. Many predicted the Wolverines would be back in the hunt for the conference title, something that hadn't happened since 1950. But not returning from that squad was the great all-around star Bennie McRae who would go on to pro fame with the Chicago Bears; fullback Bill Tunnicliff and his two backups, Ken Tureaud and Paul Raeder; and both starting ends, George Mans and Scotty Maentz. Also gone was three-fifths of their starting interior line.

It might have been that sense of tradition that kept Bump from despairing in 1962 as the losses and injuries mounted. I had met with him for an interview on the Monday prior to the September 29th opener. While using the coach's prerogative to be cautious, he seemed fairly pleased with the progress of fall drills and the attitude of the squad going into the opener with Nebraska.

His biggest problem was choosing a quarterback—he had no less than four jockeying for the position. Senior

Dave Glinka had the inside lane since he had two seasons under his belt and had played well, if not spectacularly, the previous year.

Frosty Evashevski, the son of the fabled Forest, was returning from a knee operation which had sidelined him for the entire 1961 season. At the time he had been called Michigan's finest sophomore football prospect in years. He turned out to be a much better golfer.

Another contender on the gimpy side was Bob Chandler who had ripped up a knee in the Michigan State game in '61 and retired to the injured list. He was generally conceded to have the best arm of the quartet but was suspect because of his faulty underpinnings.

There was a fourth candidate. He was a young sophomore giant by the name of Bob Timberlake.

Bob looked like a prototype for Yost or Crisler in the old single-wing days of the multi-talented tailback. One can only wonder how he would have ranked with Harmon, Chappius, or Kipke. But the single wing was gone forever and Bob was penciled in as the number three quarterback as the season began. It didn't take him long to move up.

The Wolverines did have some other bright spots that didn't go unnoticed by fans and media. Back from two years as their leading scorer was halfback Dave Raimey, a 5-10, 195-pound package of dynamite who, along with his other accomplishments in 1961, had returned a kickoff 90 yards for a touchdown against Ohio State. Raimey also had a unique high school career in Dayton. An orphan, he was raised by his grandmother until midway through his senior year when she became seriously ill. This forced Dave to move to other relatives across town. A transfer in schools also came about but Dave never missed a beat—he ended up leading both Woodrow Wilson and Roosevelt in scoring that season.

In McRae's absence in the Wolverine backfield, Raimey was expected to carry the major load in the '62 season.

So, in that final week of preparation, the major emphasis centered around the wealth of quarterbacks, the excitement of Raimey and the 6-3 mark of 1961. Bump's final words were simply, "We have a lot of new faces and it should be an interesting season in that respect." When the season ended, I don't think interesting would have been one of the words Bump would have used.

Since Bill Stegath would be doing the play-by-play that season, he asked me if I would do statistics for him since I would be in the booth anyway. After that season I gained a completely new admiration for stat men and have managed to hold onto the best in the business, Bill Swisher, who began with me in the 1963 season.

As we prepared for the opener with Nebraska, Larry Osterman, a Nebraska native, arrived from Kalamazoo and dropped into the booth.

"Hey, you know the Cornhuskers are going to kick some Wolverine tails today, don't you?" he smirked.

But Larry knew that Nebraska had staggered through six consecutive losing seasons and hadn't won a conference championship since 1937 when it was known as the Big Six. To attempt to turn this around, the school had brought in Bob Devaney who had just won four Skyline titles in five years at Wyoming. He, of course, was no stranger to the state of Michigan having served as an assistant to Biggie Munn and Duffy Daugherty at MSU for four years. This had followed a spectacular career as head coach at Alpena High. As we all know now, Devaney didn't just turn the program around, he brought it to the top and made the Cornhuskers a yearly choice for national championship contention.

I interviewed Bob on Friday afternoon as he brought his team out for a look at the stadium. I remember how convivial and charming he was as we chatted in the stadium tunnel. After our interview, he asked if I would go with him into the visitor's dressing room.

"Wouldn't you think the University of Michigan could do a little better for visiting teams than this?" he said, gesturing to the pegs on the wall, the cramped quarters and the leaky plumbing. He shook his head and smiled, "Oh well, maybe it will fire us up a little more tomorrow." I don't know if Bob read 21 years later that Sam Wyche had made the same complaints to the media covering the Indiana-Michigan game.

Despite Devaney's arrival, the oddsmakers weren't impressed and made the Cornhuskers 13-point underdogs, much to the concern of Bump Elliott. Part of the downgrading of the visitors stemmed from the fact that even in those days their size didn't stack up to Big Ten standards. Two of their lineman barely made the 200-pound mark with their center Don Stevenson possessing the only bulk at 251.

Observers dismissed Devaney's claim that he was looking for mobility and not size as a ploy to prepare the folks back in Lincoln for another long autumn. A couple of facts had escaped the experts however. Devaney had moved Bill "Thunder" Thornton back to his regular position as fullback after former coach Bill Jennings had wasted him at halfback for two years. Along with this switch, Devaney got quarterback Dennis Claridge back after a year of forced retirement because of academic difficulties.

But none of these thoughts were in my mind as I looked

out from the booth at the crowd of 74,000 that had come out on a warm and sunny afternoon to open what they were sure would be a glorious season. At that moment, I was relishing the fact that I wouldn't be broadcasting this game. I was excited enough just being there.

Nebraska received the opening kickoff, failed to move and punted to the Michigan 27. Raimey scooted around the left side for nine. Bill Dodd carried for eight and when Glinka hit Jim Ward on another pickup of nine, Michigan was in Nebraska territory.

"Hey, this is going to be a fun season," I figured as I chalked up the gains on the stat sheet.

But Michigan also stalled and Bump sent Joe O'Donnell back to punt.

Now, Joe really was a story in himself. At 230 pounds he had to be the biggest punter in Michigan history. In high school at Milan, Joe had been an all-state fullback. He played briefly at that spot for Bump before being shifted to guard where he became one of the best in the Big Ten. In the previous season's opener against UCLA, Joe went down with a broken arm that wiped him out for the season. Then, early in spring drills, Joe managed to break the same arm again. Without preparation, this season Joe had been moved over to right tackle where the Wolverines had been hit hard by graduation—he thus was manning his third position in a Michigan uniform. Joe would go on to produce an outstanding play for his scrapbook the following season. Back to punt against SMU, Joe found nobody on defense rushing and tucked the ball under his arm to go 52 yards for a touchdown. "I always told Bump he shouldn't have moved me out of the backfield," he informed the press after the game.

Joe went on to play some excellent pro ball, giving the

town of Milan the rare distinction of supplying two pro stars – O'Donnell and Bill Laskey.

So, in came Joe to punt and Nebraska had the ball again at their 24. But not for long. On the first play, Willie Ross fumbled and O'Donnell recovered at the 29.

Carries by Dick Rindfuss, equally at home at halfback or defense, Dodd and Raimey moved the ball to the 14. But that was it and when Glinka missed a wide-open Harvey Chapman in the end zone it was fourth and seven. Dodd then came in to attempt a field goal but when the kick sailed wide, Michigan was left with nothing to show for their great break of moments before. Again Nebraska couldn't move but Michigan's subsequent drive petered out at the Cornhusker 33 as the first quarter ended.

It seemed just a matter of time before Michigan would sustain a drive and start wearing down the underdog Huskers. After all they had run 22 plays in the first period to Nebraska's 10 and had spent most of the period in Red and White territory. So as the second quarter got under-way the crowd was in an impatient but relaxed mood.

While most of Michigan's defensive preparations had centered on stopping the throwing of Claridge and the running of Thornton, little was known about the rest of the Big Red backfield. The Wolverines got a crash course on the next series, however, as a young lad named Dennis Stuewe woke everybody up. Stuewe – sidelined by injuries over much of his first two years – took a pitchout from Claridge and streaked down the far sideline for 42 yards before Chapman could haul him down. Three plays later, Stuewe gathered in a screen pass and danced for another 20 yards to the Michigan 14. Two plays later he scamp-ered into the end zone and Nebraska led, 7-0.

Michigan quickly rallied behind Raimey's running and

a 23-yard pass from Glinka to Chapman that moved the ball to the Nebraska 8. There, after dropping back to pass and finding no one open, Glinka raced around the right side for a touchdown. But Glinka's two-point conversion pass attempt to Chapman fell short and Nebraska carried a 7-6 lead at the end of the first half.

Midway into the third quarter came the key play in the game. Nebraska punted to the Michigan 17 and the Wolverines offense prepared to take over. But wait a minute—a flag back at the line of scrimmage. Offside, Michigan. Nebraska first down at the Michigan 45. They wasted little time. Dave Thiesen took a pitchout and started a sweep around the right side. With the defense closing, Theisen put on the brakes and heaved a perfect strike to wide-open Jim Huge and the Huskers were at the Michigan 15. Five plays later Thornton thundered over from the one. Jim Conley blocked the conversion attempt and it was 13-6, Nebraska.

After an exchange of fumbles, Nebraska took over at the Michigan 27. Five plays later Claridge shot over from the six and Nebraska held a 19-6 margin.

That prompted Bump to try another quarterback as he brought in Evashevski and Frosty quickly moved them to the Cornhusker 26. Timberlake replaced Evy at the start of the fourth quarter and completed the drive with Rindfuss carrying it over from the four. Bump also decided at this point to let Timberlake take over the PAT chores and Timbo put it through to make it a 19-13 game.

Since there were still 12 minutes left Michigan still appeared to be very much in the game. Five minutes later however, Nebraska still had the ball and through the running and throwing of Claridge had marched to the Michigan 16. Thornton took care of the remaining distance as he pounded across for his second touchdown of the afternoon. And although there was still a half of the quarter to go, it was over. Bump tried his fourth quarterback of the day in Chandler but the Wolverines failed to get past the 50-yard line the rest of the afternoon. A shocked and subdued crowd filtered out of the stadium with a score of Nebraska 25, Michigan 13 blinking overhead. It was a tremendous opening for Devaney and his underdogs — one that launched the team from the midlands as a national power. But what about Michigan? I couldn't believe they weren't better than they looked today. Well, shoot, one game doesn't make a season and they could turn it around next Saturday against Army.

Prior to practice each Monday, Bump met with the press in back of Yost. I wondered why he seemed a bit surprised to see me there. Later I learned that I was the first member of the electronic media to show up at these gatherings. In later years, these sessions would become more formal — a lunch at Webers for about 30 media people. But in 1962 there were just four of us.

The questioning went quickly. I had done a lot of listening and little talking. If I had just continued to do that, I would have been a whole lot better off.

Practice that week seemed pretty intense to an onlooker although Bump and his coaches didn't appear to be any more highly charged in their actions on the practice field. And the following Saturday it seemed to pay off as Michigan rebounded with an impressive 17-7 win over Army.

The mood was euphoric in the booth as we all envisioned the start of something big. Stegath got so carried away he even let me on the air for a wrapup at the end of the game.

The victory over Army was quickly overshadowed by

the disquieting news that the Russians had established a major missile network in Cuba. All week long the world seemed to teeter on the brink of all-out war. It would be resolved the following weekend when John Kennedy announced to the nation that the Soviets had acceded to all of the US demands.

Bump had closed down drills to the general public that week but still allowed the media carte blanche. I noticed that Bump was running from an unbalanced line at times and using Timberlake as a halfback. I mentioned this to Hollway.

"You're not supposed to notice that," Bob smiled.

"Don't worry, Bob, I'm not going to race up and tell Duffy."

"No, I didn't think you were," he glared, "but keep it to yourself, okay?"

I agreed but wondered who on earth I would come in contact with that could possibly care.

For most Michigan fans, the victory over Army had kindled the hope that this would be the year that the long winless streak against the Spartans would be snapped. The Wolverines hadn't beaten State since 1955, a game I had watched from the MSU broadcast booth. But this was not one of Duffy's stronger teams and as the week progressed so did Michigan's optimism.

But that Saturday, the Spartans bolted ahead quickly when they scored a touchdown off a fake field goal attempt. That play prompted Stegath to jump up from the microphone and assault the wall with his fist.

"Gee," I mumbled to myself, "I thought I was taking this hard."

George Saimes, Sherm Lewis, and company went on to completely dismantle Michigan 28-0, the second straight year they had humiliated their intra-state rivals by that score.

The next week was worse. Ron DeGravio passed them into submission, 37-0, at Purdue.

Minnesota made it three straight shutouts with a 17-0 pasting before the Homecoming grads in Ann Arbor.

Despite the strain, Bump continued to display remarkable poise and composure in dealing with the press. He refused to be drawn into a verbal tug of war with a pair of columnists who were questioning his ability to coach. After the Minnesota game, Wally Weber burst into the athletic office waving the paper containing the latest offending column.

"This man is trying to start a war," Wally boomed. "He's a danger to society and has to be stopped."

To the suggestion that Bump should be replaced, Fritz Crisler icily replied, "Bump is the coach at Michigan and will remain so as long as I am here."

End of quote.

It was during this period that I moved into Bump's doghouse for an extended stay. With the benefit of hindsight, I can see why. Being inexperienced and unsure of myself I asked the wrong questions at the wrong time. Bump must have felt that I should be in another line of work, preferably in some other state. And I looked no older than his players. So he avoided me for years to come. He was still accessible for interviews but it was clear he was not dealing with his media favorite.

Had I been in Bump's shoes, I would have felt the same way. Considering the pressures of that 1962 season, he was fully justified in being wary of a green newcomer. I have always regretted I did not get off to a better start with one of the nicest people in the universe. Fortunately, with the passage of time, that relationship changed — I always look forward to meeting Bump along the Big Ten trail.

Against Wisconsin the following Saturday, Michigan scored a pair of touchdowns to break the scoreless streak. They were far too little, however, as the eventual Big Ten champion rolled to a 34-12 victory.

This was probably the Badgers' greatest team, sparked by the Ron Vanderkelen-Pat Richter combo that shredded secondaries around the conference. That particular afternoon, Richter had a field day with the Michigan pass defense, especially one poor Wolverine defender.

The following January, I was seated at a luncheon next to Bob Ufer as the discussion turned to Michigan football. Unaware who Bob was, a gentleman across from us brought up the Wisconsin game and the throwing of Vanderkelen.

"I was listening to the game in the car," the man said, "and this announcer was just ripping one Michigan defensive back for allowing all those passes to be completed. I thought if I was his father I'd be looking for the announcer with a shotgun."

Ufer flashed a sheepish grin.

"That was me," Bob admitted, "I guess I was a little rough on him but I got awfully tired of watching Richter catch the ball that day."

We all did.

Things finally improved. Bump continued his eerie domination of brother Pete by nipping the Illini, 14-10. A crowd of less than 48,000 turned up for the final home game of the season.

The real shocker against the Illini would come the next season, however, as Bump almost cost Pete the championship. That Illinois team included Dick Butkus, Jim Grabowski, and Larry McCarren, all future NFL stars. But a feisty underdog Michigan team went into Champaign and upset the top-heavy favorites, 14-8. Most Wolverines on that team agreed that it was the game that laid the foundation for the 1964 success. Illinois did recover to defeat Michigan State in the final game in 1963 to wrap up the title and make their last Rose Bowl trip until 1984.

The win over Pete provided only a brief respite for Bump. At Iowa City, the Hawkeyes dealt them a 28-14 loss to leave U-M at 2-6 on the season.

Everyone was aware that only twice in Michigan history had a team lost as many as seven games in a season. The first came in 1934 when the squad had a center by the name of Gerald Ford. And the last was in 1936. Both of these teams were under the tutelage of Harry Kipke, one of Michigan's greatest all-around stars and by far their most enigmatic coach. From 1929, his first year at the helm, through 1933 Kipke posted a staggering record—36 wins, 4 losses and 4 ties, with four Big Ten crowns. From 1934 until he was succeeded by Crisler in 1938, Kipke's teams won 10 games while dropping 22. And only five of those wins came against Big Ten teams.

With the final game coming up in Columbus, the question was could Bump avoid joining the ill-fated Kipke?

It was a strange season for Ohio State. They were 5-3 but most observers had expected a repeat of the great 1961 season which they climaxed by whipping Michigan, 50-20. That was the game that found Woody rolling up the score in the final minutes with his first team as he made his bid for the number one national ranking. Up in the Ohio State coaches' booth was a Buckeye assistant, Bo Schembechler, who was unjustly accused of being an instigator in the scheme. But as Bo would point out later, the communications between the field and the booth broke down during the second half and he became simply a spectator in the fourth quarter. Oddly enough, the captain of that 1961 team was Gary Moeller who would play a major role in molding later Wolverine squads.

The Bucks had stumbled out of the gate in 1962, losing to UCLA, Northwestern, and Iowa to eliminate any hopes of a repeat conference crown. They were also still steaming over the refusal of the school's administration to allow them to represent the conference in the Rose Bowl the year before. Woody later admitted that had a devastating effect on the team's morale. They had one day in the sun, however, as they knocked off Wisconsin, the only conference loss for the Badgers in 1962.

Despite the fact that Wisconsin and Minnesota were playing for the title that day, ABC was locked in to showing the Michigan-Ohio State game. This was in the days of the schedule being made up prior to the season without any leeway for wild-card listings. And, of course, at the start of the season it looked like a good bet for a possible title matchup. Instead, it proved to be a fitting climax for Michigan's most disappointing season in 25 years— OSU's Dave Francis ran through, over, and around the Michigan defense in keying a 28-0 win.

I had flown to Columbus on our engineer's private plane, so the trip back to Ann Arbor was a short one. But it was long enough for me to reconcile my expectations in September with the reality of November. Even though the 1962 season had been a disaster, it had given me a chance to learn the ropes without the pressure of play-by-play. And although I didn't realize it at the time, it also made the ensuing years that much sweeter. Within two years, Bump had silenced his critics by soaring to a Big Ten championship, a 34-7 thrashing of Oregon State in the Rose Bowl, and a spot in the top ten.

THREE

On The Road Again

Travel is exciting, stimulating, refreshing, educational and fun. It is also boring, nerve-wracking, frustrating, strength-sapping and a drag. I have experienced all the above — sometimes on the same trip.

In these wanderings with the Wolverines I have pretty well touched all of the corners of the country. Providence to Atlanta to San Diego to Seattle. Plus the obligatory Midwest stopovers in the Big Ten. Not to forget Denton, Texas or Pullman, Washington or Moscow, Idaho or Tuscaloosa, Alabama. Yes, none of these places have the likes of the Metropolitan Museum of Art or the Washington Monument or Waikiki but they do have one thing in common — people. The Las Vegas taxi driver who explained that he gave up running a drugstore in Illinois because it was too serene. The waitress in Minneapolis who revealed that Florida simply had too much good weather for her tastes. The discovery that a Greenwich Village espresso shop owner grew up 12 miles from your hometown.

61

Since most motel rooms are hewn from the same log—
one TV, one bed, two chairs, one table, one picture (early
Sears & Roebuck)—I learned early in my career that listening to people in a city was a whole lot better than listening to Archie Bunker. And what an education it has been!
Almost as much of an education as learning how quix-
otic the nation's weather and airlines can be. The greatest
challenges of my job haven't been before the microphone,
they have been before the ticket counters.

A tipoff to my future road life with the Wolverines came
on the first trip I had with the basketball squad. It was
January, 1963 and the team had opened with victories
over Northwestern and Iowa. That meant they were going to move into Columbus with a chance to accomplish
something no Michigan team had done in 23 years, open
the Big Ten season with three straight wins. So it was
with a high level of anticipation that I showed up at Willow Run airport to meet the team for the charter flight
to Ohio.

Coach Dave Strack had told me to be there at noon
for the 12:30 flight. By 12:15 I was still the only member
of the traveling party in the airport lobby and needless
to say a bit on the edgy side. When 12:30 came and still
no basketball team I decided I had misunderstood Strack
and the team was already gone. (Years later that actually
happened when Dave forgot to mention the team was flying out of Metro airport rather than Willow Run.) Just
about the time I had given up, the group came bursting
through the lobby led by the coach himself.

"Glad to see you, coach," I said as I grabbed my gear,
"I thought I'd been stood up."

He stared blankly at me, muttered something and went
up to the counter to check on the flight. Within minutes
he was back announcing to the squad that the Colum-

bus airport was closed because of weather and we probably would have to take a bus. The only problem was that the ordering and delivering of a Greyhound takes about three hours so it was late afternoon before we actually started to roll south. A fitting start to more than two decades of travel with the Wolverines.

Not all of my reversals on the road have been caused by outside elements. More than one was my own fault.

The 1965-66 season was Cazzie Russell's final year and the club had opened with an 8-1 record in the Big Ten. This was the team that defeated Wisconsin at Yost, 120-102, in a run-and-shoot NBA affair. Most of the fans wandered out of the Fieldhouse thinking it would be a long time before they would see anything like that again. Not quite. The next Saturday, Cazzie and company rolled up a 128-94 victory over Purdue. That was the only team in Michigan history to average better than 91 points a game. Seven times that season they were over the 100-point mark.

So we all were primed for the upcoming affair with the Hawkeyes in Iowa. A 9-1 record would put Michigan in the driver's seat—a 14-game conference schedule was in effect at the time. The team had left Wednesday for the Thursday night encounter but since the charter was full I was flying commercially. My flight was scheduled to arrive in Iowa at 2:00 P.M. on Thursday since I was unable to leave on Wednesday as was my normal practice. The customary route to Iowa City requires a flight to Chicago with a change to Cedar Rapids. From there you are on your own to find the needed transportation for the 25-mile journey to the home of the University of Iowa. It's not a taxing trip and shouldn't be a difficult one to arrange.

My flight to Chicago's O'Hare was on time and left

me with roughly an hour and a half before the connecting flight to Cedar Rapids. After finding the gate number
listed on the TV monitor, I went to the appropriate waiting area and quickly became engrossed in a book. I only
vaguely heard a call for boarding and was among the final
passengers to board. Handing my ticket to the stewardess,
I moved back to my seat and got back into my book. The
doors slammed shut and we were off—not only on time
but 10 minutes early.

Shortly after takeoff, the pilot came on with his customary welcome.

"Good afternoon. This is your pilot speaking. We are
now cruising at an altitude of 37,000 feet enroute to our
destination which will take us over the Quad Cities, Clinton, Cedar Rapids and Des Moines. Perhaps you will be
able to see a bit of the serious flooding the state of Iowa
is experiencing. We hope you enjoy your flight today and
welcome to the friendly skies of United."

I stared at the cockpit. Perhaps I had misunderstood
but I was certain he had said " . . . flying *over* Cedar
Rapids . . . " Now if this plane was goint to *take* me to
Cedar Rapids, wasn't it necessary to land rather than *fly
over* it?

I motioned to the stewardess.

"Excuse me, but did the captain say we're going to fly
over Cedar Rapids?"

"Yes, I think he did," was her reply. "Why, was there
something you wanted to see down there?"

"Yeah," I answered, starting to catch the significance
of the pilot's words, "I was hoping to see the terminal.
Where is this flight going?"

"Omaha. Where are you supposed to be going?"

"Cedar Rapids."

"Oh, no. Let me see your ticket, that's impossible."

She took the ticket stub to the chief stewardess at the front of the plane.

Moments later she returned with the same puzzled look on her face.

"We can't figure out what happened but they apparently switched gates and you didn't notice the new sign at the counter. But I'll tell you what. I have to work a flight that gets back to Cedar Rapids at 7:00. Stay with me and I'll get you on board."

That meant I'd be getting to the fieldhouse about five minutes before tipoff if my figuring was correct. I calculated that if the flight was supposed to arrive in Cedar Rapids at 7:00 it would be probably be closer to 7:15 with another 40 minutes by taxi to Iowa City. But I had no other options.

True to her word she got me on board the return flight to Cedar Rapids which amazingly landed only five minutes late. I raced outside the terminal, where by the grace of God a taxi was waiting.

"Iowa Fieldhouse!" I shouted to the driver. "And I've got 35 minutes before I'm supposed to be broadcasting a basketball game."

"Gee, I don't know. That's kind of pushing it."

"I've got 30 bucks that says you can do it."

There now is a beautiful, divided highway connecting Cedar Rapids and Iowa City. But in 1966 there was only a two-lane road over rolling hills sprinkled with No Passing signs. A road strictly for leisurely Sunday afternoons. Only two things weighed in my favor, the weather was cold but dry so the pavement was in good shape and most of the Iowa farmers were much more punctual about attending basketball games than I was so there was little congestion. Oh yes, there was a third factor, my chauffeur. Whether the challenge of the hunt or the 30 dollars was the inspiration, he drove the race of his life.

As we screeched up to the steps of the arena, I slapped the money in his hand and raced inside. Luckily, in those days we were still hiring outside engineers who supplied their own equipment for the broadcast rather than the one-man show now in effect. I streaked up to the balcony radio location and plunked myself down next to my engineer, John Songes, completely out of breath.

"Nice to see you," he grinned. "I thought I was going to be able to do my first play-by-play."

"You still may. It could be days before I get back to normal."

Exactly three minutes later I was on the air.

I have often wondered how I would have explained to my bosses at WUOM that I had missed a game because I overshot the destination by 400 miles.

Incidentally, Michigan didn't fare any better than I did, losing 91-82. But they came back strong to win their next three to wrap up their third straight Big Ten championship.

Guess where the NCAA Mid-East Regional was played that year. Iowa City. I had no trouble finding it.

But I wasn't to blame for the most infamous of trips, the legendary Indiana-Minnesota death march of 1982.

U-M had staggered off to a horrible start, dropping nine of their first 10 games including two in the conference. Thus, a pessimistic squad embarked for a Thursday-Saturday swing to Bloomington and Minneapolis. We landed at the Bloomington airport to a warm January sun with temperatures in the 50s. It was surely the most deceiving beginning to a trip since the Titanic left port.

The Indiana hospitality ended the next night as the Hoosiers raced to an 81-51 victory—the Wolverines' eighth consecutive loss.

The next day dawned bright and warm. Most of us were sitting in the sun waiting to board the bus when assistant coach Buddy Van De Wege joined the group. Among Buddy's other duties that year was transportation coordinator. It was a role I'm sure he could have done without that year.

"I just got through talking with our flight crew. They told me that the Minneapolis airport is closed because of high winds and blowing snow," he announced.

"Damn," Bill Frieder said. "Well, let's go out to the airport and meet our crew, maybe we can find out what's going on."

"Ah, wait a minute," Buddy said. "Our crew is still in Cleveland waiting for the weather to clear."

"Oh, for God's sake," Bill exploded, "how in hell are they going to get us to Minneapolis if they're in Cleveland and we're in Indiana?"

Buddy went off to try again and the rest of us got aboard the bus that would take us to the airport. Once we were on the bus, Frieder showed up with two announcements.

"Men, the airport in Minneapolis is still closed and our plane still isn't on the way. And I just talked with our athletic department and they said Bo is going to hold a press conference about going to Texas A&M."

Bo? Texas A&M? What what this all about?

"Apparently they're waving some big money at him," Bill said.

We pulled up to the Bloomington airport with its extremely tiny lounge. Frieder immediately jumped out to get the latest news on the weather and Bo.

Meanwhile, inside the bus, the conjecture over Bo went on.

"How much money are they talking?"

"Would he really leave Michigan for Texas?"

"Why would he call a press conference if he wasn't going?"

Eventually Frieder returned with an update.

"Well, the plane still hasn't left but they're promising they'll get going in a few minutes. So we might as well wait inside."

So we filed inside the pocket-size waiting room where we sat and munched and drank and paced and talked but mostly listened to Buddy's latest bulletins on the flight crew.

"I just talked to their dispatcher and he informed us that the plane left minutes ago."

Cheers.

Fifteen minutes pass. Buddy is back.

"Frieder just called Cleveland and they told him they can still see the plane on the ground."

Moans and groans.

Meanwhile the Schembechler situation was also getting its share of attention. One member of the media announced, "Bo is definitely going and will make the announcement in a half-hour."

Frieder was dubious.

"He might go," began Bill, "but I dunno, that's not like Bo if it's just for money."

It was now two and a half hours after we had arrived at the airport.

Finally the long-awaited charter arrived with Frieder quickly making it clear to the crew he wasn't exactly pleased over the events of the day.

After accompanying the crew to the flight operations office, Bill came back with the word.

"Minneapolis is still closed so we're going to Madison, Wisconsin."

"That's better anyway," cracked George Pomey. "They'll be easier to beat than Minnesota."

"We'll figure out later what we're going to do tonight," continued Bill. "If we can go on to Minneapolis we will, if we can't we'll stay in Madison and try to get the rest of the way Saturday."

It wasn't long after our takeoff that the brilliant sunshine gave way to a thick, gray, ugly-looking floorboard of clouds. By the time we reached Madison, our visions of an early spring had long disappeared.

A blast of Arctic air hit us as we struggled against the icy winds into the Madison terminal. While Buddy tried to find an arena for practice in case our stay was an extended one, the rest of us discovered a badly needed watering hole. Within an hour we were given the welcome news that we could get to Minneapolis after all and it was back into our icy seats aboard the charter.

As we circled the Minneapolis airport, our pilot announced that the temperature was now 15 degrees below zero with a wind chill index roughly four times that. But after seven hours of riding, waiting and flying, we willingly traded the 65-degree drop in temperature for the opportunity to complete the trip in one day.

The team departed directly for Williams Arena and a late practice session. This didn't appeal to fellow broadcaster Paul Keels and me so we opted to mush into the terminal and take our chances with a cab. By the time we made it inside we looked like survivors of Scott's assault on the South Pole. Our directions to the cab dispatcher were a bit vague since neither Paul or I knew exactly where we were and it was almost an hour before the driver found us. By the time we reached our hotel rooms, the late news was just beginning. The lead story that night was the miserable weather the Twin Cities were experiencing.

"Friend," I told the newscaster, "you don't know the half of it."

As it turned out, neither did I.

Clear skies greeted us on Saturday but the sun was an imposter with temperatures still well below zero.

Our driver was a garrulous fellow who helped load the equipment and baggage underneath. Pulling up as close to the Arena's front doors as possible he again helped to unload our gear.

"Hey, this guy's all right," I thought.

"Is it okay if we leave our personal baggage on the bus during the game?" asked Buddy.

"No problem," answered the driver. "Everything will be locked up tight."

Despite the previous day's tribulations, the team didn't play that badly as they bowed, 67-58. But it was the ninth loss in a row so it was a rather down-in-the-mouth group that ressembled in the arena lobby for the trip to the airport. Looking out to the frozen parking area we all were quickly struck by the same thought—Where was the bus?

"Buddy," said Bill, "where in hell's the bus?"

"I don't know, coach."

"Well, take a look, we gotta get moving."

Buddy bundled up as best he could against the numbing cold and made a quick exit. Ten minutes later he was back.

"I've been all around the building, Bill, and I don't see anything of our bus."

"Dammit," said Bill, "all he had to do was wait for us here. What's so hard about that?"

"I'll give the bus company a call," said Buddy, flapping his arms trying to restore some circulation.

Meanwhile the rest of the group offered some feeble attempts at humor.

"That driver did look a bit like Bobby Knight," said one member.

"Maybe it was highjacked to Miami," suggested another. Soon Buddy was back.

"The bus company doesn't know any more than we do. They can't raise him on the radio and haven't any idea why he isn't here."

At that point, Frieder delivered a line of expletives that would have impressed a muleskinner. Some of us were a little more worried about what might happen to the driver if he did show up rather than if he didn't.

A half-hour later it was apparent our driver was long gone and the bus company had agreed to find a replacement. By the time he had arrived it was roughly two hours after the end of the game. There was still the problem of our personal baggage which disappeared with the lost bus. It was decided to leave Buddy in Minneapolis until the other bus could be found (something many of us were highly doubtful of). He then would return to Ann Arbor with the missing pieces.

After cramming ourselves into our much smaller substitute bus we had journeyed about two miles up the freeway when trainer Danny Campbell cried out, "Hey, look, there's a bus parked on the shoulder up there."

Figuring the coincidence factor was rather strong, our driver pulled over and manager Greg Ruggles struggled up the bank to investigate. A quick peek inside verified that indeed the lost had been found. A long, icy, baggage brigade was then formed and shortly everything had been transferred. Since our new bus had no lower compartment we were forced to wedge in all around the luggage but at least we had regained what many of us had given up for irretrievably lost. Retracing our route, we returned to the Arena where we picked up a surprised Buddy Van De Wege and finally left for the airport.

By the time we had loaded the aircraft and strapped ourselves in our seats, three hours had elapsed from the time we assembled in the Arena. While congratulating ourselves on finally arriving, we were interrupted by a voice from the cockpit.

"Good evening. We're all set to go up here but we have a slight problem. It seems there is a 747 parked in our way which is stuck on the ice. Until he gets out of our way we aren't going anywhere."

I can't tell you much about what it takes to free a 747 from an ice floe except that it takes a considerable amount of time. With the temperatures diving past 20-below our heating system was laboring to keep it in the 50-degree range in the cabin. Eventually however we were shaken by a sudden blast of turbulence that signalled the huge jet had worked itself free.

We watched our oversized nemesis move out of the area and were gratified to hear our own propellers turning immediately. Turning—but not firing. Back came the voice from the front.

"Well, I'm afraid we have some more problems."

The long wait had drained the internal power for starting the engines. Thus an outside power unit would have to be found. By the time it was located, we were convinced our lost bus driver was at the controls. Eventually though, the power generator was wheeled up, plugged in, and shortly we heard the beautiful sound of two engines roaring at full speed.

A little after takeoff, Frieder stood at the front of the plane, staring out into the darkness.

"You know, the only thing left for us is to crash."

"Don't say that, Bill!" chastised his wife, Jan.

To all within earshot it seemed like a perfectly reasonable speculation.

Sometimes the trip is fine—it's the destination that creates the problem. For example, the Rose Bowl visit in 1978. Michigan had sailed through the season with only the 16-0 upset at the hands of Minnesota marring its record. Its opponent, Washington, had slid into the Pac 10 title at the last moment and were 13-point underdogs.

We had decided to shift our motel headquarters from the previous year because of greatly increased rates. My intrepid travel agent, Ardi Everhard, informed me not to worry—she had discovered a quaint little place that would be delighted to house our crew for a week. Ardi is easily one of the most important persons in my life. Without her adept schedule juggling, my years of globetrotting would have been complete chaos. When she said she had a place, that was it. I never hesitated for a minute.

Let's call Ardi's "find," the Cactus Arms Motel. When we arrived, we saw at once that it didn't quite fit Ardi's description. The sign spanning the entrance was ready to fall down—one end was considerably lower than the other. Once inside we noticed a number of unescorted ladies milling about. Oh well, we thought, it was Rose Bowl week and maybe the motel was the site of a major reunion of bowl queens.

A young desk clerk got us registered, though he seemed

a bit confused over my color man Tom Slade's arrival with his wife, Pam, while the other four in our party were traveling solo.

As we made our way to our rooms, we gave the place a closer inspection. There was a nice pool and what seemed to be the largest and most attractive crew of maids we had ever seen.

My room seemed pretty standard but I had taken only a few steps when I heard something crunch underfoot. It was a decidedly full-grown insect. I gingerly nudged it under my bed while looking around for others. Finding none I decided, somewhat uncomfortably, to unpack. When I went back out onto the landing, I encountered an obviously agitated Tom and Pam Slade.

"We have a crack in our wall the size of the San Andreas fault," she said.

"And there must be fifty cockroaches making their home in it," added Tom. "We're going down to the office and get moved to a decent room."

The desk clerk quickly arranged for another room. "But," he insisted, "we never have had any problem with cockroaches," he sniffed.

"I can believe that," said Pam. "It looks like you go out of your way to keep them happy."

Following a trip to the stadium to check on our broadcast location we retired to our rooms anticipating a good night's sleep. After a quick insect check I dropped off immediately. But it was only a matter of minutes before I was awakened by a commotion outside my room. I pushed aside the curtains to see a mob of people wearing Washington Huskie caps, shirts or jackets. All had jugs, mugs, or glasses and were shouting at the top of their voices something like,

"GO, HUSHKY, GO MUSHKY, WELUVYA, BEAT-MICHIGAN"

And in the nearby parking lot, another group was making laps with their purple and white festooned campers, trucks, jeeps, and cars.

A half-hour later, the celebration had, if anything, increased in size and gained in volume.

"That's it," I muttered. "I'm dialing the front office to get somebody to put down this riot."

But the desk clerk had either retired for the night, given up or was part of the celebration—no one would pick up the phone. Finally about three o'clock the revelry ceased; peace returned to Cactus Arms.

"Well, at least they'll be out of circulation for a while," I thought, figuring I could sleep until late morning. But with the first rays of sun, the next shift took over outside. And they began the same incoherent chants. Giving up, I decided the Rose Bowl press headquarters would be much more relaxing and got out of bed. A bleary-eyed Tom Slade was waiting downstairs for me.

"You look like you got as much sleep as I did," he said, as we climbed into the car.

"I thought World War III had broken out," I replied.

"The thing that worries me is that there are still two days before the game. Think they'll make it?"

"I hope not," I answered as we pulled out of the driveway narrowly missing a whooping Huskie.

They not only didn't fold, they got stronger as the Monday kickoff approached. So we simply stayed as far away from the Cactus Arms as possible until exhaustion set in and we could be assured of a few winks between the night and day shifts. We hoped the Michigan football team was getting more rest than we were.

Game day dawned cloudy and cool but without the rain that recently had plagued the area. By the time we had completed our pre-game setup, the sun broke through and a promising day looked in store. We were sharing the platform atop the stadium roof with an NBC cameraman but it was spacious and could easily fit in our four-man crew. The only problem was that there was no counter space which meant we had to hold everything on our laps—spot charts, stat sheets, press guides, even our microphones. But we were there. We were finally on the air.

The first minutes of action belonged solely to Michigan. Pushing the ball to the Washington 38, the Wolverines stalled and in came John Anderson to punt. Anderson, a devastating linebacker, rivaled O'Donell in both size and ability to pin the opposition with coffin corner kicks.

Sure enough, John's punt sailed out inside the 10-yard line and the Wolverine defense prepared to go to work. But instead of spotting the ball where the ball went out of bounds, the referee trotted back upfield and placed it at the spot here Anderson had punted. He then signalled first down for Washington at the 49 much to the befuddlement of all.

Then it dawned on us: in kneeling for a low pass from center, Anderson had fielded the ball while his knee was apparently touching the ground. Thus the ball was dead at that spot. I had never seen it called before (nor have I since).

Out came the Huskies offense. They were led by a quarterback named Warren Moon. The senior signal caller had turned in an up-and down year in leading the Huskies to their 7-4 mark. At times he had looked brilliant, at times he was just another erratic thrower. His first play was a bomb intended for Spider Gaines who just missed catching up to it at the Michigan 10. But it put the Wolverine defense on alert—it could expect the unexpected out of Washington and Mr. Moon.

With a third and six, Moon rolled out to his left and while on the run, flicked a spot pass to running back Joe Steele for a first down. Six plays later the Huskies were at the two. Moon again rolled left, but this time he tucked the ball away and shot into the end zone. The 13-point underdogs were up 7-0.

Leach, Edwards, and Davis took turns driving U-M to the Washington 49 on the ensuing series but on third and eight, Leach was tossed for an 11-yard loss. This time Anderson kept his knee off the ground but after a quarter the Wolverines had nothing to show for 15 minutes of action.

Midway through the second quarter, Moon connected on a first-down strike to Gaines and before Michigan could corral Spider he was at the Michigan 17—a 62-yard gain for the Huskies. The defense rose up to stifle Washington on three subsequent downs and they settled for a field goal to put them up, 10-0.

Moments later, Washington got the ball back on downs at their 40. Coach Don James hauled out the ancient end-around play and, at the U-M 31, Moon handed off to Gaines who scooted into the end zone. But a Husky clip nullified it and the ball was placed at the 35. Five plays later, an undaunted Moon slid over to make it a 17-0 game.

Still, the Michigan miseries wouldn't end. After getting to the Washington 31, Leach turned to hand off to Davis and lost control of the ball. Washington's huge defensive tackle Dave Browning wasted little time in jumping on it and with just a minute and a half remaining in the half, they were in business again. This time, however, three Moon passes missed and in came Carl Wilson to punt. At least so we all thought. Instead, he stepped up and fired a perfect pass to tight end Joe Stevens who legged it up to the U-M 20. Across the field I could see our Cactus Arms neighbors go into complete pandemonium. Along with them, we realized we weren't seeing a possible upset but a rout of a team that had been rated number one in mid-season. Moon filled the air with footballs as the clock ran down but his third toss ended up in the arms of defensive back Dwight Hicks. It hardly affected the enthusiasm of the Huskies, however, as they trooped off the field with a 17-0 lead.

As the second half started, Slade suggested that perhaps after having had a half to study Moon, Michigan's defense might have decided that the traditional methods weren't going to work. And on the first series for Washington, it appeared that Bill McCartney's defensive troops might have come up with the proper adjustments. A Ron Simpkins sack pushed Washington back to its 26. Moon tried to find Gaines on third and long but this time Mike Jolly beat him to the ball and returned the interception 25 yards to the Huskie 11. Finally the Michigan fans had a chance to dust off some "GO BLUE" chants for the first time on the day.

On first down, Davis went two. On second, Davis gained four. On third, Leach picked up two. On fourth, Roosevelt Smith gained zero. That's four downs and eight yards, about two shy of the first down and three short of the end zone. Later Bo would come in for some heavy fire for electing to go up the middle on four straight plays.

So the golden opportunity vanished. Two plays later, Washington had moved to the nine and all 105,312 spectators were convinced that with a third and four Moon would uncork one from his end zone. Instead he handed off to Steele who scampered for 13 yards. Moon, Steele, and Gipson then took turns carrying the ball until 10 plays later the Huskies were at the Michigan 28. On first down, Moon found the ever-faithful Gaines in the end zone to climax a 97-yard drive—Washington 24, Michigan 0.

As the Wolverine offense took the field we tried to imagine what misfortune could possibly befall them next. What fell instead was a Rose Bowl record. On the second play of the series, Leach dropped back to his 26 and hummed a bullet to Curt Stephenson at the Michigan 45. Curt shot down the far sidelines for a 76-yard touchdown play, the longest ever at the Rose Bowl and the second longest at the time in Michigan history.

So Michigan was on the board although down 24-7. But there still was 4:30 of the third quarter and all of the fourth period to go. First, however, they had to do something about the Washington offense. Unfortunately by the time the Michigan defense got on the field the ball was already at the U-M 44 as Roy Stevens galloped 53 yards up the middle on the kick-off return. Again sticking mainly with the rush, Washington moved close enough for Steve Robbins to kick a 27-yard field goal to bump the score to 27-7.

Then, early in the fourth quarter, an amazing transformation took place. The Michigan team we had watched all season long finally showed up.

Taking the ball at their 22, Michigan thundered up the field. Alternating the pass and run, Leach found four different targets. An 11-yarder to Davis made it first and goal at the two. From there Davis blasted over to make it 27-14 with just a minute and a half gone in the quarter.

Neither team could sustain a march and with 6:19 on the clock, the Wolverines stopped the Huskies again and took over at their 30. Again, passing and running brilliantly, Leach led U-M to the Huskie 32. There, on second and nine, he retreated to throw and saw freshman tailback Stanley Edwards standing all alone in the middle. Edwards had been a last-minute starter due to an ankle injury suffered by Harlan Huckleby. Grabbing the ball at the 20, Edwards raced in untouched for the touchdown. But on the extra point attempt Stephenson had trouble with the snap and failed to get a good placement. Gregg Wilner's kick sailed wide and it was 27-20.

Washington failed to get a first down for the third straight time and with 2:46 left, Michigan was in striking distance at their 42.

A 17-yard completion to Ralph Clayton; an eight-yard scramble by Leach; and an 11-yard burst by Edwards brought the ball to the Huskie eight for a first and goal with almost two minutes left. The Wolverines, treated like a demo squad for three quarters, somehow had salvaged a shot at winning.

Again Leach drifted back to pass and again he spotted Edwards up the middle at the three. The ball hit Stanley on the shoulder pad, bounced up, and resettled there. While he frantically tried to recapture it, he disappeared in a swarm of Huskies. Moments later, linebacker Michael Jackson emerged from the pileup waving the elusive pigskin. Replays showed Jackson grabbing the ball from Edwards' shoulder just before Stanley hit the ground.

So, Washington had the ball at the three with 1:21 remaining. Playing it conservatively, they ran the ball three times, forcing Michigan to use their timeouts. After a punt to Michigan at midfield, there remained 45 seconds. Considering the wackiness of this game, no one was ruling out a miracle. But a Leach aerial intended for Clayton was snared by cornerback Nesby Glasgow and the weirdest of Michigan bowl games was history.

While we packed our equipment, we watched the wild celebration on the field by the Huskie fans. Deciding our motel was not the place to be, we treated ourselves to a lengthy dinner before returning to our home away from home. We drove up to the now-familiar lopsided sign of the Cactus Arms, and realized the first challenge would be just to get into the parking area where cars, campers, and trucks had been abandoned. There appeared to be nobody around.

"Well, somebody had to drive these here," our engineer John Hendricks said, nodding toward the crazy-quilt mass of vehicles.

We started walking to the stairs at the corner of the courtyard. Then, through the open drapes we could see purple and white clad bodies draped over beds, chairs and on the floor. None showed the slightest sign of life. More of the same on the second floor. More exhausted bodies, more silence.

As I flopped down on my bed, I wondered how long the peace would last. It seemed like only moments later that I was awakened by a pounding at the door.

"They're at it again," I thought as I staggered to the door. Standing there in the blinding morning sun was Slade.

"Hey, I thought we were going to meet for breakfast at nine?"

"You mean we made it through the night without our friends waking us up?"

After getting dressed, we headed toward the corner coffee shop. The drapes were still open in most rooms. And the same spent Huskie bodies were still in the same poses.

"Do you think we should notify the next of kin?" I asked.

"Let's wait until we check out," said Slade.

As we stepped into the office to settle up our bill, we wondered if we should pay for only one night since that was all the rest we had gotten.

Instead, the Cactus Arms had another surprise.

"Wait a minute," Slade said, "this is for two rooms!"

"Yes, that's correct," the ever-smiling clerk said. "You are registered for 213 and 218."

"But I moved out of one and into the other."

"Well, it wasn't cancelled on our sheet, so we'll have to charge you because we couldn't release it for another guest."

"Listen, you clown, you couldn't pay someone to live in that cockroach-infested hole. I'm paying for one room and that's all."

"Well, I'll have to check with our manager."

The debate went on until, sensing he was outnumbered, the clerk relented.

"Have a good day," he called after us as we headed out to our car. "And come back and see us."

Over the years, on our trips to Pasadena, we always drive past our favorite motel. Each year the sign tilts a bit more. And it's still full of campers and vans. And the pool is surrounded by stunning young women. And we always wondered, have those purple and white Huskie bodies moved yet? We don't stop. But as we drive by, we do slow down.

For announcers and fans, a bad road trip is just a disappointing experience. But for a team, a trip can throw an entire season out of kilter. Case in point: Bill Frieder's first year at the helm.

The 1980-81 basketball edition was a good if not great squad. Mike McGee, ending his record setting four years, was surrounded by steady Paul Heuerman and Thad Garner, the erratic but exciting Johnny Johnson, and the Bodnar twins. It was a team that started with a rush, winning its first nine games including road meetings with Kansas and Dayton. A spot in the top 10 was the result.

Because of TV commitments, the Big Ten scheudule had Michigan opening on a Monday night in Purdue — Michigan would make three one-game conference trips on the season. It didn't seem significant at the time.

The Wolverines played well but finally bowed, 81-74, to the Boilermakers who were also under a new coach, Gene Keady. It was a loss but certainly not a demoralizing one as the Wolverines proved by reeling off seven victories in their next nine games. Included in that string were double-overtime thrillers against Minnesota and Illinois; a 55-52 overtime classic against the eventual Big Ten champion Indiana Hoosiers; another overtime scrambler over Michigan State, 79-77, and a road sweep of Northwestern and Wisconsin.

So at 7-3 Frieder felt naturally enough that his club was in contention for a high Big Ten finish. He knew that a 4-4 split over the next eight games would leave them short of the title, but it would give them a 20-7 mark overall. And that normally merits an NCAA tournament nod.

Then, the next Thursday, Ohio State moved into town. The Buckeyes had been pushed to the limit to defeat Michigan in Columbus earlier in the season, 69-63, so U-M fans figured the tables could be turned in Ann Ar-

bor. But it wasn't to be as the Bucks mauled the Blue,
105-37. A four point loss to Michigan State at East Lansing followed, leaving the Wolverines still four wins shy
of the magic 20 mark with road trips upcoming to Illinois,
Iowa and Indiana. The Illinois jaunt was a single-game
trip followed by a home contest with Northwestern. Michigan definitely needed a sweep to offset the expected pair
of losses in Iowa City and Bloomington.

A warm front had brought some unusually high mid-
February temperatures and also some impenetrable fog.
Michigan had planned to depart on their normal Wednesday afternoon charter for Champaign and return immediately following the game. But immense layers of mist
wiped out any chances the team had of getting an early
start southward. Frieder was thus left with the choice of
a seven-hour bus trip or postponing the charter for a day
and taking his chances on Thursday. He chose the latter—
no one wanted to spend seven hours on a Greyhound.

Thursday proved to be a carbon copy of Wednesday.
Dense fog, constant drizzle and unseasonably warm. As
I inched my way to Crisler Arena that morning I had the
uncomfortable thought that the long bus tour was still
in the offing.

Arriving at the arena, we learned the expected from
Frieder—all local airports were closed and our flight crew
was still at their base in Cleveland. However, the bad
weather appeared to be confined to a narrow band, with
Ann Arbor in the middle. But it meant that if we could
find a new point of departure we might still be spared
the tiring bus trip. The key was to find a new embarka-
tion point. After mulling over the possibilities for an hour
we were told that sitting in brilliant sunshine with a perfectly serviceable airport for our charter was Lansing,

Michigan. This might have been the first time that city would be looked to for help by a U-M athletic team. In another hour we were in a University bus and on our way. Sure enough, about 20 minutes out of Ann Arbor, the fog had dissipated and we were under blue skies. The aircraft was there to meet us when we pulled into the airport and little time was lost in loading and leaving. Still, it would be well into the afternoon before we arrived in Champaign which meant not much time for relaxation prior to the game.

The flight path took us to the west of Ann Arbor but we could see the heavy concentration of fog to the east as we made our way across northern Indiana. It was about that time that our pilot greeted us over the intercom.

"We have been advised that some heavy thunderstorms are now expected in the Champaign area. It would probably be a good idea to stay in your seats and keep buckled up as we get closer."

Our plane bounced along above the flatlands of Illinois with ominous gray clouds looming larger and larger. But soon we started to square up with the runway and head down.

As we started our descent, back came the thundershowers. The plane was buffeted about like a bingo number in the popper.

After a few minutes that seemed like hours of being slammed by the turbulence, the landing gear smacked onto the ground and the plane finally shuddered to a stop at the terminal. Instead of the raucous chatter that usually greeted a landing there was complete silence. Shakily, the players gathered up their bags and filed onto the bus taking us to the motel.

We wouldn't be staying overnight, but Frieder had arranged for the players to check into rooms for a couple of hours rest prior to the game. The rest of us headed to the local tavern to solder some badly frayed nerve endings. For most of the players the attempt at relaxing proved fruitless. Heuerman later said most of the time was spent staring at the ceiling while replaying the landing in Champaign. In any case it was a brief and unsatisfying respite before heading for Assembly Hall.

A sellout crowd of 16,492 had turned out to watch the battle between two teams sporting the same records in conference and overall play—9-3 and 16-5 respectively. Despite the fatigue and jangling nerves, Michigan played a steady first half, led by the red-hot McGee who poured in 16 points to push Michigan to a 33-29 halftime lead. This quickly increased to six as Johnson drilled in one of his picturesque jumpers to open the second half. But that only spurred on the Illini who raced to a five-point lead with eight minutes gone in the half. The Wolverines refused to fold.

Calling on some untapped reserves, U-M staged their own comeback. McGee's only two field goals of the second half and three straight from the free throw line from Mike and Johnson put the Wolverines up by five with just two and a half minutes remaining. Two highly questionable foul calls on Garner and Marty Bodner gave the Illini a pair of one-and-one opportunities. Mark Smith and Perry Smith converted each and Michigan's lead was down to one with a minute and a half to go.

After a timeout, Michigan came up the court looking to protect the ball but Johnson was grabbed by Range and calmly stepped to the line to knock down both. 62-59, Michigan. But Range's 20-footer found the mark and when Derek Harper's steal turned into a layup for James

Griffin, Illinois led by one. A shot by McGee missed and when Craig Tucker was fouled by Johnson you could sense the chill of defeat. Tucker made both free throws and with only 30 seconds left Michigan trailed by three.

But the fight wasn't gone. McGee collided with Derek Holcomb and although the crowd raised the arena roof, Holcomb was tagged with the foul and if Mike could convert Michigan was still alive. He did.

Still down by a point with time running out, the Wolverines were forced to foul. This time it was Range hammered by Heuerman. With the game on the line, the defensive specialist hit on both tosses to push the margin to three with 24 seconds on the clock. The dead-tired Wolverines couldn't find the mark as McGee missed an 18-footer and when Heuerman missed on the tip it was all over. ILLINOIS 67, MICHIGAN 64.

It was a thoroughly downhearted and slow-moving group of Wolverines that fell into their seats on the bus to await the return journey. However, Bill Frieder had yet to bounce into his reserved front seat. Finally he appeared. But he had some disquieting news.

"Well, the airport is still closed at Willow Run so we can't go back there tonight. The problem is they're afraid this airport is going to be shut down tomorrow too and we might not get out if we stay here tonight. So we've got a choice of taking a chance here or trying to get someplace tonight where we can get out tomorrow. What do you think?"

We talked it over, then agreed with Bill that yet another city should be added to our itinerary for this trip. At the airport we found our charter crew huddled with flight officials about our alternate destination. They soon settled on Cleveland. Since this also happened to be the home base of the crew we were a bit suspicious. But Cleveland did made sense—it was the closest airfield to Detroit not closed by the weather.

The proper flight plan was filed and within a half-hour we were again on our way. By the time we checked into the motel at Hopkins Airport it was 1:30 A.M. Also, we had no luggage since we had all planned to be back in our beds that night.

It was a motley, unshaven, and wrinkled group of players, coaches, fans, and media people which reassembled in the motel lobby the next morning. It was also a rather wary crew because the ever-present fog was back. It wasn't long before we got the expected news.

"The airport's closed here," Bill gloomily announced. "They have no idea when it's going to open up."

"What about Willow Run?"

"That's open," Bill answered. "And so's Champaign. If we hadn't listened to that damned weatherman we could have stayed there and flown back an hour ago. We're trying to charter a bus. That looks like the only way we're going to get home."

Three hours later, Frieder came over to where I was sitting and asked, "Hey, would you emcee our basketball banquet this year? It's going to be the first Monday after the end of the season."

"Sure," I said, "but will we get back in time for it?"

Finally the charter bus arrived and we spent another three hours bouncing back to Ann Arbor.

Seeing some of the paying passengers looking a bit peaked, Bill announced, "Look at it this way. Where else could you get a bus ride to Lansing, a flight to Champaign, a flight to Cleveland, and another bus ride to Ann Arbor for this low price?"

It was late afternoon when we pulled up to Crisler

Arena. Had things gone as planned the team would have held their normal Friday's practice earlier that day and been showering at the time we arrived. Sensing his squad was dragging badly, Frieder elected to hold a short and easy session and dismissed the team quickly. The Wolverines had earlier posted an easy 15-point win at Evanston over Northwestern and so the following day when game time rolled around, most of us were convinced that the three-game losing streak would be snapped.

However, it was apparent as soon as the opening tip was made that this Michigan team had not yet recovered from Champaign. Shots careened off the backboard, passes sailed well wide of the mark, and the defense was apparently still on the road somewhere. In the game's first two and a half-minutes, Northwestern had opened up a stunning 13-0 lead.

McGee picked up three fouls in the first six minutes while the team itself went over the limit just two minutes later. Frieder went to the bench for a completely new five. They did briefly get the margin down to five but it was a short-lived rally and by halftime the Wildcats were up by 16. As the team left the floor, the crowd of 10,000 wondered what had happened to a team that just two weeks earlier had been flying so high.

To kill any hopes of a quick second-half comeback by Michigan, the Wildcats picked up four points in 30 seconds to open the period. And McGee grabbed his fourth foul. Soon the lead was 20 and the boos cascaded down.

Then, Michigan mounted a slow and painful climb. A flurry of 11 straight points brought them within seven. Northwestern worked it back to 11 but a nine-point streak by U-M made it 66-64 with four minutes left. Northwestern pushed it back to four on a jumper by Michael Jenkins on a play that saw McGee commit his fifth foul.

Jenkins missed his free throw and seconds later M.C. Burton popped home a shot from the corner. Michigan was within two again. One minute later, the classy Thad Garner hooked in a six-footer and after 38 and a half minutes Michigan had finally caught the Wildcats.

The crowd was now in an uproar. Michigan had come from twenty points down to battle their way to a 68-68 deadlock. Could they sustain the effort and steal a game they earlier seemed intent on giving away?

Northwestern killed almost a minute before Jenkins spotted Rod Roberson alone under the basket. Roberson grabbed the pass, hit the layup and the Wildcats led by two. Now 47 seconds were left on the clock. Normally the Wolverines would have looked to set up the marvelous McGee but Mike was sitting on the bench forlornly looking on with his five fouls. So the Wolverines decided to run a play for Johnson to get the shot. The play went as designed but Johnny couldn't get the shot to fall. When the rebound came out to Roberson, Johnson immediately fouled him in desperation. That was it. Roberson connected on two free throws and Northwestern held on for a 74-70 victory, one of only three conference wins for them that season.

So the losing string was stretched to four. It would grow to six the next weekend with back-to-back road losses at Iowa and Indiana.

Thus ended the possibilities of an NCAA bid and a respectable finish in the Big Ten. But I've often wondered if things would have been different had the day dawned bright and clear back on that Wednesday in February.

Lest I leave the impression that trips can only lead to trouble let me point out that some journeys have been very pleasant and enjoyable. There was the beautiful winding drive from Spokane to Pullman, the site of the first round NCAA clash between Michigan and UCLA in 1975. Part of the route hugs the sheer cliffs of the Spokane Valley before it empties into the vast wheat-growing areas of Whitman County. The homes were either perched on the crests of the sharp hills or nestled at the bottom. Nothing in between. Smiling, assistant coach Jim Dutcher turned to Johnny Orr.

"See that house there, John?"

"Yeah," John cautiously replied.

"Well," said Jim, pointing to the top of the steep rise, "Six days ago it was up there."

Pullman, Washington and Moscow, Idaho are situated in what is termed the "banana belt" because of freak atmospheric conditions which bring spring about six weeks earlier to this section than the surrounding areas. Thus from 35-degree temperatures in Spokane we climbed out of our bus into 62 degrees at Moscow where the team was bivouacked. Not one complaint was heard. And the people of Pullman and Washington State University went out of their way to make things first class for the visitors. The game was something else, though — it will undoubtedly go down in Michigan annals as one of the most heartbreaking in history. The sight of C.J. Kupec's shot bouncing off the rim in the final eight seconds of regulation time will never go away. If that shot drops, Michigan pulls off one of its greatest upsets, a victory over the eventual national champion Bruins. But it didn't; the return trip to Spokane, magnificent scenery and all, couldn't erase the hurt.

Or how about the opening game football trip to Chapel Hill, North Carolina in 1965? Cozy Kenan Stadium rests in the midst of towering pines which are beautiful to behold and make the setting one of the prettiest in the nation. Unfortunately for Michigan it also happened to be a day with both the temperature and humidity in the 90s. With no breath of fresh air able to reach the gridiron through the stately firs, the field conditions were close to oven warmth by kickoff time. I started the broadcast in a short-sleeve shirt, trousers, socks, and shoes. By the third quarter our booth felt like an overheated sauna and I was in danger of arrest for indecent exposure. Michigan won the game 31-24 but was drained for weeks to come. Bump later said he learned two important things in Chapel Hill. Don't take your normal lengthy pre-game warmups when your players can hardly breathe and don't play a game in North Carolina in early September.

But my all-time favorite adventure to broadcast a Michigan game was to the Holiday Festival at old Madison Square Garden in 1964. Some people are very successful in disguising the fact they are ever impressed or overwhelmed with anything. I've never had that problem. Of course, when you're my size there is a lot of opportunity to be overwhelmed. So when I learned I would be broadcasting Michigan's basketball action in the oldest tournament in the nation from one of the most fabled sports arenas in history, I was flying.

The team was coming off its sensational win over Wichita State on a last-second jumper by Cazzie Russell that left a packed house at Cobo Arena limp. It also left Michigan in first place in the nation as the Wolverines and Shockers had gone into the game ranked #1 and #2 in the polls. The team was arguably Michigan's greatest. A tremendous gathering of talent that fashioned victories sometimes in almost preposterous ways: The Holiday Festival that year included one of those masterpieces.

We arrived in New York Sunday afternoon with opening action slated for the Wolverines the next evening with Manhattan. After settling into the hotel we pored over the papers which were wild in their praise for Dave Strack's team.

Most of the writers had already conceded the tourney title to Michigan and that didn't sit too well with Strack. For one thing, the eight-team field was made up of some top competition—Syracuse, led by the silky smooth Dave Bing; Cincinnati, an NCAA finalist for three of the last four years; Princeton, with the amazing Bill Bradley, and the hometown Redmen of St. Johns under the legendary Joe Lapchik. Not exactly a collection of creampuffs. Much of the pre-tournament ink dealt with a possible confrontation between Bradley and Russell. This was a distinct possibility since each team needed only a win in its opening game to bring about the meeting.

Assistant coach Jim Skala had managed to get tickets for the New York Knicks game at the Garden that night. I remember the feeling as we made the short five-block walk up Eighth Avenue and spotted the famous old Garden marquee. A small crowd was on hand to watch the Knicks roll over the St. Louis Hawks but I had trouble focusing on the game as I looked around at the yawning three-tiered expanse which had been the scene of so many of boxing's greatest moments. I tried to visualize the floor as it must have looked with the ringside seats and aisles, with spotlights pouring down from above, with a howling crowd awaiting the arrival of Dempsey or Louis.

At halftime I decided to wander upstairs to check out our broadcast location for tomorrow night's game. I started up the first catwalk I spotted, thinking I could take the spiraling circuit up to the second level. But instead, there was no exit to the second concourse, just more of the same walkway leading higher. Finally, I reached an exit. I stared down at the far-away floor from the upper reaches of the Garden. I decided to take advantage of the chance to walk around the perimeter. But before I had taken more than two steps I was intercepted by a beefy usher who insisted that I return to my seat below. Back down the labyrinth I went, feeling like a youngster caught snitching cookies. And I still hadn't discovered the route to the second level. So I resolved to show up a little early the next night.

Michigan's game was the first of the evening double-header — we would open the broadcast at 6:55. At five o'clock sharp I was at the press gate. In fact, I was the *only* person at the press gate — there was not a Garden attendant around. Setting down my briefcase I peered in through the tiny window in the door and could see nothing but the unlit gloom of the interior.

Fifteen minutes passed as I banged on the door with no response. A half-hour. Finally, a lock rattled, and at last a door swung open.

"Hey, you're an early bird," the startled doorkeeper said. He motioned for me to come in.

"I thought maybe I got the wrong place."

"Nope, only one Gahden, kid."

It was a good thing I allowed plenty of time. Even after getting instructions to the mezzanine, I immediately became lost again, twice. But on the third attempt, I saw the sign and entrance to the second level that I had missed before. And sure enough, after following the arrow I found the proper exit — there was the long sought-after area. I quickly found our broadcast location but much to my surprise no engineer. It was now well after six, already late for him not to be there. I called WUOM and was assured arrangements had been made with a New York station to furnish an engineer and equipment. No one knew why he wasn't there. By 6:45 with still no sign of a technician, there was no doubt we were going to have to improvise. All we had was one telephone and one announcer. But that was enough. Our engineering whiz at WUOM, Jim McEachern, jerry-rigged a system so we could broadcast over the phone itself. So, in my long-anticipated debut at Madison Square Garden, I sat there with a telephone in my hand saying, "Good evening everyone . . . "

But once the game was underway I almost forgot that I was speaking into the mouthpiece of a phone rather than my normal headset-mike. In fact I was so immersed in the play that I didn't notice the arrival of the tardy engineer until he set his case down on the counter beside me. I motioned to him to set up the amplifier and mikes while at the same time trying to concentrate on the play-by-play. As soon as a timeout was called, I hooked up my mike to his gear and broadcast the rest of the game in traditional style.

As for the game, it developed into the expected run-away in the second half. Michigan sped away from the outclassed Manhattan team and the stage was set for a semi-final duel with Princeton who had earlier defeated Syracuse behind a 36-point performance from Bradley.

Wednesday night they were literally packed into the Garden for the Michigan-Princeton clash. Spectators stood three and four deep around the upper concourse despite the fact that from many of the upper reaches only a third of the court was visible. I had noticed that in my brief catwalk tour. And WUOM had flown a dependable engineer to town for the remainder of the tourney.

By the time tipoff had rolled around, the highly partisan Princeton crowd was ready for some Wolverine hide. The Tigers didn't disappoint them—Bradley turned out to be all and more than Michigan had feared. He almost singlehandedly pushed the Ivy Leaguers to an 18-point lead midway through the second half. But then a totally exhausted Bradley committed a foolish fifth foul with 4:37 left. He bowed out to a two-minute standing ovation.

His departure didn't seem to make that much difference as with three minutes remaining Michigan still trailed by 13. A minute later it was 10—still a sizeable margin with less than two minutes on the clock. A bucket by Cazzie cut it to eight. Larry Tregoning hit a layup to narrow it to six. John Thompson stole the inbounds pass and streaked the length of the court for another layup. It was now 78-74, Princeton.

Then, in bringing the ball up the court, the Tigers were hit with an offensive foul as Gary Walters charged into George Pomey. Down the floor came the Wolverines with Pomey feeding underneath to Cazzie who hooked in his 29th point of the evening. The margin was two. Princeton again tried to move the ball up the court only to have Pomey strip the ball loose and rifle it downcourt to Thompson. John quickly popped one home and the score was tied at 78.

In less than a minute, Michigan had erased a 10-point bulge. But Princeton still had a chance with 36 seconds to go as they moved into the forecourt. The ball went to John Hummer at the baseline who swung around to shoot. But Cazzie reached out and snared the ball before it ever got into the air. Now it was Michigan's turn for a crack at winning the game in the final seconds.

Cazzie moved the ball over the time line, watching the

seconds tick off the famed overhead scoreboard. 9 . . .8
. . . 7 . . . Cazzie started to move towards the key . . . 5
. . . Cazzie soars up, up . . . 4 . . . the ball is on its way
. . . 3 . . . and through the net as the Michigan bench
explodes and an unbelieving crowd sits in utter shock.

For the second time in three games Cazzie had hit at
the final buzzer, this time to climax one of the most amazing comebacks in Michigan history.

As I wound my way through the catacombs beneath
the Garden to visit the dressing room of Michigan, I came
across the Princeton coach Butch Van Breda Kolff holding
court for the press. It was plain that Butch, whom Piston
fans would meet in a few years, was greatly upset with
the officiating which had cost him not only Bradley but
two other starters. Raging in a voice graveled by years
of cigars, Butch seared the referees. He also refused to
allow the press to interview Bradley which earned Butch
a few knocks in the next morning's editions. Dropping
into the press room to pick up the final statistics, I noticed
a tall, odd-looking gentleman pushing his way through
the waiting members of the media.

"Where are the damned stat sheets?" he demanded, and
went on to grumble about the slothfulness of the Garden
press crew.

I asked a broadcasting friend who the man was.

"Oh, that's Howard Cosell. No one pays any attention to him."

The next game wasn't on tap until Saturday night
which gave the U-M contingent three days to see New
York City. Times Square on New Year's Eve . . . Greenwich Village on New Year's morning . . . Central Park
. . . Broadway . . . Brooklyn . . . the Bronx. Inevitably,
on Saturday night, January 2, 1965, we were back at the

Garden for the championship game with St. Johns.

Despite the bowl games of the day before, the New York press had remained focused on the Garden and that evening. Michigan, number one in the country with the All-Americans Russell and Bill Buntin versus the sentimental favorites of the entire city and much of the nation, the Redmen.

Part of the pre-game ballyhoo centered around the fact that this was the last year at St. Johns for the king of New York basketball, Joe Lapchik. Reaching a mandatory retirement age of 65, Joe was being forced out after 20 years at the school. As a charter member of the Original Celtics, pro basketball's first great team and later a coach of the Knicks, Lapchik was adored by everyone who followed basketball. Most of the 18,499 that had shoehorned their way into the old arena felt this would be Joe's night. As the tall, balding man in the gray suit moved out of the St. Johns' dressing room and made his way to the floor, the roar from the stands outdid even Bradley's ovation of three nights earlier.

Joe wasn't without his resources coming into the game. His sophomore center Sonny Dove had poured in 28 points to lead them to an opening night win over LaSalle while two free throws by Jerry Houston had brought them a last-second win in the semi-final over Cincinnati. Dove had been touted as the next great East Coast star and nothing he did that night dimmed that prophecy. It probably was his finest performance to date and one the Detroit Pistons would remember when it came time to draft two years later. He would lead St. Johns to an NIT championship that year and to an NCAA berth in his senior season, a year he gained All-American honors.

Michigan wasted little time in proving that its thriller

against Princeton hadn't siphoned off any intensity as the Wolverines shot off to an early lead. Dave Strack had pulled a surprise in starting George Pomey in place of Oliver Darden and Pomey grabbed off seven rebounds in the half to lead the team in that department for the first and only time of his career. Meanwhile, Cazzie, Tregoning, and Buntin were providing the firepower to offset a 15-point performance by Dove who missed only one of eight shots in the half while scraping off 10 rebounds. Michigan led by as much as 10 with three and a half minutes left in the first period but a late flurry of six points by St. Johns made it 39-35 at the buzzer.

Michigan did have a problem though—Buntin had been whistled for three fouls in his duel with Dove who had collected but one. This brought a few grumbles from the Michigan rooters about "hometown cooking" by the striped shirts. But the Wolverines didn't let themselves get too discouraged about the officiating or the late St. John's flurry and came out firing in the second half.

With Buntin and Russell leading the way, U-M shot out to a 16-point margin, 68-52, with less than 10 minutes to go. But when Russell and Buntin got tagged with their fourth fouls, the Redmen picked up six straight free throws to narrow the gap to 10. Dove then came up with a steal and a court-long drive to slice it to eight. Another bucket by Dove and three straight by Kenny McIntyre brought the Redmen even at 70-70. With bedlam reigning and two minutes to go, Dove picked up his fourth foul as he whacked Cazzie in the act of shooting. Caz could make only one of the two. The Redmen went immediately to Dove at the baseline. The 6-7 sophomore whiz hummed in a 17-footer to put St. Johns up by one. It was their first lead since early in the game.

As U-M did so many times in Buntin's career, when in trouble they looked to the big fellow. He took the ball in his familiar high post spot, turned to drive the lane and was drilled by McIntyre. Now it was Billy's turn to get a chance for pair. He, too, could coax only one to drop. It was tied at 72 with a minute and a half left.

Jerry Houston, who had wrapped up the Cincinnati game in spectacular fashion, had been strangely quiet this game, getting only two points in the first half. Except for two quick field goals at the start of the second period, he had not been heard from. But he found a gap in the Michigan defense, shot inside the lane and canned a layup giving St. Johns the lead. Strack called a time out to plot his final-minute strategy.

With the clock reading :30, Cazzie started to make his move to the key—the spot where he had won the Wichita State and Princeton games. But McIntyre jumped in the way causing a collision. Steve Honzo reached behind his head, signalling an offensive foul on Cazzie. It was his fifth.

With St. Johns in control, Pomey was forced to foul Houston who this time could manage only one successful free throw that left the New Yorkers up 75-72 with just 28 seconds left. Tregoning quickly misfired from well out but Pomey tapped in the rebound to bring Michigan back within one. Nineteen seconds left.

Now St. Johns sat on the ball and Michigan again had to foul. This time it was Dove who was sent to the line for two. But the evening of battling Buntin had taken its toll as the 19-year-old star spun his first off to the right. Still, a second free throw made would insure his team of at least a tie.

The crowd hushed for one of the few times all evening as Dove's next shot arched high, banged off the front of the rim, and bounced crazily up the court. With the seconds ticking down, there was a wild scramble for the ball. Pomey finally gained control and quickly threw it to Tregoning who crossed the half-court line ready to pull the trigger. But in the scramble for the loose ball, the clock had run out. Players and fans swarmed around Lapchick and Dove in one of the wildest celebrations ever seen on the corner of Eighth and 49th.

As I worked my way through the happy crowd outside the Garden I paused momentarily to look back at the ancient structure.

"What a fantastic week!" I thought.

Years later I found myself with some hours to kill while awaiting a Piston game at the new Garden. Reflecting back to that tumultuous week in 1964 I decided to renew some acquaintances by retracing the well-traveled route between our hotel and the old arena. As soon as I got past the hotel I knew I had made a mistake. The shops we had drifted in and out of, the restaurants, the Irish saloon where we had toasted every eastern and midwestern college known to man, were now boarded up.

Finally I crossed the last intersection and stood where I had waited for the gate to open that first night. There was no trace of the old Garden. Instead, there was a freshly paved parking lot surrounded by a prison-like fence. Not one brick of America's most famous sports spa was left.

FOUR

Zebras, Zanies, Zepp and Zahn

Does the name Jim Enright mean anything to you? How about Red Mohalik? Floyd Magnuson? Red Strauthers? Probably not, huh? Well, don't feel badly, they're not exactly household names. But they were among the top officials in the Big Ten when I broke into the conference in 1963.

Enright was especially a favorite of mine. "Jumbo Jim" was built along the lines of a beach ball and he bounced like one up and down the court until he finally had to retire when his mobility dropped drastically. Jim was one of those rare officials who became as big a favorite with the crowd as the players.

In addition to Enright's offical duties he was a highly entertaining columnist for the *Chicago Sun* and a much sought-after dinner speaker. In fact he came to Ann Arbor following Michigan's great 1965 season to be master of ceremonies for the team's banquet. He proved to be as big a hit in person as he was in print. Now, think a moment about what Big Ten official you would like to invite to emcee the next Michigan banquet. Of course, keep in mind you must provide adequate security to insure his safe arrival and departure. The point is, what has happened since the days of Enright, Mohalik and Strauthers? Has the game progressed to the stage where it is impossible to call? Do all of us just demand too much? Or is there a canyon-size gap in talent between those people and the Robinsons, Bains, and Weilers of today. I truly wonder if some of the old officials would even stay on the court if paired with some of their modern-day counterparts.

To begin with, I don't even remember thinking about the officials in the Sixties. Oh sure, there would be times you questioned a referee's sanity after a controversial call. But there might be just that one call per game that you would take issue with. Nowadays one per minute seems more likely.

I remember during a trip to Lexington and the Kentucky Invitational when the Baron, Adolph Rupp, was still on the throne. Michigan was giving the Wildcats fits with Rudy Tomjanovich shooting out the lights. As the teams came down the stretch neck and neck, a call went against Kentucky that brought Adolph popping off the bench. Michalik happened to be the closest at hand so the Baron opened up on him.

"Jeezus Kee-rist, Red!" Rupp barked, "for what I'm paying you guys how can you make a call like that?"

Never breaking stride Red shot back, "For what you're paying us Adolph, you should be glad you're even in the game."

Kentucky went on to win the shootout 112-104 and Michalik was still chuckling about the exchange in the dressing room afterward.

The fact that Red was one of two Big Ten officials working the game should tell you something about the esteem that Adolph and the rest of the country's coaches held for Big Ten referees.

I'm not sure when the deterioration began but when it did the slide was a rapid one. A quick check of box scores shows that the old guard was mostly gone by the early Seventies—that seems to have also been the start of the slippage. You may recall that beginning with the 1969-70 season the conference went to the three-official crew. Johnny Orr's comment at the time was more prophetic than either John or the rest of us realized.

"Well, as far as I can see that just gives them 33 percent more of a chance to be wrong."

I'm not sure it was as much the quantity as the quality of the new people brought in that did the damage. Within five years, the new men had supplanted the older referees and the results were evident.

By 1973, things had reached such a stage that during an Iowa-Michigan game in Iowa City, Jimmy Dutcher had to hold onto Orr's coattails to prevent him from going onto the court after an official. Johnny had tossed a towel at one of the men in stripes ("I was just trying to get his attention") and was apparently bent on following it. For that he was given his first technical of the season. Meanwhile the game ended in total confusion with players, coaches, and fans pushing and shoving each other as the officials streaked to the dressing room with a second on the clock. It also provided the irrepressible Dutch with one of his classic lines. Asked about his part in restraining the enraged Orr, Dutcher thoughtfully considered the question.

"Yeah, we've been working on Johnny's towel toss all

season. He's got the distance but still needs to improve his accuracy. We'll keep working on it, though."

I'm sure since Jimmy became a head coach again he doesn't have quite the same sense of humor these days when it comes to discussing Big Ten officials.

Some people defend the current-day crop by pointing out that the steadily increasing pressure on coaches has triggered the fiery reactions from the bench and sidelines. I would point out that there were no more intense coaches in America than Indiana's Branch McCracken or Forddy Anderson of Michigan State or Ohio State's Fred Taylor. All were at the helms of teams in the Fifties and Sixties when basketball really came of age. And they wanted to win as badly as a Bob Knight or a Gene Keady, just to mention two of the Eighties' more animated coaches.

The most emotional game I have ever broadcast—the Indiana-Michigan basketball game of 1965—could have exploded at any time. Instead the duo of Lenny Wirtz and Russ Kaefer kept the lid on throughout. As a result we were treated to a classic instead of a modern-day debacle. I can recall waiting for the Michigan team to emerge from the locker room after the game. I spotted Wirtz and Kaefer threading their way through some of the heartbroken Indiana fans.

"Oh, oh," I thought. "Here it comes."

One of the longest-faced of the Hoosier rooters caught sight of the pair as they walked by.

"Hey, you guys," rasped the voice, obviously at its lowest ebb after two overtimes of yelling itself hoarse, "I think you two did a great job even if we did blow it. Good luck."

The two officials looked at each other as though they had been reprieved from the firing squad.

Contrast this to 11 years later in Bloomington, this time at the new Assembly Hall. Michigan had led all the way over the unbeaten Hoosiers (who would go on to a national title by beating this same Wolverine squad). Coming down to the final 30 seconds, Michigan led by four and had the ball with a chance to run out the clock. Phil Hubbard glided across the top of the key on the dribble when he was suddenly leveled by Quinn Buckner. The ball went one way, Hubbard the other and here was Bob Burson (later chief of Big Ten basketball officials) signalling a traveling violation on Hub. It was such a blatant miscall that even mild-mannered Dick Enberg exploded on the national telecast.

So instead of a chance for U-M to wrap it up with a one-and-one free throw opportunity, the ball went over to Indiana. Buckner came down to score with :14 to go and draw the Hoosiers within two. Steve Grote, one of the steadiest free throw shooters that Michigan has seen, was sent to the line after being fouled by Wayne Radford. This time however, Grote bounced the free throw short and when Radford grabbed the rebound Indiana was still alive. After a timeout, the Hoosiers worked the ball to Scotty May with three seconds to go. May cut one loose from the corner that caromed off the rim to teammate Jim Crews. Crews batted it up against the board to keep it alive but again failed to put it through the hoop. As the buzzer sounded Kent Benson made a final swipe at the ball sending it into the net.

Although the crowd exploded it seemed certain that Burson would wave off the tip as too late. But no way was Burson going to toy with Knight and a crowd of 18,000. The shot was allowed to stand and despite some highly energetic protests by Johnny Orr and his team, it went into overtime. You know the rest. Hubbard and Grote both were hit with their fifth fouls and Indiana kept their unbeaten streak alive, 72-67. Five hours later I sat at the motel restaurant with a still-seething Orr.

"I just can't believe it," John would repeat over and over, "Hub was killed by Buckner and those S.O.B.s wouldn't call it. We won that game, coach, (John calls everybody coach) I don't care what the scorebook shows."

A couple of years later I had an opportunity to visit with Buckner after he had joined the Milwaukee Bucks. I asked him if he recalled the play.

"I sure do," he said. "The funny thing was that we wanted to foul Hubbard because he was the worst free throw shooter on the team. I was afraid they were going to call an intentional foul when I hit him so hard. We couldn't believe it when he called traveling."

Neither could Orr.

The most irritating aspect of the entire mess was that only one week before in Champaign the tables had been reversed. Trailing by a point with 10 seconds to go, Hubbard sent up an errant shot from the circle that was rebounded by Wayman Britt who missed the tip. Johnny Robinson then batted it through as the buzzer sounded. This time however, Art White discounted the bucket with the explanation that although it had been in the air when the buzzer went off, Robinson did not have control of the ball as needed in this circumstance. There was no argument in this case from Orr who simply said, "If that's the rule I guess we lost."

It was a rule that apparently was in effect in all Big Ten arenas except Bloomington's Assembly Hall.

Maybe the oft-used cliche that officiating is such an impossible job it shouldn't be held up to scrutiny is true.

But, of course, if it is true, then we also shouldn't get too critical of general managers who cut a Johnny Unitas. Or coaches who come up with an unworkable game plan. Or a back who fumbles at the goal line. Those jobs are tough too. But to see the same people making the same outlandish calls year after year after year puts a huge question mark over the credibility of all officials. Unfair but true.

Even worse are those refs who delight in staring down a player after a horrible call. They seem to hope for a reaction in order to tag the offender with a technical. So, it really isn't a surprise that the Big Ten front office apparently now instructs its officials to race at full speed to the exits as soon as the final buzzer is heard. If things continue at their present pace, it won't be long before a lynch mob will be on their heels.

We can only hope that the cycle will reverse somehow, and that there is another generation of Jim Enrights and Red Mohaliks and Charles Allens out there just waiting to be found.

It's important that we distinguish between the two types of zanies. There is a great deal of difference between the everyday zanies like the howling Huskies of the Cactus Arms and the Wolverine zanies—the unholy trio of Dottie Day and the Ernsts who seem to drive eight million miles per year keeping up with the Michigan basketball team. The first group is really a misguided missile that sloshes from stadium to stadium, arena to arena, and diamond to diamond creating havoc and enemies as it goes. The second group—the Wolverine zanies—are people who are endowed with that priceless quality—Loyalty.

When talking about dedicated zanies like Dottie, Bud and Flo, remember that while their interest was sparked in the halcyon days of Kupec, Grote, Green, Hubbard and the rest, it has endured through the years of 7-20 records. A typical week for these crazies is to embark for Iowa City at 2 A.M. Wednesday morning—a must since they absolutely have to be there in time to meet the team during their afternoon practice session.

Then it's back to the motel to greet the players again while Florence adds to her collection of more than 5,000 player photos. From there it's on to the dining room for a good-sized steak and a discussion about the state of the team. After a night's sleep, it's up and on to the arena where they will settle in directly behind the Michigan bench to provide some much needed road encouragment. It never bothers these Wolverine zanies that they are outnumbered several thousand to one; what they lack in numbers, they make up for in intensity.

Immediately following the game they will head for the dressing room entrance to offer congratulations or condolences. Then they get into Bud's trusty limousine for an all-night ride to Minnesota or wherever to repeat the entire scenario. Not only do they seem to thrive on this schedule, they have actually enlisted a perfectly normal and lovely lady, Pat Hatch, to join their madness. Knowing the persuasive powers of these three, the group may grow further by the time they finish recruiting. Distance means absolutely nothing to this threesome. And that is fortunate since Michigan basketball schedule makers throw some pretty sharp-breaking curves. For instance, how about East Rutherford, New Jersey on a Wednesday and El Paso, Texas the following Tuesday? This modern-day band of Lewises and Clarks simply headed out after watching Michigan annihilate Rutgers to arrive on the scene in plenty of time to greet the team's plane in El Paso. And they accomplished this during one of the country's worst winter storms in decades. They probably never noticed the weather while devising a defense to handle the unbeaten Miners of UTEP.

Just to prove to Bo that they hadn't completely lost their hearts to Bill Frieder, they worked in a short trip to New Orleans for the Sugar Bowl on the way home. What the heck, it was kind of on the way.

They are absolutely the most lovable loonies Michigan athletics have ever known. May their wanderings never cease.

Some other zanies, however, aren't quite so lovable. Some universities are of the opinion that the most direct way to instill fan fervor is to take the loudest, raspiest and crudest individual they can find and hand him the public address microphone. Thankfully, the Big Ten has kept this to a minimum although there is one character at Minnesota who almost makes up for the rest. His voice can best be described as a cross between a 747 jet and W.C. Fields. Before the football Gophers moved into the new Metrodome, we were always treated to the situation of having the P.A. speakers perched directly outside our booth at old Memorial Stadium. Many times it was simply prudent to quit talking until our maestro of the mike had completed his play-by-play. I often wondered if he considered the spectators incapable of digesting what they saw without his running commentary or whether he just assumed all were afflicted with serious eye problems. At least the new stadium seems to absorb his tones to a much more manageable level.

Running him a close second is the joker in South Bend

who strings out the syllables of the starters to such length
that it's almost impossible to tell the player's name by the
time he's through. When Orlando Woolridge was still on
the team you could break for a commercial during his
intro and still have time to spare before our friend finally
got it out. I always felt he had no peer in this department
until Michigan took part in the Sun Bowl tourney where
the University of Texas-El Paso announcer even exceeded
his Notre Dame counterpart.

Some zanies are completely harmless, although a little
tough to comprehend. During one of my trips to Columbus with the basketball team, I was visited by a gentleman
who offered his services at halftime. He explained he was
the inventor of the Possession/Points/Power ratings —
PPP, as he called it. This, according to him, was the most
accurate system devised to gauge a team's true worth.
Well, it *sounded* interesting. So, at the halftime break I
had this authority on hand. As I recall, the interview went
something like this.

"Paul, you have a rather unique system for assessing
a team's proper strength. Maybe you could tell us a little
something as to how it works."

"Certainly, I'd be glad to." Here he pulled out a gigantic
graph with lines shooting upwards, downwards, sideways
and diagonally. "You see, when a team has the ball they
have a chance to score two points. Right? And the other
team can stop them from scoring, right? So when a team
has the ball in the other team's forecourt I give them a
possession rating of two because they can score two. Now
they might only get one maybe on a free throw or none
so that total is put into their point column while the two
remains in their possession column. Now when the other
team moves into their forecourt the exact same thing hap-

pens only I also keep the former team's defensive points since they have the opportunity to stop the other team so they might get two or none . . . "

By this time I'm sure my listeners were lost—I know I was.

And on he went.

"So you see if a team takes the ball up the court 45 times and scores 64 points while they hold the other team to 55 points on their 45 possessions, my rating of 1.7 would show that they are a dominant team since the normal rating would be one, of course."

Of course.

Thinking I might be able to politely ease him out, I moved into what I thought was my closing remark.

"Well, thank you very much, Paul, it was truly enlightening to hear about your system and I'm sure we'll want to keep a close eye on what happens here tonight."

"I'm glad you asked about tonight because here is how the first half went according to my ratings . . . "

And off he went again.

He finally allowed me to break in with the second half of play while promising to come back and join me the next time I was in Columbus.

During our commercial break prior to the second half tipoff, I turned to my engineer, Larry Donald, who worked for all visiting Big Ten stations.

"What did he say, Larry?"

"Don't feel badly," Larry grinned, "nobody else has ever figured it out either."

One day in Ann Arbor, I happened to be in Dave Strack's office when I brought up the subject of my off-the-wall interview. As soon as I mentioned my interviewee's name, Strack said, "Oh, my God, that guy sends every coach in the country reams of material about their team. I got some on my desk right now. Nobody can make head or tail of it."

Sometimes a team will emerge with a touch of lunacy much greater than the sum of its parts. For instance, there was no one individual on the 1968-69 basketball team that could be described as zany. But that has to be the zaniest team I have ever broadcast. It had a respectable record of 13-11 overall and 7-7 in the Big Ten but there was nothing else even close to the mid-point on that club.

You knew it was going to be a different type of season when the Wolverines opened conference play with back-to-back overtime wins over Iowa and Indiana. Before you jump to conclusions however, the two victories excited absolutely nobody for the simple reason that the Hawk-eyes and Hoosiers were headed for eighth and tenth place finishes respectively that year. Any year that these two teams settle to the bottom of the league you know it's an odd season.

This was Johnny Orr's first year as head coach of Michigan — maybe Dave Strack had sensed a year earlier what was coming. I'm convinced that 80 percent of Orr's hair disappeared that season. It wasn't that the team was bad — in fact at times they were very good. But that was the problem. Johnny had absolutely no clue as to which team was going to show up on any given night.

This was the great Rudy Tomjanovich's junior year and any team with Rudy on it was going to be in most games. He was simply amazing whether he was banking home a 23-footer, hooking one in from the key, batting back a teammate's miss or outfighting guys five inches taller for a rebound. Rudy's season ranks with the best any Michigan player will have regardless of how many centuries they play the game in Ann Arbor. He averaged nearly 26 points per game, finishing second only to the scoring machine from Purdue, Rick Mount. He nailed over 15 rebounds per game to top the conference in that department, including 30 against Loyola to set a Michigan mark. His 48 points against Indiana tied Cazzie for the all-time game scoring record and his 21 field goals in that game was another new Michigan standard.

And incredibly, Rudy did all this while playing out of position. Since at 6-7 he was the tallest player on the team, Orr had no choice but to stick him at center and hope for the best. Rudy still found time to slip away into the corner to hum home those one-of-a-kind howitzers that never seemed to arch an inch. Rudy once explained that because he had learned to play the game on a playground with low-hanging wires, he didn't dare loft the ball. I don't think anyone ever suggested that he change.

During Rudy's sophomore season, he was introverted to the point of seclusion. He was very careful with his words and took part in none of the horseplay that is customary on road trips. But by his junior year he started to open up and while never leading the team in speeches, his intelligence, decency, and warm personality shone through. That such a likeable player should have his NBA career shortened by another player's roundhouse right uppercut is one of the game's most grim ironies.

Had Rudy been born four years earlier, imagine a front line of Darden, Buntin, and Tomjanovich with Cazzie in the backcourt. But it was Rudy's destiny to hook up with teams that struggled to make it to the .500 level. In fact, the 1968-69 edition was the only one of the three teams he played with that would break even. But they were never dull.

Combining with Rudy up front was the pair of Dennis Stewart and Bob Sullivan, both high school All-Americans from very different backgrounds. Stewart came from the rough-and-tumble environment of Steeltown, Pennsylvania while Sullivan grew up in a very well-to-do neighborhood of Manitowoc, Wisconsin. Their games on the court were just about as far apart and consistency was neither's strong point. Sully should have been playing guard at 6-4 but was pressed into a forward slot after Rudy moved to center. Sully, like Denny, could shoot the ball and had the ability to suspend himself in air about as long as any Wolverine I can remember. Unfortunately for Bob he would at times decide to dish the ball off rather than take the shot — as a result the ball would sail off the head of another Wolverine or into the crowd.

But Sully shouldn't be singled out for this transgression, it was one that the team specialized in throughout the year. Orr would hold his head in despair as the offense would come firing up the court only to have five players seemingly going in five different directions.

The backcourt included steady Dan Fife, who took over the starting position although only a sophomore, and who would eventually become one of Michigan's finest captains. But as a first-year man, it was hard for Danny to put a tether on his older teammates. Teaming with him was captain Kenny Maxey, who came out of Chicago Carver High two years after a fellow named Cazzie Russell graduated from the same school. Maxey had the quickness of Cazzie but never quite harnessed it to the same degree. But he was exciting and at 5-9 would punish his bigger opponents on defense with his all-out effort. His offense was just as lively but at times he tended to confuse Rudy, Danny, and the others almost as much as the opposition.

Maxey's great moment came during the Illinois game at Crisler that year when somehow he managed to tie up the ball with Illinois' Les Busboom. (I told you it was a crazy year.) Busboom stood 6-4 which gave him roughly a 7-inch height advantage for the jump. (This was before the Big Ten officials lost the art of throwing up the ball for a held ball situation.)

Just prior to the jump, Stewart had almost decapitated Sullivan with a pass he never saw coming and that scattered a few spectators behind the Michigan bench. So the fans were still murmuring about that line drive when Maxey stepped in against Busboom. Up went the ball but Maxey never moved as Busboom soared into the air and, expecting some competition, strongly batted the ball. It rocketed about ten rows up in the same area where Stewart had awakened them a minute earlier. While Maxey and his teammates doubled up in laughter, the crowd began to vacate that vicinity.

Also typical of that team was that as soon as they regained possession Maxey fed a beautiful pass to Sully who streaked in from the side and laid it through. Michigan ended up winning in a thriller, 92-87.

There must have been something about Illinois that sparked the craziness that year. In the rematch in Champaign, Michigan again took the game to the Illini with everything clicking. Passes were on target, Rudy and Stewart were shooting the eyes out of the basket and the Wolverines seemed on their way to a staggering upset over the eventual Big Ten Runnerups.

On one trip down, moving into the forecourt, Stewart got the ball in his favorite spot on the side and fired. Down it went, without drawing a bit of iron, well into the nets. The scorekeeper even flashed two points. But in the most bizarre fashion I have ever seen, the ball suddenly spun back up out of the net, through the rim, and dropped back onto the court. The players, coaches, fans, and at least one broadcaster I know were completely flabbergasted. When Johnny Orr could regain his senses, he insisted to the officials that the shot should count since it had gone all the way through the rim and into the nets. Suffice to say, he lost the argument. And Michigan lost the game, 100-92.

This was also the team that scored 100 points or better on five different occasions, a mark exceeded only by the rampaging '65-66 squad. The difference is, of course, that the '65-66 team won all of its triple figure games; the '68-69 team won three and lost two.

One of those losses came at Chicago Stadium as the Wolverines met Loyola of Chicago as part of a doubleheader. The Chicago fans must have thought they had gotten their dates mixed and were sitting in on an NBA contest between the Bulls and Pistons. The Ramblers broke out to a 49-39 lead in the first half as the teams were hardly waiting to get over the center court line before firing. When they weren't shooting the ball, they were throwing it away—there were 24 turnovers during the first half alone.

Michigan rallied in the second half behind the phenomenal shooting of Sullivan to send it into overtime at 89-89. Nowadays, the strategy during an extra period is usually to protect the ball, take a shot only if the shot clock is about to run out or when it's a lead-pipe cinch. This was heresy to that club—they peppered away as though they were in the opening minute of play. Normally 11 points in overtime is enough to keep you close or win you the game. It didn't do either for the Wolverines as Loyola poured in an incredible 23 points to win in a cakewalk. At one point an exasperated Johnny Orr called a timeout and waited for his troops to gather around.

"Men, I just want to ask you one question. Can somebody please tell me what offense it is you're running? I've never seen it before and from the way you're playing I don't think you have either."

Sullivan had his greatest night as a Wolverine with 31 points while Rudy chipped in with 29. Just to put this in perspective, Sully and Rudy scored more points between them than the entire Michigan squad scored in 10 of its games during the 1983-84 season.

Three games later, Sullivan climaxed his up-and-down season at Iowa in the rematch of their opener. In that first game, Bob had hardly seen action, being used exclusively as a sixth man by Orr who went with his starters almost all of the way in the 99-92 win. But two games later, John decided to stick the acrobatic Sullivan into the forward spot opposite Stewart. With three minutes to go in the game, Michigan was leading 84-75 with Sully almost perfect from the floor, hitting on 7-of-9 shots.

A nine-point lead at the 17:00 mark is normally cause for a bit of relaxing for the coach but Johnny knew better with this fun-loving bunch. Three turnovers, three fouls and 10 points later Iowa had taken an 85-84 lead. After a missed Stewart jumper and an Iowa rebound the Hawkeyes were in the driver's seat with seconds showing on the clock. But the Wolverines of '68-69 always were at their best when trailing—they had the Hawks right where they wanted them.

As Chad Calabria crossed the 10-second line on the dribble, everyone knew he would be looking for Glen Vidnovic, an 86 percent free throw shooter. Since Michigan was in an obvious fouling situation, sending Vidnovic to the line would just about lock it up for Iowa. Sure enough Calabria fired the ball to Vidnovic coming across the middle. However, the fellow they called "Stick" never got the ball as little Kenny Maxey, who qualified more as a "Twig," shot in front and grabbed the ball. In one motion, the Michigan captain flipped it down the court to Sullivan who gathered it in at the half-court line and drove the distance for the layup that gave Michigan an 86-85 victory.

A bemused Johnny Orr just sat in the locker room shaking his head. "Coach, I don't think I'm going to make it," he sighed as he watched the celebration. "These guys are going to be the death of me."

But Johnny survived. He not only survived, he also went on to win 209 games at the helm of Michigan before moving on to Iowa State. But he never had a group like his first one. Maybe for John's sake, we should all be thankful.

Zepp and Zahn? Okay, maybe it's a little devious to use this pairing as a way to talk about Michigan baseball, but I ask you, has there ever been a pitching staff in history—majors, minors or college— that had a pair of starters beginning with Z? As a matter of fact, until Kurt Zimmerman came along in 1983, Bill Zepp and Geoff Zahn were the only players ever to earn a Michigan baseball letter that had Z as their leadoff last name letter. That both were good enough to move into the major leagues was just another strange twist in this Wolverine baseball believe-it-or-not saga.

But as for Michigan baseball itself, there has been nothing strange about it. In fact, as a comparatively small and

loyal band of fans know, there may be nothing more relaxing than sitting in the stands at Fisher Stadium during
a warm May afternoon.

My first experience with Michigan baseball, however,
did not involve sitting in the stands. In the 1960s and early
'70s, the broadcasters and writers were perched in what
Red Barber called the catbird seat. But at Fisher this was
literally true because we sat on the roof, in what passed
as a press box. It wasn't the most spacious facility in the
country but it sufficed for the rather small media contingent that covered the games. Our broadcast booth was
on the extreme end of the box, directly behind home plate
and separated by a partition from the baseball writers.
Since there was no screen above the facing of the roof,
we were treated to the excitement of hitting the deck when
a foul ball would scream directly into our booth. One
afternoon in a game with Michigan State, Spartan out-
fielder John Dace sent three fouls rocketing upstairs that
sent engineer Stan Dilley and me scrambling for safety.
We flinched on every swing of the bat for the rest of the
game.

Eventually the broadcast locations were moved downstairs in the stands as the roof was declared unsafe. Stan
and I could have told them that. But I will admit that
a lot of the challenge has gone out of broadcasting the
game without the thrill of ducking baseballs.

There were also a few other rough spots in doing Michigan baseball. One season, engineer Ralph Johnson and
I went down to do a single game between Michigan and
MSU. It was a gorgeous early May day with the temperature around 65 degrees and a brilliant sun overhead. We
had packed a basket of sandwiches and soft drinks (baseball broadcasting is rather low key) and were prepared

to spend a lazy spring afternoon at Fisher. For the first five innings it was exactly that as we sat in our short-sleeve shirts enjoying the rays that would wander into our booth. We complimented ourselves for being so farsighted as to schedule a broadcast for a day such as this.

Then ominous clouds began appearing to the west over Michigan Stadium. By the sixth the temperature had dropped 30 degrees. One of those unpredictably (or at least unpredicted) cold fronts raced through Ann Arbor. There was no rain but there was plenty of wind and a gray, sullen sky. Well, we figured we could tough it out for another inning as we rubbed our goose-pimpled arms. Unfortunately, the Spartans had tied the game in the sixth and after seven innings it was still deadlocked, 3-3. Inning after inning dragged by. And upstairs, by degrees, Ralph and I turned progressively bluer. By the 10th inning, my teeth were chattering and I really wondered if I could keep up a coherent account. By the 11th inning, I prayed for someone to end this nonsense.

In the bottom of the 12th, with hypothermia beginning to set in, big Jim Steckley stepped to the plate for Michigan and mercifully powered one over the left-field fence. As I recall, I never talked Ralph into going back to Fisher with me to engineer another baseball game.

With the short collegiate season in the midwest, Big Ten coaches are reluctant to cancel games because of mundane things such as blizzards, downpours or tornadoes. So, as you might expect, weather has been an important and controversial factor in broadcasting Michigan baseball.

While the national anthem was being played at Kobs Field in East Lansing one sparkling spring day, a driving snowstorm hit with such force that the tarpaulin covering the temporary press box was blown off. Coaches

Danny Litwhiler of Michigan State and Moby Benedict of Michigan were kind enough to at least wait until the field could be seen before they went ahead with the game.

The final game of the 1975 Mid-east regional at Eastern Michigan was halted in the ninth inning by one of the truly high-powered storms to rip through southeastern Michigan. While Dave McKay and I cowered for shelter in the stands, the wind and rain ripped sideways across the diamond and streaks of lightning lit the sky. At least the drenched crowd was kept entertained. Although we had been given weather warnings all during the oppressively hot and sultry afternoon, we were still unprepared for the suddenness of the first jagged streak and thunderous boom that accompanied the flash. You never saw a broadcast wrapped up so quickly. Somehow, sitting with yards of electrical equipment wrapped around our bodies, while 8 million volts of electrical force zapped around the sky, stimulated us. Michigan came back the next day in beautiful conditions to play a scoreless ninth and concede the regional crown to Eastern.

A doubleheader between Michigan and Indiana to decide the title was completed under a near monsoon with my scorebook looking like Howard Cosell's toupee by the end of the second game.

Weather also played a minor part in the 1980 College World Series which produced one of Michigan's most memorable games. The Wolverines had been scheduled to meet California as the final game of the first round which would have made it an 8:00 P.M. start that Saturday night in Omaha. However, a heavy rainstorm moved through the area early that afternoon, delaying play for almost four hours and shoving back the schedule. Thus Michigan found themselves coming out Sunday afternoon to lead off that day's activities. The kicker was that the loser would have to return immediately to face Clemson in a loser's bracket contest. This didn't seem too major a problem at the time but as the game developed it became a much larger consideration.

Michigan coach Bud Middaugh had started freshman ace Scott Dawson against the Golden Bears and Scotty, with a 9-1 mark on the year, got into instant trouble. A single, double, and Dawson's error gave the Bears a quick 1-0 lead in the first. Michigan got the run back in the third and went ahead with another in the fourth. Dawson couldn't hold the lead, however, as California jumped on him with three straight singles in the bottom of the fourth and Dawson was replaced by Steve Ontiveros. The Bears managed another run before Steve could put out the fire and it was a 3-2 game after four. And with California starter Chuck Hensley ripping through the Michigan batting order with little trouble, it looked as though that one-run lead might be enough as after six innings, Michigan still was down by that 3-2 count.

Greg Schulte opened the seventh with a walk and advanced to second on a sacrifice. George Foussianes went down swinging to bring up the Wolverines record-setting power hitter, Jim Paciorek. Jim had been held hitless in three trips that day but immediately snapped the streak sending a Hensley fast ball rocketing over the right-field fence to give Michigan a 4-3 lead. It also sent Hensley to the showers—a move that California coach Bob Milano was severely questioned about later.

Meanwhile, Ontiveros had done a masterful job in relief, allowing but three hits in shutting out the Bears, but in the bottom of the eighth the roof caved in on the big O. After a single, walk, sacrifice, and another single scored

the tying run, Bud Middaugh decided that was it for Steve—
he brought in seldom-used Joe Wissing. With runners at
third and first, Joe gave up another single and the Pac
Ten champs were back on top 5-4 and runners at first
and second. That was all for Wissing as another freshman
sensation, Scotty Elam, trotted in from the bullpen. Scotty
finally slammed the door after loading the bases but the
Wolverines came up for their final whacks needing a run
to tie.

Jeff Jacobsen was the scheduled leadoff man in the
ninth but Bud opted to go with pinch hitter Pat Balaze.
(Although a light hitter then, three years later Jacobsen
would hit .360 and lead the team in RBIs.) Balaze did
his job—he worked reliefer Mitch Hawley for a walk and
was immediately replaced by pinch runner Dave Nuss.
A sacrifice by Schulte moved Nuss to second. When Chuck
Wagner ground out, Foussianes was left to ward off
defeat. The Michigan captain promptly lined a shot to
left, scoring Nuss. Michigan was still alive. Paciorek then
smacked one down the left-field line into the corner. Middaugh, coaching at third, never hesitated as he frantically
waved Foussianes around third with the go-ahead run.
Speed, however was never George's main suit, and a perfect relay cut him down by 10 feet at the plate leaving
the score deadlocked at five.

Out for his second inning of work, Elam got himself
into all kinds of trouble in a hurry. The first two California batters walked and advanced on a sacrifice. An intentional walk loaded the bases and again Michigan was
looking down the barrel of a smoking gun. But Elam came
back with a strikeout of Michael Buggs which brought
up leadoff man Lyle Brackenridge. After falling behind
0-2 to the hitter, Scotty came back to draw even. On the

2-2 count, Brackenridge sent a bouncer down to Tony Evans at short who went to second for the force and Michigan had survived.

As the Bears trotted out onto the field in the 10th, it started to register in the minds of everybody that the loser of this game was going to have some problems recovering. The game already had taken three hours with no end in sight. Gerry Hool opened the Michigan 10th with a frozen rope into left-center and the Wolverines had the tie-breaker at second. Two outs later, it was still there with Evans at the plate.

Through Middaugh's lineup changes, the pitcher was scheduled to hit in the ninth slot which meant he would be following Tony unless a pinch hitter was forthcoming. But to our surprise, Bob Milano decided to pitch to Evans rather than force Bud's hand into leaving Elam in to hit or yanking him for a pinch hitter. Evans wasted no time in showing Milano what he thought of his disregard for Tony's hitting as he sent a drive just inside the bag at third that scored Hool easily with Tony pulling into second with a double. With Michigan now leading 6-5, Bud allowed Elam to hit for himself and on the first pitch Evans stole third.

Dusting himself off, Tony paused for a brief chat with Middaugh in the coaching box. It was soon clear what the conversation was about as on the next pitch Evans set sail for the plate. Elam tried his best to give his shortstop some help as he swung wildly at the pitch but to no avail as Tom Colburn put the tag on the sliding Evans and Michigan had to be content with a 6-5 lead going into the bottom of the 10th.

Elam, who had been shaky in his two innings of action, immediately got himself in another jam. He dealt the leadoff hitter Dan Driscoll a base on balls. Things got even stickier a minute later as Hool fielded Jeff Ronk's bunt and threw late to second attempting to cut down Driscoll. So with nobody out, the Bears had the tying run at second and the winner at first. Another bunt moved the runners up and put Michigan in trouble again. It also brought Middaugh out of the dugout as he brought in his fifth hurler of the day, Mark Clinton. It had been expected that Clinton would be the starter in Michigan's second game but Bud had no thoughts of any game but the present one as he signalled his senior righthander in from the bullpen.

The first hitter Clinton faced was Greg Zunino and Middaugh was presented with a choice. He could put Zunino on to load the bases but this would bring up left-handed hitting Tom Colburn. Bud decided on his second option. And then he made a decision which would change the outcome of the game — he motioned for his infield to play back at their normal depth rather than to pull in for a play at the plate. On the first pitch to Zunino, it was quickly apparent that Bud's move was right because the little third baseman sent a bouncer to the left of short-stop Evans. Tony glided over, scooped and threw the ball in one motion to the plate where Hool made the tag on Driscoll for the second out. Had Evans been playing in on the grass, the grounder would have been by him and the game very possibly would have been history. As it was, Clinton now had to face the tough Colburn with runners at first and third. A quick pair of strikes put Colburn in the hole but on the next pitch he reached out and punched a line drive over Evans's head to left to again tie the game.

So back to work went Clinton to face Kelly Wood with

the winning run now standing down at second. Wood laid into a Clinton fast ball and sent a shot towards left field. But the cat-like Evans leaped to his glove side and speared the drive. It was into the 11th inning in a game that would take its place among the greatest in College World Series history.

As luck would have it, Clinton was the leadoff man in the 11th and with the pitching staff drained there was no one else for Middaugh to turn to. The coach elected to let Mark hit for himself. Clinton quickly proved he wasn't a complete stranger to the plate as he bounced a ground ball towards second base which took a crazy hop off Ronk's chest. Michigan had the leadoff man on. However Mark proved to be a better hitter than baserunner. He found himself trapped off first on Schulte's bunt pop-up to third and was erased before he could scramble back to the bag. So instead of Michigan having the go-ahead run at second with one out, it was now a bases empty situation with two down. California hurler Dave Granger couldn't stand the prosperity—he proceeded to walk both Wagner and Foussianes to bring Paciorek to the plate. That was it for Granger and Milano summoned his top reliever, Glenn Newton, who would become California's fourth, and the game's ninth pitcher.

As Newton raced in, the public address announcer informed the packed house that the game was now four hours old but added that it seemed only half that length. Sensing that they were about to become a part of history, the fans rose as one in a standing ovation. Whether it rattled Newton or not is unknown, but his first pitch to Paciorek was in the dirt which sent Wagner to third and Foussianes to second. It also prompted Milano to decide that he wanted no part of the devastating Paciorek and motioned Newton to walk the big slugger and pitch to Hool. Gerry's double in the 10th had been his first hit of the game and when he waved futilely at a pair of wide-breaking curves Milano's strategy looked good. After missing with two more breaking pitches, Newton came back with his fifth in a row. But this time Hool was ready and he slammed a twisting line drive to left that eluded Driscoll and rolled to the wall. As the Michigan dugout exploded, Wagner, Foussianes and Paciorek all came pounding across the plate and Michigan had a 9-6 lead.

In any other baseball game, a three-run lead in the bottom of the 11th might have been cause for a sigh of relief but not in this one.

When Clinton walked the leadoff hitter, the worst fears of Michigan fans again seemed to be coming true. A force-out brought some momentary relief but when Bracken-ridge and Driscoll tagged back-to-back singles, it was 9-7 with runners at first and third. Ronk brought home another run with a sacrifice fly to narrow the margin to one but the Bears were down to their final out again. And just as in the 10th, they refused to go meekly. Another single advanced the tying run to second and put the winning tally at first. And in another replay, it was Zunino once more at the plate with a chance to knot the count. About this time, the same thought was coursing through the minds of spectators, players, writers, and broadcasters— "How long can this go on?"

The thought that one of these teams would have to return to the field shortly after the completion of this game was a horrifying one. Which team would draw the short straw?

The answer was quickly forthcoming as Zunino jumped on Clinton's first pitch and sent a high fly ball to right

that Paciorek gathered in as his Michigan teammates pum-
meled each other.

Finally, four hours and 15 minutes after it started, the
final game of the first round of the 1980 College World
Series was over. Few people would complain that it hadn't been worth
the 24-hour wait. A total of 34 players had seen action
in the marathon which saw 17 runs and 30 base hits. The
final line score was MICHIGAN 9 14 2, CALIFORNIA
8 16 1. But the most incredible statistic was: Left on base,
California-18. It must have seemed to Bud Middaugh that
his pitchers spent the entire day pitching with the bases
loaded and three-and-two counts to the hitters.

Reflecting back on the game, I wonder how the players
would have staggered through another game and if I could
have made it through another broadcast had Michigan
lost and been forced to return immediately.

A couple of post-game developments turned out to be
almost as intriguing as the game itself. First of all, California somehow managed to come back and actually defeat
Clemson in the nightcap of that Sunday's twinbill. Secondly, Mark Clinton came back the next day against
Miami of Florida and pitched a sterling five-hitter before
leaving in the eighth inning. Only a couple of defensive
breakdowns prevented Clinton from registering his second
win in two days as Michigan bowed 3-2. Quite a series.

However, my favorite recollection of Michigan baseball
came one day during the '70s prior to an otherwise un-
eventful afternoon. And it had little to do with the game.
While making my way to the Wolverine dugout, I noticed a shapely co-ed seated in the front row directly
behind the Michigan players. I could tell I wasn't the only
one to spot her — one of Moby Benedict's group was earn-

estly involved in trying to persuade a teammate to bring about an introduction.

"Look," said the budding Casanova, "You just toss me the ball a little high and I'll let it hit the dugout and go into the stands. Than I can chase it down and meet her on the way back."

His partner in crime wasn't that convinced.

"What if I hit her with it?" he argued, "Moby'll have my butt in a sling."

"Hey, there's nobody there but the chick," retorted the other, "And you don't have to throw it hard, just kind of bounce it soft off the top."

After a few more minutes of pleading, with the rest of the squad eagerly listening in, our Romeo finally got his buddy to agree to one wild toss.

The throw was perfect, high and wide, just to the left of the Dolly Parton look-alike. The only problem was that at the moment, the boyfriend (a Bubba Smith look-alike) had settled next to his girl just in time for the errant throw to bounce off his chest.

As the rest of the team doubled up in laughter, the two culprits fled to the dugout where they argued about who was going into the stands for the baseball. They finally agreed to send the ball boy, figuring the 260-pound lineman might be a sucker for kids. As far as I know, they didn't duplicate the stunt again.

Zepp and Zahn would have loved it.

FIVE

That Championship Season
(Part I)

According to the experts, your first love is always the truest and strongest. Others may come, but none will ever nudge the first out of your heart's center court. And I guess that's the way I feel about the first Michigan football and basketball champs I watched. Oddly enough, both came in the same year, 1964.

It would be stretching a point to say that the 1963-64 cagers took everyone by surprise. Michigan basketball fans had been salivating for a full year as they awaited the great freshman class of 1962 to join the fun. This was the fabulous five of Oliver Darden, John Thompson, Jim Myers, John Clawson and, of course, Cazzie Russell.

The previous season, fans would come out two hours early simply to watch this freshman team play the "M" Law Club or Med School or whatever competition they could drum up. Freshman coach Tom Jorgensen would watch his fledglings in action and wonder how he would fare if he took this squad into the Big Ten. Head coach Dave Strack would have settled for Cazzie but the freshman eligibility rule was still more than 10 years down the road. So it wasn't until 1963-64 that these talented youngsters came of age—and so did Michigan basketball.

Not that Strack didn't have some pretty decent material coming back to integrate with this highly touted sophomore group. First and foremost was Bill Buntin. Billy was listed at 6-7 although he looked no taller than 6-5½ Cazzie when he and Russell stood shoulder to shoulder. But nobody ever bothered to tell Bill he was giving away three, four, and five inches every game. Bill would go out game after game and outfinesse a 6-10 Mel Northway or 6-9 Fred Thomann or overpower a 6-7 Earl Brown or 6-8 George Peeples. And he could toss in that beautiful 15-foot hook over anybody in the country. The year before he had led Michigan in just about every category—including smiles. He was always smiling—in warmups, on the plane, in the motel lobby, wherever he was he was happy. And yet, he had a lot of burdens. Trying to support a family while splitting studies and basketball is not easy but Bill handled it with aplomb. Just like he handled Big Ten centers. The only center who held his own with Billy was Ohio State's two time All-American Gary Bradds. But Bradds gave everybody problems.

Bill was equally deft with a pool cue. When Caz was first brought to Ann Arbor, he was naturally introduced to Buntin who gave him a complete tour of key campus sites. One stop was the Union poolroom where Bill gave Cazzie a few pointers in eight-ball.

"I told him the only way he was going to get even was

to come back to U-M in the fall and practice," Bill grinned.

Bill could also deal a mean hand of cribbage. He always came equipped with board and cards waiting for his favorite patsy to show up. Me. Bill may have been the world's jolliest soul but this didn't prevent him from taking every advantage presented to him at the card table. In cribbage, each player is supposed to tally his point total at the completion of each hand. If he miscounts, the other player may catch the omission and add it to his total. Bill would watch like a hawk as I counted out my points: "Fifteen, two; fifteen, four; fifteen, six; and a run of three for nine . . . "

"And a pair, that's two for me!" he would gleefully announce.

"Wait a minute," I would tell him, "you never gave me a chance to complete my sentence."

"Yes, you did," he would claim while pegging the additional points, "you dropped your voice."

"Well, I was just looking over the rest of my hand."

"You should have done it all at once like I do."

No wonder he never lost a rebound. He never gave the other guy a chance to go after the ball.

And did he get the boards! There is a great photograph on the cover of the 1963-64 program of number 22 sailing through the air under the other team's backboard with the ball pressed firmly between those two giant paws. Bill is about two feet off the floor while Jim Myers and three Iowa players stand and stare.

Bill's total of 1,037 rebounds stands as the second best in Michigan history, exceeded only by Rudy Tomjanovich's 1,039. But there is a footnote to Rudy's total: In the final game of Rudy's career any ball that landed within a 20-foot radius of him was automatically awarded to

Rudy T. as a rebound. That wouldn't have bothered Bill. He was used to being nagged about rebound credits by Darden who always accused Bill of siphoning off rebounds that rightfully belonged to Oliver. And Ollie, who had the wryest humor on the team, also felt Cazzie stole a few boards because of the inability of the scorers to tell them apart.

"We all look the same to them," Ollie would kid Buntin, "and when they aren't sure they just give them to you out of habit."

Darden did have a point. The trio did appear to be "carved out of the same block of marble," as one Kentucky sportswriter put it. And they all wore double numbers: Buntin #22; Russell #33 and Darden #55.

Oliver's greatest line came at the end of the NCAA regional matchup with Loyola. Glancing at the stat sheet, Darden looked over to Bill who had collapsed in front of his locker.

"Hey, look at this, Billy. Tregoning outrebounded you!"

"What?" barked Bill rousing himself out of his exhaustion.

Sure enough, there it was in black and white, Tregoning 14, Buntin 13. This was about double Larry's normal board total per game. It was also the only time all year that the 6-5 Ferndale junior, built like a matchstick and as white as the shower room walls, had topped Buntin on the boards.

"Hey, wait a minute, this can't be," grumbled Bill.

"Sure it can," chirped Tregoning, "I was tough tonight."

"It's just like I told you," Darden said, "they really can't tell us apart, even Trigger."

Buntin also had an incredibly delicate touch on his shot. If the opposing center chose to play him belly up at the high post where Billy tended to hang out, Buntin would put the ball on the floor and head for the hoop. If that prompted the opposition to play him soft, Bill would simply send up a jumper or his devastating hook and everybody would start running to the other end of the floor. And at the free throw line that year he was second only to Cazzie.

Unfortunately for Bill, "second only to Cazzie," was a phrase he would hear for the rest of his U-M career. Not from his teammates—they were well aware of his worth. But from the well-meaning fans and from a not-so-well-meaning media.

"People thought I was mad when Cazzie arrived," Bill once told me. "I wasn't mad, I was glad he was here to help me win some games. There were never any problems between us. He would come to my house, I would go to his. We were friends."

Cazzie was aware early of the possibility of conflict.

"I told Billy that there was nothing I could do about what the writers would write. I told him that we would have to keep doing what we always did and not pay any attention to it."

Regrettably, Billy got very bad advice upon gradua-tion. The Pistons were almost obligated to draft him be-cause of his immense popularity in the Detroit area. They knew, as did anyone else who had given it any thought, that his future would have to be at forward in the NBA. But with his marvelous touch, he surely could have made it in the pros. But shifting positions is tough, so when the draft was held and Buntin turned up on the Piston list, it was important for him to get as early start as possible. However, when the offer came from the Pistons it was rejected out of hand by Bill's advisors.

"No way," they told him. "Just hold on and they'll up it to proportions you deserve."

But the Pistons, feeling they were taking a gamble in

the first place, refused to increase the offer. Thus, when Bill should have been attending rookie camp for a badly needed indoctrination he was sitting home putting on pounds. Lots of pounds. Finally, after disregarding his advisors' last-ditch argument to sit out the season he settled for the original offer. And then he reported to the Pistons very late and badly out of shape. Under those conditions, no wonder he never could get started. Eventually he was released.

Shortly afterward, while playing on the backyard courts where he excelled as a youngster, Bill Buntin suffered a fatal heart attack.

All of his former teammates and coaches were there on that hot summer day for Billy's funeral. Each was shocked that this smiling, easy-going muscle man was gone at the age of 27.

Strack's only seniors on that team were a pair of under-sized over-achievers in the backcourt, Bobby Cantrell and Doug Herner. Herner had lost his starting role to Cazzie but never lost any enthusiasm for playing. Oddly enough, in his final game as a Wolverine, he regained his starter's job when Cazzie couldn't play because of an injured ankle. Herner reverted to his former play-making brilliance as he led the team with 10 assists in a 100-90 victory over Kansas State in the NCAA third-place contest. On a club outstanding for intelligence, Herner might have owned the quickest mind of all.

If Doug had the quickest mind, Cantrell probably had the quickest mouth. Absolutely nothing intimidated him, including opposing 6-10 centers who towered over him by a good foot. Bobby seemed to be at his best when faced with a challenge. The bigger the challenge, the tougher he played. In mid-December, Michigan awaited the ar-

John Henderson – a ballet dancer in cleats.

(Courtesy University of Michigan Athletic Department)

Ron Johnson – His five T. D. performance
against Wisconsin may never be equaled.

(Courtesy University of Michigan Athletic Department)

William Laskey – Bill Laskey didn't
catch many passes but hit a lot of
people who did.

(Courtesy University of Michigan Athletic Department)

Wally Weber – "The Wizard
of Words"

Fritz Crisler – A Michigan legend.

Chalmers "Bump" Elliott – Coach of the '64 champs.

Bennie Oosterbaan – Michigan's greatest athlete and nicest gentleman.

The tank from Toledo – Jim Detwiler. Air Force game, 1964.

(Courtesy University of Michigan Athletic Department)

The fun-loving captain of the '64 kings – Jim Conley.

(Courtesy University of Michigan Athletic Department)

Bill Buntin – Michigan basketball came of age when this man showed up in Ann Arbor.

(Courtesy University of Michigan Athletic Department)

Gordie Bell in flight.

The man with the Golden Arm –
Rudy Tomjanovich.

The giant lefthander from
Holland – Victor Amaya.

The fiesty Rick Sygar – at home on
offense or defense.

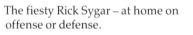

(Courtesy University of Michigan News Service)

The Cincinnati Comet – Carl Ward.

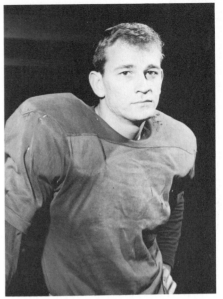

(Courtesy University of Michigan Athletic Department)

The preacherman – All American quarterback Bob Timberlake.

(Courtesy George Fenton – Photography)

Geoff Zahn – One-half of the z combo.

(Detroit Baseball Club)

Bill Zepp – The other half.

George Pomey – Mr. defense of the
'64 champs.

The delightful destroyer – Oliver Darden.

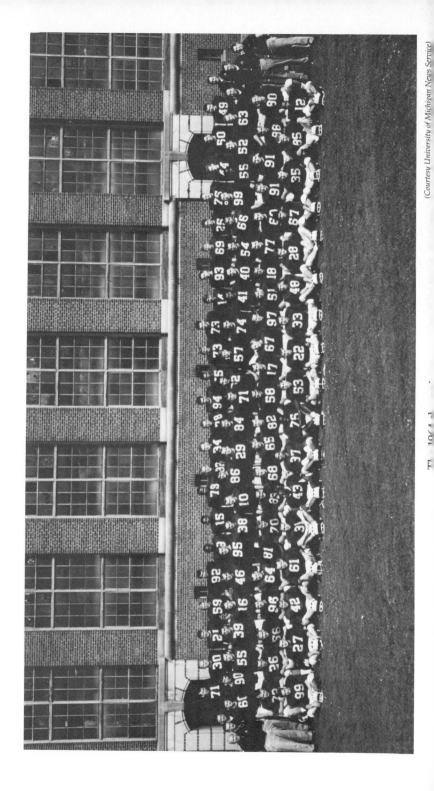

(Photo by Bob Kalmbach)

A longer-haired Steve Grote on the muscle.

Anthony Carter – Nobody has ever done it better than A. C.; 1982, Wisconsin.

Mel Anthony chewing up the Middies.

(Photo by Malcolm W. Emmons)

Johnny Orr. Tall John – M's winningest basketball coach.

(Photo by Bob Kalmbach)

The amazing Rich Leach – eluding another would-be tackler.

(Photo by Bob Kalmbach)

Rickey Green – Quicksilver – again has left the pack behind.

rival of their high-scoring neighbors to the west, the Broncos of Western Michigan. The pregame buildup centered on the matchup of Western's Manny Newsome and Michigan's Cazzie Russell. The Broncos had already topped the 100-point total twice in their first four games, including 102 points against the nation's number one team, Loyola of Chicago. Much of that was due to Newsome who carried a 35-point average into Yost Fieldhouse that evening. There were many who thought the old arena would see a new individual point total set that night. They had forgotten to check with Cantrell who was no stranger to Newsome. The two had locked horns during their high school days with Cantrell coming out of East Chicago and Newsome from Gary. During warmups the two briefly met at midcourt.

"No 35 tonight, Manny," cautioned Bobby.

"Screw you," Newsome tossed back.

"See you later," flipped Cantrell as he drove for the basket in the layup drill.

When the ball went up to open the game, Cantrell jumped into Manny's back pocket. Everywhere that Manny went, Bobby was sure to go. If Manny brought the ball up the court, Cantrell started mugging him by the time he reached the time line, forcing him out of his dribble and making him give up the ball. And once he gave it up he was unlikely to get it back because Cantrell almost draped himself around Manny's shoulders like a stole. Midway through the first half, Newsome's point total was exactly zero and the high-powered Bronco offense had managed a feeble 13 points. By the time the first half was over, Michigan had blasted to a 52-34 lead with Manny contributing four points.

The second half was more of the same. During one time

out called by a harassed Western coach Don Boven, who turned up in the Bronco huddle but Cantrell, standing right next to Manny Newsome, of course.

After Michigan rolled up a 30-point margin, Strack mercifully pulled his starters and Newsome finally got a chance to toss in some jumpers. His 20 points still left him well short of his average and the 104-81 shellacking would be the worst his team would suffer that season. And Cantrell?

"I've faced tougher."

Confidence was not a problem with Bobby Cantrell.

In the final minute of the gut-wrenching NCAA regional game with Loyola, the Ramblers' Ron Miller went to the line for two key free throws. Miller, a street-wise kid out of the Bronx, was their top scorer and an 80 percent shooter from the line. Cantrell casually strolled next to him as Miller prepared to shoot.

"Make these and I'll kill you," he politely announced.

Miller never came close on either.

I was later to arrange for Bobby to be my halftime guest of the 1965 all-time classic with Indiana at Bloomington. Bobby had gone back to his high school alma mater as coach and was attending the game as a spectator. This is the game that will be discussed as long as Michigan basketball is talked or written about. After the teams left the floor at halftime, with Michigan down 50-44, I patiently awaited the arrival of Cantrell. Five minutes passed. No Bobby. Ten minutes. Still no Bobby. Back onto the court came the teams and there, racing back from the locker room with the Wolverines, was Cantrell. Following the game in the tumultuous Michigan locker room I found Bobby beaming along with everybody else.

"Hey, I'm sorry I stood you up at halftime," he apologized. "I just had to come in here and give them some boosting."

I understood.

Michigan never had a more dedicated captain.

The hero of that game in Bloomington was Larry Tregoning who stepped to the free throw line with time running out and banged home a pair of tosses to climax the incredible comeback and send the game into overtime. The amazing part about that was that Trigger was the worst free throw shooter on the team.

But it wasn't free throw shooting that brought Trigger to Michigan. I remember the first practice I attended the previous year at Yost. I had heard about Buntin, Cantrell, Tom Cole and the famed freshmen. But watching the Wolverines warm up, I quickly zeroed in on the skinny white kid knocking down those 20-footers.

"That's Tregoning," smiled Jorgensen, who was standing next to me. "He can flatout shoot, can't he?"

He sure could and my impression never changed. There weren't a lot of points left to go around on that team after Buntin and Russell got their share but "Trigger" Tregoning was never bashful about trying to pick up what was left over. When Larry got into a streak, he was absolutely beautiful to watch. Nor was he shy about going to the board—although with the Russell-Buntin-Darden trio working over opposing rebounders, Trigger usually found his roughest competition from his own teammates.

Trigger had that perpetual scowl that made him look rough and rugged. But that was strictly a mask because he was pleasant and friendly. Trigger's biggest problem was that he was more susceptible to wild swings of performance level than anyone on the team. A case in point was the three-game set near the end of the season.

Against Indiana in Ann Arbor, Tregoning had probably his finest game of his junior season—he hit 9-of-12 floor shots, grabbed 10 rebounds and eventually cost the Hoosiers the services of Tom VanArsdale who picked up five fouls trying to guard him. Two days later in Minneapolis, Trigger could connect on only 3-of-14 shots from outside and 1-of-3 from the free throw line. On to Wisconsin where Tregoning missed only once all afternoon from the floor as he also outrebounded Darden for one of the few times all year. Tough to predict, never dull to watch.

Tregoning's junior teammate and buddy George Pomey was as steady as Trigger was erratic. At 6-4, Pomey was used at forward or guard by Strack depending on the situation. However, with Cantrell and Russell at the guards—backed up by Herner, Thompson and Clawson—there wasn't much time available in the backcourt. As a result, George usually found himself up front. The following season, things would be reversed, with George taking over outside as Cazzie's running mate.

Pomey would never dazzle anyone with his offense. And he couldn't rake in a one-handed rebound. But that wasn't what that team was lacking. Defensively, he was as tough as Cantrell which was saying it all. This would be proved even more so the following season when Pomey moved to a starting guard role. In 1963-64, Pomey would mainly back up Darden and Tregoning, with occasional stints at guard. He was a close runnerup to Herner when it came to game smarts and later became a member of the Michigan coaching staff.

This then was the nucleus of the team that welcomed the highly touted kids aboard when they began practice that fall.

But there's something wrong about identifying Oliver Darden as a kid. Like the other four newcomers, Ollie was only 19 years old when he made his debut as a Wolverine in December but you would have a hard time convincing people of that fact. Especially people like Lou Hudson or Dick VanArsdale or Dave Schellhase who had to bang heads with him. A muscular 6-7, Darden appeared to be literally walking on air when he soared above the rim to spear a rebound. Woe unto any opponent or teammate who wandered too close when Ollie was scraping the ball off the backboard. It was for good reason that they called it "Bloody Nose Lane" and I would have to speculate that Darden might have edged Buntin when it came to handing out nostril restructuring.

Once, while strolling through the Indiana fieldhouse, the U-M players spotted a machine used to test jumping ability. The bar had been set at its highest point for storage, somewhere well above 10 feet. Still dressed in their street clothes, some of the players took a shot at touching the bar but fell considerably short. Oliver then stepped forward and loftily announced, "You guys are awful."

With that he crouched and shot straight up, past the bar and grabbed the top of the machine.

If, on this team of strongly assertive players, there had to be selected a single enforcer, Darden would have to be given the title. Yet, his wit, intelligence, and banter made him a positively great antidote to the endless hours of monotony on the road.

Ollie's mere presence on the court was usually enough to insure order. One testimonial to that effect was offered by the Buckeyes' Bill Hosket. During a hard-fought Ohio State-Michigan game in Columbus, a brief flurry erupted featuring Hosket and Cazzie Russell, two of the unlikeliest players to try to mix it up. It ended in a hurry as they simply grabbed each other and held on. I later saw Hosket and kidded him about that fracas.

"Listen, if I had known Cazzie was such a pussycat I would have at least tried to throw a punch," he laughed. "Because when we both ended up with the Knicks, I found out he was as much of a coward as I was. The main thing I wanted that night in Columbus was to hold onto Cazzie to keep him between me and Oliver Darden. I didn't want anything to do with Ollie."

Not many of Hosket's counterparts did either.

Because of his intense play, Darden was prone to foul difficulty, sometimes rather early in the game. But Ollie didn't let that change his style of play. His foul total was tops on the team although Cantrell, as you might expect, ran a close second. But, as with rebounds, Oliver claimed mistaken identity. At least occasionally he might have been right. Some officials may have been as misled as Ollie's opponents about his fierce demeanor.

The second sophomore, Jim ("Shag") Myers, never scared anyone but his barbers. By later-day standards, Myers was well cropped, but on a team that featured Pomey's crewcut, Tregoning's German butcher cut and Herner's Princeton, "Shag" was probably a fitting handle. He was a neck-and-neck contender for Buntin's smile leadership which was fortunate since he was the main target for teammates' jibes. That might have been because he was about the best-liked player on the team.

Because of Darden's frequent visits to the bench with foul difficulties, Myers saw more action than Strack may have visualized for his 6-8 smooth-shooting Ohioan. The tallest player on the team, he weighed in at only 200 pounds. Despite the boyish countenance and slender frame,

Jim wasn't timid about pounding the boards—he finished fifth in rebounding in spite of his limited duty. But his shooting, a strong feature of his high school game, never came around that season although it would improve markedly in his next two seasons. Shag would invariably hear from his fellow Wolverines when they would spot a 2-for-7 field goal reading by his name in the game statistics sheet. Shag would grin and get back to the crossword puzzle.

The pair of Johns—Clawson and Thompson—could almost be considered as a tandem. Both hailed from Illinois—Clawson from Naperville and Thompson from Pontiac. Both were outstanding backcourt men in high school and both had been highly sought-after recruits. Clawson would eventually end up in the front court for Strack but in 1963-64 he shared the backup guard role with Thompson and Herner. Clawson was by far the taller of the two at 6-4 compared to Thompson's 6-0. Thompson was the better ball handler, Clawson the better shooter. Neither would see extensive duty and their stats were almost identical for the year. Having been All-State players in Illinois, it must have been difficult for each having to watch most of the games from the bench but neither seemed to have any problems adjusting. Like Darden and Myers they also had another problem to deal with. And all four of them handled it with great class. They had to live for three years in the shadow of Number 33.

Whether or not you agree that Cazzie Russell is the greatest basketball player ever in Michigan history, it is hard to argue with the premise that his debut in a Wolverine uniform was the most eagerly awaited event in modern U-M times. Cazzie and I arrived on the Ann

Arbor scene about the same time, the fall of '62, but his coming seem to be a bit more heralded than mine. Apparently everybody knew about this marvel out of Carver High who had narrowed his choices to Iowa and Michigan before casting his lot with Dave Strack. For a town as starved for basketball success as Ann Arbor, it was a fantastic coup.

Assistant coaches Jim Skala and Tom Jorgensen, Chicago boys themselves, had done most of the leg work in corralling Cazzie. They began watching him in his high school sophomore year. Jorgy once told me that, oddly enough, he wasn't greatly impressed with Cazzie until his senior year.

"He was still erratic, not the polished player that some of the other kids on the court were. I really thought that Donnie Freeman was the best player in the state until Cazzie came on so strong his last year."

Freeman would go on to an outstanding career with Illinois but would never approach Russell in national acclaim.

Skala used to chuckle about his meetings with Cazzie when he made his official visits to the U-M campus.

"Everytime the subject of Yost Fieldhouse came up I would always shuffle around in my pocket and pretend that I couldn't find the keys to the front door. There wasn't any way I was going to show Cazzie that place before he signed."

And Cazzie never did see Yost until he enrolled that fall. But I'm not sure it would have made that much difference. His dad recalled his thoughts during the period when Cazzie was making up his mind on where to attend school.

"I just kept thinking Ann Arbor, Ann Arbor. Never

had seen it, didn't really know that much about it but I just felt there was something there that was right for Junior. I can't explain it but I knew he would end up in Ann Arbor."

Cazzie, Senior, had called it correctly and thousands of Michigan fans were eternally grateful.

It is always dangerous to label someone the best or the greatest or the most popular. But I must say that in my 23 years of broadcasting Michigan teams, only one other player comes close to having the charismatic love affair with Wolverine fans that Cazzie did. Anthony Carter.

Cazzie could orchestrate the media and the fans like a maestro. His outgoing, bubbling personality captivated people as much as his twisting, gravity-defying jumpers or reverse dunks during warmups that would send the crowd into a frenzy. I always enjoyed chatting with Cazzie but never really knew if he was naturally that gregarious or just very publicity minded. But I had no trouble giving Caz the benefit of the doubt since he was such an avid conversationalist and so eager to learn about everything.

Some athletes shy from the spotlight, preferring to perform without the roar of the crowd pushing them to greater heights. Cazzie's All-American counterpart Bill Bradley was a classic example. But not Cazzie. He basked in the attention and affection from the stands and nobody ever worked harder at improving his talent in order to continue to deserve the acclaim.

Yet, oddly enough, basketball was only second choice for the young Cazzie Lee Russell, Jr.

"I always loved baseball. When I was young I would go outside by myself and stroke a baseball all over the vacant lot out back. I would pretend I was Bob Elson (long time White Sox announcer) and broadcast the game while I hit. I really wanted to become a major leaguer."

He excelled on the diamond in high school and was seriously considering concentrating on the sport in college. His high school coach cautioned him, however, that while he was in line for an attractive scholarship offer for basketball, not many baseball scholarships were given to black high school players. He wisely accepted the advice. But he never gave up his love for the summer game. As a matter of fact, he and Buntin played in the recreational league during their vacation periods in Ann Arbor. Imagine Dave Strack's nightmares over the thought of his two stars bending a leg at a 90-degree angle trying to score from second on a single.

Cazzie may not have seen the inside of old Yost Fieldhouse before he enrolled but he sure made up for it once he got there. It was almost impossible to walk into the Fieldhouse at any time of any day and not find Cazzie perfecting his moves. He would enlist the aid of any bystander in his efforts to become the best.

Number 33 was never satisfied with resting on his performance from the previous game. If he was 11-of-17 from the floor and 7-of-8 from the line he would fret over his seven misses.

So, these higher visibility players, along with the less-heralded Doug Greenwald (as good at the cribbage board as Buntin), Van Tillotson, the delightful Charley Adams, and the fiesty Tom Ludwig were the Wolverines of 1963-64. And this was the club that would ignite the basketball fires in Ann Arbor and before they were done, would fan them to an inferno.

Now, what about the man who directed them? `

First of all, was Dave Strack the director or was he

simply a figurehead? Were Jim Skala and Tom Jorgensen the behind-the-scenes brain trust? These questions were asked often during Michigan's three-year ascendency. Frankly, I never understood why these questions were raised. No more than I did when such later questions were posed in relation to Johnny Orr and Jim Dutcher. Or Johnny Orr and Bill Frieder. Despite his less-than-placid nature, Strack was certainly smart enough to involve two young and solid assistants in the program. I have always been mystified as to how a fan can determine how much input is the result of the head coach and how much is divided among his aides.

A much more pertinent question was, how good a coach was Strack? His first three teams at Michigan went 8 and 34 in Big Ten play, ending twice in the cellar and once in eighth place. Next, Buntin and Russell showed up. Strack's next four teams posted a 43-13 mark with three championships along the way. Then Cazzie left for the Knicks and Strack's next two teams came in 8 and 20. Clearly, when Strack had the talent he won and when he didn't he lost. His obvious mistake was in not bringing in replacements for the stellar class of '66. When they all departed at the same time, it was a disaster. And it no doubt hastened Strack's move into the associate athletic director's role. Still, that really begs the question: was Strack a good coach?

One segment of Michigan fans insisted that anyone could have coached a team of that caliber to a conference championship. All that was needed was somebody to hand out the basketballs in practice and provide the alumni with preferential seating.

I don't think so. It certainly wasn't a team of difficult personalities that would cause a coach a morale prob-

lem. However, it was a team that needed firm guidance —
all that high-powered talent could have exploded into
chaos if not properly harnessed. And this Strack did well.

He also realized that this was a team that wasn't going to torture too many people defensively but could overpower and outboard most teams they would meet. As a
result he gave them a loose rein in using their obvious
advantage at the offensive end of the court. Now, you
can say it didn't take a genius to turn Caz, Buntin, Tregoning and the rest loose, but more than one coach has screwed
up in trying to mold a team to his coaching philosophy
rather than vice-versa. If Skala and Jorgensen were instrumental in this decision, so be it. Strack would have
been foolish to disregard their expertise and if there was
one thing Strack was not it was dumb.

The one valid criticism that might have been made was
that he sometimes adjusted too slowly to game situations.
A couple of players later suggested that perhaps a game
could have been salvaged if Strack had reshuffled his personnel to keep pace with the opposition's strength. With
his multiple-choice lineup maybe he did sometimes go too
long with a pat hand. But remember, during three magic
years, he lost an average of only five games a year. Any
coach would have had problems departing from such a
successful format to do a bit of experimenting. Still, Strack's
fellow coaches thought enough of him to name him as
the 1965 NCAA coach of the year.

In personality, Strack was considered a bit unusual by
some. One of his later assistants once told me in exaspera-
tion, "I never know what to expect when I come in to
work. He might say 'Hi', he might say nothing, or he
might laugh and kid with me for a half an hour. It really
takes a little getting used to."

That sums it up pretty well. Maybe it was the pressure of being thrust into a cauldron of fan and media hysteria after the serene years of crowds of 500.

Maybe it was the fact that he was no longer given the luxury of losing even one game without his motives or strategy being questioned. Or maybe he was just basically a reticent individual who enjoyed his family and friends while tolerating the rest of us because it was his job. I suspect it was probably a combination of all three. Added to it should be the possibility that some of us in the media just aren't all that likeable.

(Later, it would be a whale of an adjustment to make when Johnny Orr took over in 1968. I probably had more conversations with John in his first month on the job than I did in six years with Dave.) I don't mean to imply that I had any problems with Strack, I simply had no relationship with him at all. Surprisingly, after he departed for Arizona, we had some lengthy and warm visits. I'm sorry he couldn't have stopped to enjoy himself just a little more during his glory years in Ann Arbor.

Like Strack, Jim Skala and Tommy Jorgensen were former Michigan basketball captains which gave the team a troika probably never before and never again achieved. Both had labored through three years of mediocrity during their respective tenures, Skala under Ernie McCoy during the '50-51-52 period and Jorgy under Bill Perrigo from '54-56. Things were so tough in Skala's senior year that he led the team in scoring with a whopping 11.6 average! Both were as outgoing as Strack was introverted as they regaled us with stories of the days of the frustrating Fifties. One of Jorgy's funniest had to do with a trip to Northwestern during Perrigo's tight budget administration. The team had flown to Midway and caught cabs for the 20-mile journey to Evanston. As the cab's meter ticked away, Perrigo got more and more shaky. Finally, Perrigo could stand it no more.

"He told his driver to pull over to the curb and hauled all of us out of our cabs," said Jorgensen, "and we ended up walking the rest of the way to our hotel with our bags."

So the cast of characters had been chosen. The producers and directors were set and the critics were ready with their pens. The curtain would soon go up on a production that would run for three years to nationwide rave reviews.

But when the curtain rose, one of the co-stars was missing. Dave Strack had suspended Bill Buntin just prior to the season's first game with Ball State in Muncie.

What Buntin's transgression was will never be known because Strack committed himself to everlasting silence on the matter and Billy is gone. In any case, Michigan basketball followers were dismayed to learn that their great pivotman would not be making the trip to Indiana for the meeting with the Cardinals. But nobody was more stunned than Cazzie.

"For six weeks we had planned to get off to a great start and suddenly Billy isn't there," Cazzie said. "I didn't know what to think."

Even without Buntin's suspension, it was an opener tinged with gloom. One week before, John Kennedy had been assassinated in Dallas. This had caused the Ohio State-Michigan football game to be postponed to the following Saturday. That in turn had set up an unprecedented football-basketball doubleheader for November 30th. A number of other games had also been set back which meant the Michigan-Ball State opener hardly got a nod in the sports sections.

But as Cazzie put it, the team was well aware of the absence of their big fellow. The conversation on the plane to Indianapolis mainly dealt with the assassination — everyone had a tough time dealing with the events of the past week. There was little of the customary joking and jiving and a rather grim and tense U-M squad took the court that Saturday night.

Strack started Myers in place of Buntin, along with Darden and Pomey at the forwards. Cazzie and Cantrell manned the backcourt and 2:38 into the game Cazzie tipped in his own missed shot to record the first of his 2,164 points. But the Wolverines couldn't shake the smaller Cardinals and trailed at halftime, 41-40. The second half began the same way and the teams were tied at 65-65 with eight minutes to go. But eventually the superior firepower of Michigan asserted itself. Cazzie and Myers started popping from the outside to send Michigan off the court with a 90-75 victory. Russell finished with 30 points in his debut while Myers had an equally impressive beginning with 22, his high for the year.

Monday night the team returned to Yost for their first appearance before the home fans who surprisingly numbered only 5,300, about 2,500 shy of capacity. The win over Ball State and the subsequent number eight national ranking had not yet triggered the fanatical response that this crew would soon inspire. For Russell, the home opener against Tulane was not what he had envisioned as his varsity introduction. His first field goal didn't come until the first half was more than 10 minutes old, a half in which he managed only three points. His 13 total points would represent the lowest Ann Arbor total of his career. But truthfully, his team never missed him even though Strack extended Buntin's punishment and again started Myers in the pivot.

Then, with seven minutes gone in the game, the crowd came to its feet as Big Bill stripped off his warmup suit and checked into the lineup. Four minutes later, Buntin hooked from the key to climax a surge that shoved Michigan from a two-point lead to a 19-5 margin. There was no struggle the rest of the way with Michigan capturing a 73-47 win. The 73 points would represent the Wolverines lowest total of the year. Buntin had regained his rightful role in the middle; it was role he would never relinquish again. He ripped off 15 rebounds and posted a game-leading 20 points. Billy and his smile were back and the Michigan title train was on track.

Nebraska proved to be no more of a test despite the absence of Cantrell because of a sprained ankle. Herner took over without missing a beat as Michigan raced to a 9-0 start and steadily pulled away. Strack did some more shuffling as he inserted Darden and Myers at the forwards in place of his Tulane pairing of Tregoning and Pomey.

It was also evident from the crowd of 7,100 that basketball had made its impact. In these days of arenas seating upwards of 18,000, a figure of 7,100 might not sound like a big deal. But let's review the situation. First of all, I was always very skeptical of announced crowds at Yost. As I recall, the fire marshall had dictated a maximum of around 7,800 for the ancient arena. Before 1962, a maximum limit never mattered. With the crowds (and that is a loose term for the earlier years) that showed up in those days, there could have been a blazing inferno at midcourt and almost everyone would have had an exit to themselves to get out. Thus I suspect that sports information director Les Etter used his own system in computing the attendance during the Cazzie years — although I never knew exactly what it was. However, I would have been surprised if on any given night the total was less than 9,000. But even if only 7,100 were on hand, they *sounded* like 71,000. Long pent-up emotions of long-suffering basketball fans gushed forth in a raging flood.

And there was no attempt at sophistication, for beginning with the Nebraska game, the fans went nuts every game for three years.

By the Nebraska game, a large hand-painted sign had been unfurled in the balcony which read, "*FIRST BY THE FIRST.*" For a team which had never even made a visit to the top 20 in their long history, it was quite a lofty goal. But to the frenzied rooters that fought off the pigeons at old Yost, it was well within reach.

Of course, the Wolverines weren't above doing all they could to fan these fires of fanaticism, even during warm-ups. As soon as the team set foot on the court, the din started — by then the fans anticipated the electrifying layup drills. Now mind you, these were not the run-of-the-mill drills where a player would go in and softly lay the ball off the glass and through the net. These instead were some of the wildest all-out, slam-bang drills you will ever see. One after another they would come, Buntin slamming home a one-handed jam that would rattle the rafters; Darden roaring in with a two-handed smash calculated to put the rim to its severest test; Tregoning, Myers, Pomey, Clawson — on they would come, each with a twist or flair until it was Cazzie's turn. Starting his takeoff at about the foul line, Number 33 would soar in an arc towards the basket with the ball cradled in his left hand. Then just as he started to lose altitude he would shift the

ball from left to right and suddenly power it through the
nets while twisting his body in a half circle. Thus Caz
would touch down outside the baseline looking back up
the court.

The crowd joined in by counting off the jam dunks until
eventually it would be the turn of Herner, Cantrell, or
Ludwig who would have to break the string. The crowd
never held this against the small-sized trio but pity one
of the bigger Wolverines who broke the streak. Michigan
fans of 1964-66 must be thankful that the NCAA didn't
come along with their asinine "no-dunk" rule in warmups
until years later.

Johnny Orr used to remark wistfully that if he had had
the old Yost crowds at Crisler it would have meant three
or four more victories a year for him.

Soon it was time once again for another trip into Indiana for Michigan. But this time they had Buntin in
uniform and they knocked off Butler, 80-70, in Strack's
home town of Indianapolis. Buntin not only was in uniform, he was also about as perfect as he would get, hitting 11-of-12 shots from the floor to key the victory.
Butler's veteran coach, Tony Hinkle, asked Strack, "How
come you didn't leave him home this time?" A lot of coaches
would echo his thoughts over the next two years.

This pushed Michigan into a 7th-place ranking na-
tionally and set up the Western Michigan match between
Cantrell and Newsome.

Michigan's lopsided victory over the Broncos rocketed
them into third place in the AP rankings and prompted
Western coach Don Boven to comment, "They should
take the club into the NBA right now." Strack said, "I'm
not disappointed in our progress."

Michigan didn't have to wait long to put their lofty

rating on the line—the next Saturday who showed up but
the fifth-rated Blue Devils of Duke. Any time two teams
in the top five square off, there is bound to be national
interest, but the situation in Ann Arbor was getting serious.
Ticket manager Don Weir and his staff were completely
overwhelmed as students and staff jockeyed for tickets.
And for the first time in history, scalpers were hawking
basketball tickets and getting their asking price. Following this wild bout with the fans, Don instituted some
guidelines which didn't satisfy those who were shut out,
but at least restored some semblance of order.

I found out how far along Michigan basketball had
come as I prepared to pull into the press parking lot that
Saturday evening. Flashing my pass, I started to move
through the entrance to the lot off State Street. My path
was quickly blocked by a gate guard.

"Sorry, you can't go through without a parking pass."

"A parking pass? I've never needed one before."

"Yeah, I know but you've got to have one now."

"Well, where do I get it?"

"They're selling them for $25 at the Athletic Office."

"Selling them? Since when do broadcasters and writers
have to pay to get in?"

"I can't help it, those are the rules."

Waiting behind me was Charley Adams, one of the free
spirits on the team.

"Hey, don't you know who that is?" he yelled out of
his car window.

"Yeah, I know who he is," growled my friend, the guar-
dian of the lot, "but he ain't going nowhere without that
pass."

So much for fame.

After parking about five blocks away I stalked into the

Fieldhouse to find Les Etter, whose office was responsible for the passes. By the time I found him, he already was being besieged by other members of the media who were being asked to fork over 25 dollars for the privilege of covering Michigan basketball.

"I know, I know," Les protested. "I tried to tell Fritz that it wouldn't work but he thinks we should charge everyone."

"Les," said Pete Waldemeir of the *Detroit News*, "you tell Fritz if he wants his games covered he had better forget about charging the press for parking."

Apparently Les convinced Fritz—the following week we all got our passes, free of charge.

(I just hope this doesn't give Don Canham any ideas.)

By 6:30, Yost was packed to the bursting point. The crowd was later announced at 7,251 which brought some loud guffaws from press row.

"I guess Les just counted the ones he could see on the other side," cracked one writer.

Every other publicity man in the world has at one time or another been accused of padding attendance figures. After that night, Les must have secretly envied them.

Like Michigan, Duke had its own one-two punch in a pair of future NBA stars, Jeff Mullins and Jack Marin. And that duo combined with a pair of 6-10 pivotmen, Hack Tison and Jay Buckley, to give the Blue Devils a formidable front line. Michigan hadn't seen one player all year long close to 6-10 let alone two. "This could cause some problems," said Dave Strack.

Buntin stepped into the center circle against the towering Tison and served an early notice. He shot into the air over the Duke center and batted the ball directly to Cazzie. Russell quickly drove to the top of the circle—

and surprisingly missed the jumper. But roaring out of the pack came Buntin to drive the miss back home.

Tison shook his head in disbelief all the way back up the court. Buntin never let up throughout the game as he grabbed 18 rebounds. That, along with Cazzie's 15 gave the terrible twosome only two less than the entire Duke squad. Meanwhile, with Duke ganging up on Russell, Tregoning stepped forward to have his best scoring half to date as he fired in 13 points, mostly from long range, to propel Michigan into a 38-30 margin at halftime. It could have been Trigger's night for a 30-point performance but with the second half only four minutes old, Larry picked up his fifth foul, three coming in rapid succession. His departure proved more costly for Duke than Michigan—it prompted Cazzie to take charge.

Russell had been held to a mere two points in the opening half, a performance that no one expected to continue. Quickly canning three of his textbook jumpers to open the second half, he spurred Michigan to an 11-point lead by the time Tregoning had fouled out.

As Trigger came off the court to a standing ovation, he slumped down beside Darden who slapped him on the knee.

"Pretty cheap way to get an early rest, Trig," kidded Oliver.

"They'll never miss me," Tregoning said as he settled back to watch his teammates pour it on.

He was right—Cazzie continued to explode. What he didn't do Buntin did—the two ran off 10 points in three and a half minutes and it was all over with 12:00 to go. Michigan had a whopping 20-point margin before a shocked and delirious crowd. The final 83-67 score stunned everybody including Dave Strack. If any one game could

be pointed to as putting Michigan on the national basketball map, it was this one. In dominating the fifth-ranked
Blue Devils, the Wolverines definitely had arrived.

After a brief break for Christmas, the team headed west
for the Bruin Classic, easily the most impressive field of
any holiday tournament that year. No less than three of
the top 10 teams in the nation were involved. By the luck
of the draw, number three Michigan would face number
10 NYU in the opener while the other Big Ten team, Illinois, tangled with sixth-rated UCLA.

NYU featured Barry Kramer and Hap Hairston, another pair of future NBA performers. After their classic
against Duke, however, the Wolverines didn't appear worried about tangling with another All-American tandem.
In fact, the chief topic of conversation on arrival was the
great weather, a welcome relief to the frigid climate they
had left back in Michigan. Strack said, "I hope they just
remember what we're out here for."

They remembered all right. But so did NYU. The Vio-
lets were just starting to erase the stigma of the school's
point-shaving scandals of the Fifties. They were not as
powerful as they had been during their glory years when
they were perennial visitors to the NCAA or NIT tourney
but like Michigan they were not averse to pounding a few
bodies.

It was quickly evident to Michigan that this was going to be a rugged test. Hairston poured in 23 points in
the first half on a combination of short hooks and jumpers. It didn't make any difference who Strack put on him,
Hairston ate them all up. At the same time Buntin was
struggling through the poorest half of his career; he failed
to score a single point. However, Kramer wasn't having

much better luck — he managed merely four. As a result, Michigan still led at halftime, 39-37.

The second half started the same way, Hairston hitting from every angle. But Cazzie and Buntin started opening up for the Wolverines. Still Michigan dropped behind and was forced to play catchup until finally with seven minutes gone they climbed back on top, 50-49. Although it was close the rest of the way, the Wolverines never let the New Yorkers regain the lead and finally pulled away for an 83-74 win. Hairston ended with 35 points while Cazzie tallied 26. Buntin had come on with 12 in the second half to give the West Coast fans a glimpse of the true abilities of the magnificent Wolverines.

UCLA had knocked off Illinois in their opener and was set to meet Michigan. Feeling that his team might need a little diversion after facing two top 10 teams in a row, Strack took the squad of a tour of Disneyland. They romped through the Magic Kingdom like third graders on a holiday. Watching Darden and Buntin wedge their frames into the tiny boats was a highlight of the season. After four hours of the Matterhorn, Frontierland, the Haunted House and the Jungle Cruise, Strack herded his forces back to the motel to recover for the meeting with the Bruins the following night.

Like Michigan, UCLA had raced to a 7-0 season mark. But unlike the Wolverines, it was finesse and not strength that keyed their attack. Johnny Wooden had arrived in Westwood back in 1948, bringing to UCLA his philosophy of high-speed basketball on both offense and defense. His teams would press from the opening tip. However, until 1962, his squads lacked the talent to be a national contender. But in that year, he moved his club into the final four for the first time in his career. The Bruins bowed to the eventual champs from Cincinnati but their appetites had been whetted. Before he was done, John Wooden would satiate those appetites better than any college coach in history.

By 1964, Wooden had corralled a pair of guards that pioneered the long line of All-Americans that would pass through Pauley Pavilion.

Walt Hazzard must have been designed and assembled by Wooden in his laboratory—he was that perfect for John's team. A premier ballhandler who couldn't be loosened from the ball by a pickax, he was such a pinpoint passer that he probably made everybody else on the team 25 percent better. If all else failed, he would simply shrug and fire the ball in himself—his 19-point average attested to his shooting skill. On defense, he was even better, as he probably forced more turnovers than any other player in Bruin history. When double-teaming the ballhandler in the backcourt, Hazzard must have seemed a foot taller than his 6-2 to his opponents.

The second number of that talented pair was Gail Goodrich, who appeared to come out of Central Casting. And he was as fast as Hazzard and an even better shooter. If left unguarded, in an instant he would be by his man with the ball headed for the hole. Michigan would get more than their share of misery from this 6-1 junior in the two meetings they had.

UCLA had no starter over 6-5, giving Michigan a height advantage at four of the five positions. This wasn't anything new to the tournament hosts, however, since they only cared how fast you ran, not how tall you were. Five minutes into the game, Michigan wondered whether they were in a track meet or a basketball game. The UCLA full-court press proved devastating to Michigan who often couldn't even get the ball up the court to get a shot away. Meanwhile, the Bruins were running at will, picking up layup after layup to easily make the Wolverines their eighth straight victim, 98-80. Only Darden could find the key offensively as the muscular Detroiter scored a season-high 25 points, second only to Goodrich's 30.

"Ollie just scared 'em to death," cracked Adams.

The fast-paced UCLA attack completely nullified the Buntin-Russell duo—they combined for only 19 points. Some critics thought the Disneyland adventure had drained the team before they ever hit the floor.

"That's ridiculous," snapped Strack. "I don't think we have to get up for every game like you do in football. It was too much to ask that our team get up for Duke, NYU, and UCLA in a row."

The size of the final margin shocked most observers, including Illinois coach Harry Coombs. After his team gave the Bruins a much tougher tussle, losing by four points, Harry predicted, "They are so quick they might not lose a game all year."

How right he was.

Michigan still had another game to go on the coast, however. Although Pitt wasn't in the category of the last three foes, Strack's crew could ill afford to repeat the UCLA debacle. Strack needn't have worried. Buntin reverted to form and dominated both the scoring and rebounding columns while his team pulled away late in the first half to win going away, 95-80. Billy and Caz were named to the all-tournament team along with Hazzard, Goodrich, and Hairston.

One other item came out of the week of action on the West Coast. Darden and Tregoning stepped forward as the outstanding pair of frontliners alongside Buntin. Strack now had his regular starting five for the remainder of the season. And it was goodbye Disneyland, hello Ann Arbor.

Before they could turn their attention to the Big Ten there was the matter of a New Year's Eve game with the University of Detroit. The Titans had roughed up the Wolverines the previous season, 83-70. Not many of the players were happy about seeing them in 1964 at Yost Fieldhouse. Charley Adams, who may have trailed everybody in playing time but led by a mile in female acquaintances, looked especially glum as he trooped into the locker room.

"Isn't it against the law to have to play a game on a holiday?"

"Charley, New Year's Eve isn't a holiday," Darden informed him.

"It is to me," Adams grumped. "Nobody will even recognize me by the time I get to the party."

"Well, why not just spend a nice quiet evening with your girl at your place?" Thompson suggested.

"I can't," Charley said. "The party's at my place."

One of the Wolverines who was ready for action that night was Buntin. The normally placid Billy was still seething over his performance on the West Coast that had some western writers questioning his ability to deliver in big games. He also recalled the meeting the year before where he had been outplayed by the Titan's Dick Dzik in the Detroit romp.

Tregoning took one look at Buntin and nudged Herner.

"Look at Billy," Trigger gestured. "He might not need the rest of us tonight."

He almost didn't.

Dzik had been moved to a forward with John Schramm taking over at the pivot. Three and a half minutes into the game, Shramm posted low on Billy, took a pass and swept around him for an early layup. As Buntin clapped his hands in disgust Strack bounded off the bench.

Billy nodded as he shot Schramm a menacing look while they trotted down the court. It was the last point Schramm would score all night.

At the five-minute mark, Michigan led by only a point and Darden, who was paired against Dzik this time, was already in foul trouble having collected two in the first three minutes. The entire team seemed to be having problems shaking off the jet lag plus having to play their fourth game in a six-day span. It was at that point that Buntin staged his own party on the court. Two hooks from the key, two jumpers from the base line, two tip ins and a free throw later, Michigan had a 26-17 lead. Of those 26 points, Billy had 16. The margin grew steadily and when big number 22 hit a layup to close out the first half scoring, Michigan was up 59-38 — and Buntin had 22 points. That seemed to convince most people that Bill could still play the game although U-D coach Bob Calihan probably didn't need quite such a graphic illustration. Buntin turned the scoring chores over to Cazzie in the second half and Russell was equal to the challenge as he ripped in 20 points to finish with a season high of 36, seven more than Buntin.

Bill's backup, Doug Greenwold, also popped into the Michigan record book briefly. His jumper at 2:11 gave Michigan a 111-79 lead, smashing the previous high-water mark for a Wolverine squad. Strack started clearing his bench with seven minutes to go which got Michigan's great tackle Bill Yearby into his only game of the season. Yearby, who had been a fine basketball player in his Detroit prep days, twice clobbered Dzik as the Titan star tried to drive on him—Yearby's antics had the Michigan bench in stitches.

As Dzik shakily went to the free throw line after Yearby's second foul, the droll Darden yelled out to his fellow Detroiter, "Atta boy Yerb, he hasn't gained a yard on you yet."

The final 117-87 score was a great springboard into the Big Ten season.

The first conference foe would be the Wildcats of Northwestern who had a rather unique parlay. Included on that squad was a future unique Wildcat coach, Rick Falk, and a Davis Cup tennis star, Marty Riessen. Falk was the bigger problem as far as the Wolverines were concerned— his 27-point average placed him high among the Big Ten scorers. But Falk hadn't stepped onto the court against Bobby Cantrell that season.

By the midway point of the first half, Falk had managed to connect on one lone jumper against the fiery defense of Michigan while also drawing two charging fouls as he banged into his ever-present shadow. However, the Michigan captain was paying the price for his aggressive work on Falk. With still about eight minutes to go in the half, Cantrell picked up his third foul. Falk took advantage of Bobby's departure by scoring 10 points in the remaining portion of the period. Still, Northwestern lagged by a dozen points at halftime as Buntin had another of his typical first-half surges. Moving into the corner against the Wildcat zone, Billy hammered home 18 points while grabbing seven rebounds to lead Michigan to a 45-33 lead at the break.

The second half proved to be even tougher for Falk — Cantrell returned to shut him down without a point over the first nine minutes. However, the Wolverines were not so lucky against another Rick, this one named Lapossa. Bedeviled by three fouls in the first half, he had tallied but seven points, five coming from the free throw line. But with his team trailing by 11, the 6-3 forward caught fire. In slightly over two minutes, Lapossa pumped in 11 points on a combination of hooks, jumpers and layups. Suddenly the Wildcats had cut the lead to four and were back in the ball game. Compounding the Wolverines' problems was the fact that Darden had picked up his fourth foul early in the half trying to guard the elusive Lapossa and was replaced by Myers. But Shag had little success and Strack moved Trigger onto the hot Wildcat. The move paid off, Lapossa not only cooled down, he also picked up his fourth foul just seconds following his scoring binge. With Michigan still up by only five, it was Tregoning's turn. Three baskets by the Ferndale junior, combined with buckets by Cazzie and Pomey, sparked a Michigan 10-2 spurt that settled the issue.

The opener went into Michigan's win column, 85-73. Falk, who could get only one field goal on Cantrell in the second half, finished with 17 — 10 points under his season's average — while Lapossa tallied 29 to lead all scorers. Russell nipped Buntin for the Michigan honors, 23-22, with Tregoning not far behind at 18.

Checking the stat sheet following the game, Darden gave Trigger a mischievous glance.

"Hey, Trig, your man scored 29 points!"

"What do you mean my man?" Tregoning replied. "He only got two against me!"

"Yeah, but that's only because I wore him down for you," Ollie sniffed, "he was exhausted by the time Shag and I turned him over to you."

While everybody was commenting on his tenacious job of guarding Falk, Bobby Cantrell quietly brought it to everyone's attention that he had only three less field goals than the Northwestern scoring star on eight fewer attempts. Falk could only be happy that this was the lone meeting between the teams that season.

The following Saturday found the team in West Lafayette, Indiana for a meeting with Purdue. The Boilermakers, outside of their great scorer, Dave Schellhase, did not possess much talent. They weren't expected to mount a serious threat against the nation's fourth ranked team. But they were about to get some help from an unexpected source.

The U-M headquarters was the Morris Bryant Inn, a typical midwestern motel. But attached to the living quarters was its restaurant, famed throughout the state for its smorgasbord. For a paltry $4.50 (remember this was 1964) one could partake of a panoramic offering of meat, poultry, fish, vegetables, salads, breads and desserts. Friday night found the Wolverines mounting an attack on the overloaded tables like Donner Pass survivors. I think Strack knew he was in trouble when Buntin wobbled back to his table for the third time with yet another selection of pie ala mode.

It was a decidedly green-tinged group that took the floor at the old Purdue Fieldhouse the next day. After a listless first half which saw them only holding their own, Michigan did manage to creep in front midway through the second period to eventually put it away, 77-70. A great deal of credit went to Pomey, who took over for the ailing Tregoning, and contributed 15 points. George had been one of the more prudent eaters the night before— apparently it paid off.

Cazzie, bothered by stomach cramps all game, hit only 5-of-17 from the floor and finished with 17 points. Coming down the stretch, however, it was the two enforcers who made the difference as Darden and Buntin combined for 27 rebounds and 38 points. Despite his miseries, Buntin missed but 3-of-10 shots outside and was 9-for-9 from the free throw line. It would have been hard convincing Purdue he wasn't healthy. Nonetheless, the next time Michigan visited Purdue, Strack found another motel.

While not impressive, the win upped Michigan's mark to 11-1 overall and 2-0 in the conference. And it propelled them back into a third place spot in the national rankings. It also set up an early duel with Ohio State who also had jumped off to a 2-0 mark. Walking through the dressing room before the OSU game, I noticed a number of signs bearing only numbers—75-68, 72-57, 89-64, 80-58, 99-52, 106-83. Each was encircled with a large red magic marker. Puzzled, I asked Skala for an explanation.

"Those are the scores of the games we've lost to Ohio State over the past four years," he answered. The last Michigan victory over the Bucks had come in 1959.

Especially keyed up was Buntin who would be facing the Big Ten's two-time scoring king, All-American Gary Bradds. Named as the nation's top player of 1963, the 6-8 great out of Jamestown, Ohio would set a new conference record in four point categories that season. His 33.9 scoring average would stand as the best in Big Ten history until the fabulous Rick Mount came along to smash it five years later. However, his amazing string of six straight games of 40 points or better that year remains a Big Ten standard. Buntin was well aware there wasn't a whole lot he could do about holding down Bradds' point production but he was determined to match him at the other end of the court.

The overflow crowd (announced at 7,350) was treated to a tremendous first half as the Wolverines used their running game for several fast break layups. Buntin even picked up three himself as the lead man on the break en route to a 12-point half which Bradds matched for the Buckeyes. But the difference was in the rest of the casts. Cazzie gathered up 16 points of his own while Bradds had little support as Michigan pushed to a halftime lead of 41-29.

The Wolverines never let up in the second half. Taking a clue from UCLA, they continued to run the Bucks ragged. There was no doubt left as Michigan amassed an 82-64 victory, their greatest margin in a win over Ohio State to that time. Buntin and Bradds ended the game stalemated at 27 points, surely a great achievement for U-M's number 22. But Cazzie also ended with 27 points and added a game-high 13 rebounds (although Darden would later insist that at least five belonged in his column). Ohio State coach Fred Taylor, who had seen the best in Lucas, Havlicek, Sigfried, and the rest, could only shake his head.

"Look at the fast breaks they were getting," he said. "When a guy 6-7 takes off up the floor to lead the break, you known you're in trouble."

That pretty well summed it up.

The win pushed Michigan up another notch — number two in the national ranking behind UCLA, a spot they would occupy for most of the remainder of the season. When Minnesota moved into Ann Arbor for a Thursday night affair, another packed house was treated to a new look for the Gophers. For the first time in their history, Minnesota had a black player in their regular lineup. They had in fact, *three* top black sophomores in Lou Hudson, Tony Yates, and Archie Clark who would make Minnesota a force for three years. With 6-8 Mel Northway in the middle and 6-6 senior Bill Davis joining Hudson up front, the Gophers were a threat to any team.

Strack had worried publicly about a possible letdown after the emotional Ohio State win. He hoped that his team would realize they were playing a team every bit as good as the Buckeyes. The Wolverines took him seriously and, led by Buntin, came out firing.

(It was eerie how this team would follow roughly the same pattern in sharing the scoring load. Buntin tended to be a speed horse who would dash out of the opening gate and hit the double-figure mark before the other team knew what had happened. Cazzie, meanwhile, was more of a distance runner who would open slowly, then pour it on down the stretch. Tregoning and Darden picked up a high percentage of their points in the mid-portion of a half, providing Ollie had behaved himself and not bloodied too many noses. But in retrospect there was a perfectly good reason for this scenario. The opposition was naturally keyed on Cazzie. They concentrated on trying to stop him early. Because Russell played the low post in the 1-3-1 offense a great deal, this meant a lot of sagging by the defense. Quite often this opened up the middle and Buntin was a master at taking full advantage of it. This would force the opponents to beef up their efforts on Bill which naturally opened up the wings where Darden and Tregoning spent a lot of time. Cazzie would patiently wait until he knew he would find his openings with the defense spread more and then bury it. The Minnesota game was a classic example.)

Nine quick points by Buntin pushed Michigan to a 13-9 lead. Tregoning and Darden then teamed for six. After three picturesque jumpers by Russell, Michigan had a 25-14 bulge. The closest the Gophers could come after that was 10 points when they ran off a string of six straight at the end of the period to make it a 42-32 count at halftime. And, as if to show their coach that he needn't have fussed about a letdown, the Maize and Blue also played the first 20 minutes without a turnover.

The Gophers narrowed it to seven midway through the second half before Cazzie and Cantrell put on a jump-shooting clinic, running off 10 points between them, and Michigan coasted home, 80-66.

For the first time that season, however, a team had been able to stay with Michigan on the boards—the Gophers' 46 rebounds were only two shy of the Wolverines while Davis edged Darden for individual honors, 16-13. But when you turn the ball over only four times in a game, you can withstand a little enemy muscle. The Gophers also learned the hard way what the other Big Ten teams would discover. Fouling Buntin and Russell wasn't the answer. Bill, with the blacksmith's build and the surgeon's touch, dropped in 9-of-11 from the line while Cazzie followed with 7-of-8.

Two days later the Wolverines were climbing onto the bus for a trip to East Lansing and the first of home-and-home games with the Spartans. After their back-to-back victories over their two main contenders for the conference championship, the club was jovial. Insults and barbs flew fast and furious. One of the targets was Doug Herner who was offered a security escort inside Jenison Fieldhouse by his teammates. The previous season, Herner had returned to his hometown to hit a shot at the buzzer to give Michigan a 72-71 win. Doug had been hassled every time he touched the ball by the Spartan fans who had never forgiven him for forsaking them. Tregoning suggested that perhaps Doug should walk in between Darden and Buntin.

"That way, they'll never see you, Herns," Trigger assured him.

Herner made his way safely to the dressing room along with the rest of the team. But on the court there was no guarantee of safety for anybody that day.

A crowd of over 12,000 had shoehorned their way into Jenison while thousands more had tuned in on regional television. A few years later the East Lansing fire marshall would limit the capacity of the old arena to 10,004; but this day they were standing 10 deep around the perimeter. Most of them must have thought they had taken a wrong turn and ended up at Spartan Stadium—the contest they saw was that rough. Following the game, Cazzie would comment, "Those officials weren't calling anything under the basket. But you don't complain about it, you just clear it out of there and go on with your business."

It was also a game of streaks. The Spartans ran off eight straight points five minutes into the game to go up, 14-8. Four came from Pete Gent, their leading scorer, who went on to fame as both a Dallas Cowboy and a best-selling author. Gent also picked up a couple of quick fouls as he hacked both Darden and Cazzie. And in the first minutes of action, Stan Washington also leveled Cazzie. This apparently aroused the Chicago All-American into a reversal of his normal pattern and he went on a 15-point scoring binge that helped Michigan take a 27-16 lead midway through the half. That only provoked MSU into another eight-point splurge which brought them back within three. From there on out, it was a trade-off and when the first half horn sounded, Michigan had a slender 40-38 margin.

Cazzie and Buntin, playing the entire 20 minutes, had piled up 29 of those points between them. Both took full advantage of their frequent trips to the foul line, hitting 13-of-15 attempts. The Spartans had surprised Strack with their dominant rebounding, outboarding Michigan 33-25 in the first half, and that was a major concern since the Wolverines' 32 percent outcourt shooting was far below their normal standard. Thus MSU was getting a much heavier crack at the boards than usual.

The streakiness continued into the second half. Michigan held a one-point lead two minutes into the period when Cazzie came on with an eight-point burst to vault Michigan to a 58-46 lead. Egged on by the boisterous Jenison crowd, the Spartans slashed back with nine in a row. So, with less than nine minutes remaining, it was back to a one-point U-M edge. Buntin, who had been staging an all-out duel with the Spartans' 6-9 Fred Thomann, was off to another of his slow second-half starts; no points over the first 11 minutes. There was nothing wrong with his rebounding, though, as he had matched the massive Thomann board for board.

With Michigan hanging on to that slender 60-59 lead, Buntin connected on a foul line jumper. That broke his drought and he quickly came back with an offensive tip in, soaring over the top of both Thomann and Gent to mash it home. This inspired Cazzie to run off a string of six points but the Spartans kept pace and another sizzling finish looked inevitable.

"No way," Buntin told his teammates, "just get me the ball."

They did—with devastating results. Cantrell fed him a picture-perfect pass in the lane and Bill roared around Thomann to lay it through. Seconds later Darden scraped off a missed MSU shot and fired an outlet pass to Cantrell. Bobby whipped it across court to Cazzie who dribbled down the left side as the Spartans desperately scrambled back. Cazzie drifted into the air and spotted the runaway truck wearing number 22 sailing down the middle. Billy picked up the pass in midstride and—carrying Gent on his back—rammed the ball into the nets. As his teammates swarmed about him, Billy flashed that infectious grin, tossed in another free throw to complete his three-point play, and broke the Spartans backs.

Just for good measure, the next time down, Big Bill went to the fourth weapon in his arsenal, the hook, for two more. And that was the ball game. The final barb, though, came as Herner checked into the game for Cantrell and proceeded to score the final bucket on a driving layup with seconds to go to give Michigan a final victory margin of 14 points, 91-77. Russell, who like Buntin, again went the full 40 minutes, finished with 34 points. Billy backed him with 25. And although Michigan was outrebounded for the first time in the season, Buntin took individual honors with 13. An awed Jim Skala studied the final stat sheet shaking his head.

"How can Strack play a young kid like that for forty minutes?" he grinned. "Doesn't he know that he can't stand up to that tough a pace?"

The rematch was set for the following Saturday at Yost and this time both the crowd and the Wolverines were ready. The 7,950 fans (officially) had shown up in a belligerent mood. Apparently they had felt from game reports that the Spartans had been overly aggressive in their treatment of the beloved Blue. This was rather ironic, considering the fact that there was nothing Buntin, Darden, Cantrell, and the rest loved more than a no-holds-barred, saloon brawl. But Michigan fans were very protective of their darlings and brooked no physical assault by the opposition. They responded with thunderous cat-calls and boos for the Spartans from the time the Green and White stepped on the court until the final buzzer. This didn't deter the Spartans from throwing their weight around, however, and Michigan answered in kind with 49 fouls being called and three players fouling out.

It was apparent from the start that Michigan did not like having been outrebounded in the first game. Darden and Buntin seemed intent on outboarding the entire MSU team by themselves. Amazingly, they almost did it. The main competition for each of them, as usual, was each other. After one bruising collision under the basket, Buntin loped up the floor massaging his arm.

"You got to stop banging into me so much," he instructed Darden.

Ollie just shrugged his Atlas-like shoulders and trotted up the court to see what mayhem he could create at the other end.

Before the half was over, Buntin had the masses screaming for more—he poured in 23 points, grabbed 10 rebounds and held Thomann to five points and four rebounds. Darden, however, went him two better on the boards, snapping off 12 as the two of them accounted for five more rebounds than the Spartans combined. As a result, Michigan shot out to a 53-37 lead at halftime. Cazzie's 16 points almost went unnoticed because of the Buntin outburst. It was one of the few times that Bill would upstage him.

Moments into the second half, Darden banged into

State's Bill Curtis and picked up his fourth foul. But Strack decided against yanking his muscleman and a minute later Darden wiped out half the players on the floor catapulting over the basket to tip in a missed shot by Cazzie. And although Spartan coach Forddy Anderson screamed mightily for an offensive foul, none was forthcoming. Moments later Darden again collided with Curtis, although this time it was Curtis who drew the foul while Strack held his breath. It began to look as though the Darden-Curtis bout was going to over-shadow the game itself. However, within three minutes, two other problems moved to center stage. First, the fiesty Cantrell had drawn his third and fourth fouls just four minutes into the period. Then, two minutes later, came the crusher—Buntin collected his fourth and fifth personals within an eight-second span. Strack was wringing his hands and the Yost mob was now in an ugly mood.

As the crowd littered the floor with paper cups and even a deck of playing cards, Strack brought in the taller but lighter Myers to replace the banished Buntin. Thomann, who had managed nothing against Buntin in the first six minutes of the half, took quick advantage of the switch scoring six points, forcing Shag into a couple of fouls in the process. The Spartans had cut a 16-point deficit to nine. When Darden drew his fifth foul with six minutes to go, things were tense for the Wolverines. But somehow that seemed to spark Michigan more than it did State. George Pomey, replacing Darden, spearheaded a drive that carried the Wolverines out to an 87-68 edge—the Spartans were put away. With two minutes left, Strack cleared his bench and again it was Herner who salted away the final two points in a convincing 95-79 victory.

Buntin, scoreless in the second half, had to settle for

second-place honors to Cazzie's 25 and trailed Darden in the rebounding totals, 17-13. (The Spartans finished with 39 as a team.) Commenting on his quick exit, Buntin had trouble keeping a straight face.

"Yeah, I had visions of a big day after the first half. And I thought I was being nice out there!"

The following day, Michigan took their bruises onto a charter plane at Willow Run en route to a place where they had never won — OSU's St. John Arena. As a matter of fact, no Michigan basketball team had won in Columbus since 1947. The Buckeyes were coming into the game after a loss to Michigan State had dropped them to 3-2 in the Big Ten and 8-7 overall. Michigan, with their 6-0 conference mark, could put a serious crimp in Ohio State's hopes of defending their conference title. But Michigan was running into the hottest scorer in the nation, Gary Bradds. The Buckeye strongman was in the midst of his record setting streak of 40 points or better for six straight games. Michigan had *held* him to 27 in their first meeting but had no illusions about a repeat performance in Columbus.

Trailing by one at halftime, 42-41, U-M came out slowly in the second half and Ohio State marched up by five. The Wolverines cut it back to one several times but were unable to stop the amazing Bradds who ended up with 42 points, almost half the Buckeyes' total. OSU needed them all as they eked out an 86-85 win. Thus the Bucks stayed alive and Michigan would have to wait until Cazzie's senior year before they could register a victory at St. John.

The next Saturday, Michigan faced much the same task as they journeyed to Assembly Hall in Champaign for a meeting with Illinois.

Michigan hadn't posted a win at Illinois in five years and were getting their first look at the year-old arena which had replaced the ancient, legendary home of the Illini, Huff Gymnasium. Both teams had only a single loss in Big Ten play but in a quirk of scheduling, the Illini had met only four conference foes to Michigan's seven. The game also brought two of Illinois' most illustrious high school players together—Michigan's Russell and the Illini's Donnie Freeman. Since most Illinois fans had assumed Cazzie would stay within the boundaries of his native state to play his collegiate ball, his defection to Michigan was not greeted warmly. The veteran Illini coach, Harry Coombs, was still so upset over Cazzie's decision that he responded to a request for eight tickets by Caz's high school coach Larry Hawkins by sending him two unreserved seats—the Illini do not take basketball lightly.

It didn't help the crowd's mood when Michigan controlled the opening tip and quickly got the ball to Cazzie who canned a 10-footer to open the scoring.

Illinois had, of course, watched UCLA chew up Michigan in the Bruin Classic. That left Coombs with the same impression as a lot of other coaches in the Big Ten—the only way to stay with Michigan was to zone press them. The 1-3-1 that Coombs employed did cut down on Cazzie's ability to get the ball at the base line. As a result, with the Illini defense sagging underneath, Buntin found himself more open. To say the big fella took advantage of it would be a gross understatement. Hooking from the side, leading the fast break for layups, tipping in missed shots, Buntin did it all. He almost matched his MSU heroics with a 22-point first half. Buntin's counterpart, Skip Thoren, was having almost as much fun; the stringbean pumped in 17 points to keep the Illini within five points at halftime. It was an iron-man act on both sides with Coombs going with his starting five the entire 20 minutes while Strack substituted only Pomey for Darden.

Unlike the MSU game, Buntin had not gotten into foul trouble and that spelled trouble for Illinois. And with the Illini still sticking to their zone, Buntin came out firing again after the halftime break, scoring his 30th point of the game just four and half minutes into the second period. Still Michigan led only 50-49 when they finally decided to give their superlative center a little help in the scoring column. First it was Darden who ripped off eight points to push Michigan's lead to six. Then Russell started to open up outside with three jumpers, two layups and three assists to Buntin. Michigan began pulling away. By the time the last die-hard Illinois fan had conceded, U-M owned a 93-82 win and a 7-1 record in the Big Ten.

Buntin's 37-point performance would rank with the best of his career. Cazzie contributed 28 and Darden 17. Buntin was 16-of-31 from the field, prompting Darden to inform Bill: "Cripes, when you shoot 31 times you *should* score 37."

"Well, *somebody* had to," Bill countered. End of discussion.

The next Saturday against Indiana, Michigan would be much more democratic in passing the points around.

Despite the presence of Tom and Dick VanArsdale plus a third future NBA star, Jon McGlocklin, this was not one of Branch McCracken's stronger squads. Only 1-7 in the conference, the Hoosiers' main problem was that they had no height. McGlocklin at 6-5 was their center. Fans who watched him later as an outstanding guard for the Milwaukee Bucks might have trouble accepting this but Jon was indeed a versatile young man. He was one of the few players in Big Ten history to see action at each of the three positions.

Along with his other 6-5 frontliners, the Vans, Mc-Glocklin could score. The trio finished in the top 13 scorers in the conference but they had little help from the back-court and were hammered on the boards by every team they faced. The following year, McCracken would bring in Tom Bolyard to play the pivot and things would be different.

Michigan wasted little time in exploiting the height differential. Despite facing yet another zone, the Wolverines raced to a 13-2 lead. Meanwhile, Strack had surprised the Hoosiers with a zone defense which limited Indiana to a lone field goal by McGlocklin in the opening four and half minutes. Holding the VanArsdales down for a long stretch was, of course, impossible. Everyone knew they would explode at any moment. Stopping Tom and Dick from scoring was no easier than telling them apart. They were a broadcaster's nightmare and a coaches' dream. And even McCracken had his problems when they first showed up. After calling Tom by Dick's name and vice-versa about five times, Branch finally stopped practice. He tossed Dick a red wristband, told him to put it around his ankle and warned him never to show up to practice without it.

Taking over with their team 11 points down, the Vans paired for a 19-point splurge as the Hoosiers cut the lead to four. It was at that point that Bobby Cantrell started to exact his measure of revenge. Like thousands of other Indiana high schoolers, Bobby had dreamed of playing for IU. Upon his graduation from East Chicago, Cantrell called McCracken for an invitation to come visit.

"Don't bother," Branch told the 5-10 sparkplug, "you're too short to play at Indiana."

Reverting to his earlier days as a shooter, Cantrell popped in three straight jumpers, each of which he followed by racing past the Indiana bench shaking his fist at the gray-haired McCracken. He never let up all day, finishing with 19 points. On one of his last trips up the floor, he punctuated his fist-shaking by yelling, "How short am I now, Branch?"

In one of Michigan's most balanced scoring attacks of the season, both Buntin and Russell finished with 23 points while Larry Tregoning tied Cantrell's 19. The rebounding was as lopsided as everybody expected with Michigan holding better than a 2-1 margin — all Wolverine starters but Cantrell finishing in double figures. Since Michigan didn't pay a return visit to Bloomington that year, it was Cantrell's final shot at the man who felt he didn't measure up to Big Ten height standards. Final score — Michigan 99, Indiana, 87.

Mammoth Williams Arena in Minneapolis was next up for the Big Ten leaders where a packed house of 17,019 would greet the Wolverines. Whether this was a factor, or whether Michigan was just due a bad game is unknown. But there is no doubt that this was their worst performance of the Big Ten season. Ten turnovers in the first half alone made the Gophers' task an easier one as they seemed to take advantage of every Michigan miscue with a bucket. Midway into the first half, the Gophers had a 10-point bulge. By halftime it was 18 and the rout was on. The final of 89-75 told the whole story.

No less than six Gophers finished in double figures while only Russell and Buntin were able to dent Minnesota's defense — they tallied 26 and 22 points respectively. Buntin did command the boards with 18 rebounds but that was the only bright spot as Michigan fell into a first-place tie with Ohio State, both at 8-2 with Minnesota close behind at 7-3.

It was a glum-looking Wolverine crew that filed onto their charter late that evening. They realized they could afford no further debacles such as this one if they were to stay on track for a Big Ten title.

Seated across the aisle from me, Cazzie pounded one huge fist into another repeatedly as he replayed the game in his mind. Little did he know what lay in store Saturday in Madison.

The game itself was predictable enough—the last-place Badgers offered only token resistance to the obviously fired-up Wolverines. U-M outscored Wisconsin 21-5 in the final seven minutes of the first half to open up a 51-26 lead. Cazzie almost equalled the Badgers' output by himself, pouring in 20 as the overflow crowd of 13,217 gasped in wonder at his moves. By the middle of the second half, with Michigan leading by 35 points, Strack started yanking his starters. Unfortunately, he didn't get Cazzie off the floor quite quickly enough.

The play was one Michigan had run a hundred times. Caz hit Cantrell with a pass and headed low to the baseline. But as Russell made his cut, the Badgers' Bob Johnson bumped Cantrell sending Bobby in turn reeling into Cazzie with all three players tumbling to the floor.

Trainer Jim Hunt raced onto the floor toward the pileup where Cazzie was holding his left ankle in obvious pain. Hobbling with Jim to the bench, he spent the remainder of the massacre with ice wrapped around his foot watching his teammates sew up a 103-59 decision, the largest margin for Michigan in their Big Ten history. It was little-used Charley Adams who put them over the century mark for the third time on the season, a fact he didn't allow his fellow Wolverines to forget in the locker room. The win, Michigan's 18th of the year, also tied the former high-water mark for a Maize and Blue Squad set back in 1919. But the subdued winners were much more interested in the condition of their Chicago sophomore.

Michigan did get one break—a full week off before their next game in Ann Arbor against Illinois. By midweek Cazzie could report that his foot and ankle were sore but usable. The biggest problem that Cazzie faced was the novelty of the injury.

"I had never had to be taped in my life," he lamented. "And I felt restricted by the wrapping."

The Illini had fallen on evil times since the first matchup with Michigan and no longer entertained title hopes. They did remember the previous season, however, when an upset loss to Michigan cost them the clear-cut championship over Ohio State. The first half was almost a carbon copy of the earlier game in Champaign with Michigan establishing an early lead but never enough to threaten a runaway.

The Illini narrowed the gap to just three points with only a minute left in the half before baskets by Pomey, Darden, and Cazzie lengthened the halftime lead to 45-38. Cazzie appeared tentative in the early going but closed with a rush. Darden again found the Orange and White defense to his liking—he either penetrated or shot over the Illini zone for 13 points to tie Caz for halftime scoring honors.

Early in the second half the teams traded baskets—then a familiar U-M problem reappeared. With four minutes gone, Buntin suddenly incurred fouls number three and four in a 30-second span. With Billy gone, the Illini caught fire and twice moved within a point. Especially troublesome was guard Jim Vopicka who had seen little action in the first game between the two. But with Bill McKeown out with a broken wrist, Vopicka had taken over the other starting guard role opposite Tal Brody. With Brody having little success against Cantrell, Vopicka popped in three baskets over Russell.

With eight minutes to go and Illinois still putting on the pressure, Strack decided he couldn't afford to sit Buntin down any longer and back came Billy, four fouls and all. It paid off as a combo of Buntin, Pomey, and Darden working inside eased Michigan out to a 12-point lead with three minutes left.

Then, just as everyone started to breathe a bit easier, Buntin shot into the lane, collided with Thoren who was also playing with four fouls and was tagged with his fifth. Although Strack bitterly protested the call, big number 22 was gone for the day and the question was, did Michigan have enough of a cushion to withstand his absence?

Two minutes later, the question was still unanswered because both Freeman and Vopicka connected on one-and-one free throw situations. The Illini crept back within four. Russell and Thoren traded layups and it was 85-81 but now with only 39 seconds remaining. That forced the Illini to foul but it was another 26 seconds before they could get to the man with the ball as Russell, Cantrell, and Pomey did a brilliant job of playing keep-away. Finally, Vopicka nailed Pomey who stepped to the line with 13 seconds showing and flipped in two free throws to salt the game away.

The game, sent through the Midwest as the Big Ten game of the week, gave thousands a good look at the superb Russell at his best. He not only led everyone in scoring with his 28 points but also came up with two key steals during one late Michigan splurge. It prompted Strack to tell Bill Flemming during a postgame interview, "This just proves that Cazzie is the most versatile player in the country."

Almost overlooked in the garrison finish was the fact that Caz had broken the year-old season scoring record set by Buntin in 1963. His 28 points put him at 539 on the year, five better than Bill's of the season past.

Darden had again been tremendous with 19 points and 13 rebounds. Pomey and Cantrell had been instrumental in keeping the Wolverines in front during Buntin's first absence with Bobby popping home three long range jumpers. But none seemed to resent the massive media attention on Russell. As Darden would later say, "We knew what roles we had to play and that was it. Why worry about it?" Darden did have to put up with some jawing from his buddy Buntin following the game. Ollie had hit on a 20-footer at the buzzer to send Michigan off the court an 89-83 winner but also gave him the runnerup scoring honors by one over Bill.

"No way was that shot in time," growsed Billy. "You hadn't even thought about shooting when the horn went off."

"That just makes up for all the rebounds they give you that belong to me," Darden shot back, "and besides it was in plenty of time, I have a sixth sense about those things."

"That's six more than I thought you had about anything," chimed in Charley Adams.

It was a loose bunch of Wolverines who clambered aboard their North Central charter headed for Iowa City and their date with destiny the following Friday.

Going into the final weekend (remember, it was Saturday-Monday play back then) here was the scenario: Ohio State, by virtue of having played an additional game, was a half game up on Michigan with an 11-2 mark compared to the Wolverines' 10-2. While Michigan would be meeting Iowa, the Buckeyes would be winding up their season at home against Michigan State. Michigan, however, had their finale on Monday back in Ann Arbor against Purdue. Two wins for the Wolverines would wrap up an NCAA berth since it would assure them of at least a tie with the Bucks. At that time, the conference decided their NCAA representative by eliminating the most recent participant in case of ties. Since Ohio State had been to the tourney in 1962 in comparison to Michigan's last visit of 1948, Strack's crew was in — if they could close out with a pair of victories. Of course, an OSU loss would mean only one Wolverine win would be needed.

Just looking at the records, it didn't appear that the task of Michigan that evening would be all that difficult. The Hawkeyes were laboring through a dismal season, having posted only 3 wins against 9 losses in conference play. Their offense was dead last in the Big Ten, averaging just 74 points a game. That would seem rather substantial in a later era but consider that Michigan's 86 points per game total was good enough for only third place behind Michigan State and Ohio State. No 45-second clock was needed in 1964.

Iowa's other problem was that they had no rebounding. Despite a front line every bit as big as Michigan's, the Hawkeyes were next-to-last in Big Ten rebounding totals. Just as an example, Buntin himself outrebounded George Peeples and Dave Roach put together and they were the two top Hawkeyes in that category. So, at least on the surface, it seemed that the advantage was overwhelming for Buntin and his teammates in their only meeting with the Hawks that season. But unfortunately for the Wolverines some extenuating circumstances came into play.

Iowa's popular coach and former captain, Sharm Scheuerman, had announced a week earlier that after the season ended he would be leaving the coaching ranks to enter private business. Since this was the Hawkeyes' final home game of the season, it meant Michigan would be walking into an arena filled with fans and players bent on making Sharm's last formal appearance a memorable one. The crowd left no doubt as to its feelings when they gave Scheuerman a standing ovation upon his pre-game introduction.

The gesture wasn't lost on the Iowa players either — they roared out of the gate looking more like UCLA than the ninth-place team in the Big Ten and by midway through the half they had opened up a 10-point lead. Michigan fought back to move within a single point late in the period only to have the Hawkeyes come up with a five-point blast in the final two minutes to leave the court a 40-34 leader.

It was an incredible half in many respects. First of all, Buntin and Russell accounted for *all but four* of the Michigan points as they split 30 right down the middle. Cazzie had not had a good shooting half, however, with a feeble 33 percent mark from the floor — the same average as the Michigan team as a whole. Only the fact that the two of them hit 12-of-13 from the free throw line saved the club from total disaster. But the real shocker came on the boards where Michigan held a razor-thin 16-15 edge, half of Michigan's total going to Cazzie. Amazingly, Buntin grabbed but three, being outboarded by Iowa's

6-0 guard Andy Hankins, who picked up four in the period. Unless Michigan could do something about turning these statistics around, Sharm's final night on the Iowa sidelines was going to be a joyous one.

A quick jumper by Cantrell (his only bucket of the game) and three straight layups by Buntin and Russell brought Michigan even with just two minutes gone. But then the drought set in as the Wolverines went without another field goal until another layup by Cazzie seven and a half minutes later. But the Hawkeyes were having their own problems, reverting to their early season point ratio and at the midway juncture of the second half it was a deadlock at 49. Then, almost imperceptibly, Michigan began to inch ahead. Much of this could be credited to the fact that the two officials, Red Mohalik and Russ Kaefer, were being very active in their calling of fouls. And, as in the first half, Michigan was cashing in at the line while the Hawks took four consecutive free throw attempts without a point to show for it.

The story could be told in the gap between the 8:15 mark and the 1:56 clocking. During that period of over six minutes, Michigan managed only two baskets from the floor, both on layups by Buntin. And yet because of the free throw shooting of Russell and Bill, Michigan increased a lead of 53-50 to 63-54. Of such things are champions born. The 69-61 final score was the lowest point total of the year for Michigan. The 33 percent shooting was also a low for the year with Cazzie struggling through a 7-for-23 evening. However, his 17 rebounds were tops on the year and almost half of Michigan's total of 40. With his 27 and Buntin's 28 points, the titanic twosome had accounted for almost 80 percent of Michigan's output.

But a win is a win and the Wolverines swarmed into

the locker room knowing they were just one victory away from at least a share of their first basketball crown in 26 years. They were also aware that if Michigan State could pull a longshot and upset the Buckeyes, the Wolverines would be tournament bound. Immediately Jim Skala became the most popular person in the room as he pressed a small radio to his ear, trying to pick up the scratchy signal from Columbus. We had been informed over the public address system during the course of the Iowa game that Ohio State had led at halftime, 46-39, so no one held much hope for a Spartan comeback. Suddenly Skala barked, "MSU's up by one with a minute to go!"

Whoops and hollers erupted while others tried to gain some semblance of order to allow Skala to go on listening.

"Damn," Skala growled. "Bradds just hit for Ohio; they're back up by one."

"How much time?" Buntin anxiously inquired.

"Couldn't hear," Skala muttered.

"I can't take any more of this," Strack said, jumping up and heading back out to the arena. "Come get me when it's over."

The other murmurs died to an eerie silence as all eyes were riveted to Skala and the tiny receiver jammed to his ear.

"Wait a minute!" he yelled.

No one breathed.

"Gent just hit a jumper . . . it's all over, State won it, 81-80!!"

As soon as Skala's words had bounced off the walls, a series of hair-raising screams started loosening the tiles in the shower room. Darden and Buntin grabbed one another like crazed lovers and went bouncing off the lockers yelling, "We did it! We did it!"

Cantrell jumped up on a locker room bench and began waving a towel over his head like a shipwrecked sailor signalling for a rescue aircraft.

Pomey and Tregoning pounded each other as Jorgensen embraced Skala with such vehemence that Skala's poor radio went flying like a bullet across the room.

Meanwhile, Strack, who had learned the news from manager John Phillips at courtside, had bounded back onto the scene. He was instantly engulfed by his players. It was indeed a night of triumph for Dave, a man who years before had been called insane by some of his friends for campaigning so strenuously for the Michigan job.

"Why do you want to go to a place where they only care about football?" they asked him.

"Because I think I can win," was Dave's reply.

On March 7, 1964, before 12,300 hostile fans in the old Iowa Fieldhouse, Dave Strack proved to everyone that he had known what he was talking about.

Just as a footnote, March 7th of that year also proved to be one of the most victorious days in University of Michigan history. Not only did the basketball team capture a share of the conference title but three other Wolverine teams—track, wrestling, and gymnastics—went on to do the same that evening. And that's not counting Al Renfrew's hockey squad which wrapped up the WCHA crown that night en route to an NCAA championship. Certainly a night to remember for fans of the Blue.

Before they could turn their attention to the NCAA tournament, there was, of course, the matter of closing the regular season with Purdue. The Boilermakers, as they had proven earlier at West Lafayette, were not a team to be taken lightly. They were in a two-way battle for fourth-place honors with Michigan State which prompted

Strack to announce, "We feel we certainly owe State something and will do what we can to give them fourth place."

But more than that, the Wolverines wanted to be known as *THE* Big Ten champions, not as an entry with Ohio State in the record books. They already had won more games both overall and in the conference than any other Michigan team in history. They had scored more points and drawn more spectators than any previous club. But it wasn't enough. They wanted the whole nine yards.

One other sidelight to the game also piqued the fans' fancy: The number two, three, and four scorers in the Big Ten would be on the floor in Schellhase, Russell, and Buntin. Since Schellhase led Cazzie by only 15 points coming into the game, there was speculation that with a great evening, Russell just might slide by the Boilermaker star into the runnerup spot. Not a likely happening but enough to capture some media attention.

Midway through the first half, however, it was apparent that Cazzie not only was going to have a problem catching Schellhase but that his Wolverines were going to be hard pressed to stay with Purdue. Obviously laboring on his sore ankle, Cazzie had only a single basket in the first 10 minutes while Schellhase had pumped in four jumpers to help his club to a 10-point lead. Only the steadiness of Buntin and Darden kept Michigan close as Strack continued to shuffle his personnel in hopes of finding the spark. Darden, like Cazzie, was nursing a banged-up ankle after being fallen on by a teammate in practice.

With only a minute remaining in the half, Caz connected on his second jumper of the period and added two free throws shortly thereafter to slice the margin to three. This lasted only six seconds as Mel Garland fired in a desperation shot at the buzzer to up the Purdue margin to 43-38 as the teams left the floor. Schellhase had outscored Cazzie 12-6 but the big thorn in Michigan's side was Boilermaker guard, Bob Purkhiser. The 6-2 converted forward had led everybody in the first half with 15 points which was just about his game average over the 1964 season.

Opening the second half with two quick buckets, Schellhase served notice that the Boilermakers didn't regard the first period as a fluke. With six minutes gone, Michigan still found themselves down by seven. But as had happened so many times before in the year, Michigan's smoldering haystack suddenly burst into flames. Cazzie's three-point play brought them within four, a jumper by Darden and a layup by Buntin off a fast break cut it to one and finally a 15-footer by Cazzie put Michigan on top 56-55 to the hysterical delight of the Wolverine faithful.

From that point, the lead bounced back and forth. A seven-point burst by Purkhiser shoved Purdue back in front by five. But Cazzie came back with his own six-point tattoo to return the advantage to Michigan by three with 4:40 to go. Two and a half minutes later Cazzie hit his 21st point of the half to re-establish the lead at three. Hustling the ball up the court, Purdue's Garland moved to the top of the key, looking for either Purkhiser or Schellhase. Neither was open and finding himself free in the circle, Garland put it up. As he reached the top of his jump, Russell brushed by, sending the shooter off-stride. Immediately, Floyd Magnuson went up with his right arm signalling a foul on Cazzie but worse for Michigan, down came the ball through the nets, only the second field goal for Garland of the half. Moments later he calmly dropped in the free throw and it again was a tie game.

Michigan went to a control offense, taking over a

minute off the clock while looking for their shot. They got it when Buntin freed himself for a hook at the baseline. But the shot bounced off the rim and when Purdue captured the rebound, the crowd braced itself for the worst. And it was the unexpected nemesis, Purkhiser, who applied the coup-de-grace. Disdaining any attempt at a final-second shot, the Bluffton junior cut loose with a 16-footer that dipped through the nets perfectly and carried with it Michigan's hopes for an unshared title.

The Wolverines still had a chance to gain a tie with 30 seconds showing on the clock but again misfired. Purkhiser grabbed the rebound, was fouled by Buntin and hit two free throws to salt it away. A frustrated Cantrell, playing his final game at Yost, hit on a meaningless jumper with four seconds to go to make the final score 81-79. Grabbing the ball after the buzzer sounded, Bobby heaved it well into the balcony as if to sum up his teammates' feelings.

Thus the Wolverines would have to be content to wear the mantle of Big Ten co-champions into the NCAA Mideast regionals in Minneapolis. But it wasn't the loss to Purdue or the sole claim to the title that was the major concern of Dave Strack. He had two worries: Cazzie's foot and Loyola of Chicago.

Michigan would need every available source to counter the defending NCAA champion Ramblers. Only Jerry Harkness had departed from the previous year's crew that had sprung a 60-58 overtime upset over Cincinnati to gain their first NCAA crown. Rated eighth in the nation this year, the Ramblers lived up to their nickname with a run-and-shoot offense that averaged better than 91 points per game with four starters averaging in double figures. In guard Ron Miller and 6-7 center Les Hunter, Loyola had their own Russell-Buntin combination and many observers felt this double pairing would be the key to the game.

But at least Strack could formulate some game plan to combat the Chicagoans. However, as far as Cazzie's throbbing foot was concerned, there was nothing he could do but sit and hope. Trainer Jim Hunt had applied all his expertise in trying to bring the injured tendon around but there was just so much that treatment without prolonged rest could accomplish. In three days, the Ramblers would be waiting. On Friday the 13th.

The site of the regional was not a spot harboring happy memories for Michigan since it was Williams Arena where they had been handed their worst conference loss of the year. But during Thursday's workout, Darden found some encouragement from that earlier debacle.

"Don't worry, guys," Ollie explained, "we left a lot of points here the first time through. All we got to do is pick 'em up this time around."

Darden was right. The two teams started out as though they would use up their point quotas in the first five minutes.

The Ramblers got their running attack going in a hurry and with Hunter picking up four buckets in two and a half minutes, the defending champs shot to a 12-6 lead. But Loyola's deadeye shooting cooled in a hurry and a new one-two punch for Michigan emerged.

Larry Tregoning had not had a good outing on his first trip into Williams Arena but appeared to be well on his way to making amends—he grabbed every rebound within reach. Even Darden and Buntin couldn't stay with him on the boards. So Darden turned scorer and popped in half of the first 14 points Michigan collected. Trigger then banged in a pair as Michigan completed a 12-2 spurt for a four-point lead.

The Wolverines continued to improve their margin with

a couple of crowd thrillers included in the streak. First, Tregoning scraped another rebound off the defensive board to ignite a two-on-one fast break. The two Wolverines happened to be Buntin and Cantrell, a Mutt and Jeff combination that gave the fans and Loyola a decided shock as Bill displayed his surprising quickness.

Moments later, with Loyola on the attack, Vic Rouse drove to the side of the lane and launched a 12-footer. The ball got about two feet out of his hand when it came ricocheting back in the opposite direction as Darden soared through the air to swat it past Rouse's ear. The ball bounced into the hands of Miller who tried his luck. It wasn't any better. Like a hawk tracking a rabbit, Ollie spiked Miller's shot into the crowd which now sounded like a Yost gathering. A badly shaken Miller didn't try another shot until the final seconds of the half. The Ramblers' leading scorer found himself with but four points at halftime and his team found themselves on the short end of a 43-36 count. Miller wasn't the only member of the defending champs having his scoring difficulties as the tough little Loyola playmaker Johnny Egan had to contend with an equally tough little battler in Cantrell who limited the fiery Egan to a single basket in the first half.

Meanwhile, Cazzie, who found two and three men around him every time he touched the ball, was off to a typically slow start with a mere four points. But Buntin was again in rare form as he pounded in 16 points while combining with Trigger and Darden to put a virtual vise on the backboards.

With a minute gone in the second half, Hunter took a pass in the key and headed down the lane. But before he took two steps, Darden caught him on the arm—it was foul number four for Ollie. Myers checked in for Darden and when Buntin and Tregoning tallied back-to-back buckets Michigan led by 13 and Darden's absence didn't appear noticeable.

The Wolverines blew a golden opportunity to stretch it further as twice on fast breaks they failed to collect on layups. This gave the Ramblers a second breath and with Miller finally coming alive with eight points, Loyola carved the lead down to five. Strack called a wise timeout and within two and a half minutes Michigan had jumped it back to 11.

Cazzie was showing flashes of earlier brilliance with six of the string. But within a space of 30 seconds, the enthusiasm on the Michigan bench quickly turned to gloom. First, Myers left the game with an injury after fouling Hunter which turned into a three-point play for the big center. Then in rapid-fire sequence, Buntin and Tregoning were tacked with their fourth fouls of the game despite the anguished cries from the Michigan bench and partisans. So with still half of the second period remaining, the front line of the Wolverines was saddled with four fouls apiece and a key replacement was on the bench with an injury. Immediately Strack called another timeout to confer with Jorgenson and Skala. Their decision was to hold tight with their foul-ridden crew and continue to play their game.

Buntin took Strack seriously. He got the inbounds pass at the key and rumbled down the lane to lay home the ball over Hunter. This time there was no foul and when the same occasion presented itself a minute later he repeated the performance to push Michigan back in front by 10. However, the foul problems were costing Strack's five dearly at the other end of the court as the troubled trio of Buntin, Darden, and Iregoning could only offer token resistance. Loyola took full advantage of the situation to go inside to Hunter, Miller, and Rouse with devastating effect. Hunter especially worked over the Wolverines down low and much to the dismay of Strack was whistled for only one foul by the officiating pair of Lou Bello and Phil Fox.

Except for one of the most courageous performances in Michigan history, the Ramblers' surge might have carried them over the top. But wincing with almost every step, Cazzie Russell kept the cards from collapsing until re-inforcements arrived. First a driving layup, then another plus a free throw for a three-point play and finally another move underneath that made him cringe in pain but also gave him two more free throws. With under three minutes on the clock, Michigan still was ahead, albeit by just a point.

A free throw by Cantrell upped the score to 77-74 with two and a half minutes to go. Loyola fired up the court, but the irascible Tregoning, risking a fifth foul, reached around Hunter to spear the ball and raced down the floor at the head of the pack. Slicing into the lane he pulled up with a 12-footer that was perfect.

On their next trip to the forecourt Loyola's Egan misfired on a jumper and when Buntin nailed the rebound Michigan had the ball and a five-point lead with only 1:30 to go. Egan quickly fouled Cazzie who dropped in two more from the line. A long spinning shot by Rouse brought the margin back to five but Cantrell converted one of two from the line for a 82-76 lead with 1:10 left. Egan again missed but Hunter was there to bat it down for his 25th point of the evening.

The Wolverines took 30 seconds off the clock before

Egan could finally grab Russell. It was a necessary move but it cost Loyola the services of their great playmaker — he had picked up his fifth foul, all in the final half. The first to shake his hand was Cantrell who could recognize in Johnny Egan a soulmate in intensity and desire. Cazzie, with his 85 percent free throw average, was not the player the Ramblers wanted to foul but they had no choice. But Russell proved that he was only human — his free throw spun away into the arms of Rouse and the Ramblers were still alive, barely.

As soon as he neared the circle, Rouse put the ball in the air; it bounced off the rim but came straight back into his hands. Before he could put it up again, Tregoning knocked the ball away as he had done in the key situation moments before. But this time, Trigger failed to get the benefit of the doubt from Lou Bello, who whistled him out of the game with his fifth foul. Rouse, who was as bad a free throw shooter as Cazzie was great, proved that statistics can be meaningless as he canned both ends of a one-and-one. With 22 seconds left Loyola had come back within two, 82-80.

No one in the old barn was seated as Michigan pushed the ball up the floor against a full-court Loyola press. Cantrell crossed the time line and fired a cross-court pass to Cazzie. But the pass never arrived as Jim Coleman intercepted. Driving down the court, he laid the ball through the nets to the hysteric screams of the Loyola rooters. But the screams had covered up the whistle of Phil Fox, who had called travelling on Coleman just moments after he had picked off the pass — it was Michigan's ball again with :10 on the clock.

Russell whipped the ball to Cantrell who was immediately grabbed by Hunter who joined Egan and Tregoning on the sidelines with five fouls. Bobby Cantrell, with only 25 attempts on the year, really hadn't been given much of an opportunity to establish a meaningful free throw percentage. Yet, all the Wolverines felt they had the right man at the line. Cantrell, like Steve Grote of a later era, took very little time shooting free throws and had hardly been handed the ball by Bello when the first shot swished through the net. The second toss was a carbon copy of the first and Michigan had their first NCAA tournament victory in history.

As soon as the horn sounded, every Michigan player tried to hoist Cantrell on their shoulders. It was Michigan's greatest victory on the court to that time and certainly one of the most thrilling of any time. Strack didn't know whom to congratulate first. Buntin had been his usual rock — 26 points, 13 rebounds despite playing the final 10 minutes with four fouls. Russell had gained the admiration of everyone with his gutty 21-point performance on one leg; Darden had led them out of the blocks before the fouls did him in; Tregoning with his matched pair of 14 points and 14 rebounds plus his great defensive play. And, of course, Bobby Cantrell.

The one sobering thought that crept into the locker room was simply this: in 24 hours they would have to come back and do it all over again.

The team that Michigan was scheduled to face in the Mideast final was a team no one expected to be in Minneapolis to start with, let alone the final. The Ohio University Bobcats had won the Mid-American championship on the final day which gained them the dubious right to meet Louisville in the preliminary round of the NCAAs. A 71-69 overtime win over the Cardinals propelled them into the regionals where they were expected to be the sacrificial lambs for Adolph Rupp's third-ranked Kentucky Wildcats. It ended up the other way around as Ohio slaughtered their southern neighbors, 85-69, to set up the championship match with Michigan.

So the problem that the Wolverines were presented with was trying to come back from a highly emotional win over Loyola to meet a team that for the third consecutive game would be heavy underdogs. But two teams from the Bluegrass state had just discovered that taking the Bobcats lightly could prove to be fatal.

Personally, I had a few problems of my own. The combination of Minnesota weather and a cold had merged into a budding case of laryngitis which wasn't aided by the tenseness of the Friday night broadcast. Saturday morning I frantically searched for a nearby drugstore. Finally finding one, I stocked up on every remedy which promised relief and spent the remainder of the afternoon writing notes to my engineer, Jim McEachern, my sole source of sympathy. When I signed on the broadcast that evening, I wondered if I was going to be able to sign it off two hours later. As it turned out I did—but the final minutes of play-by-play were tortuous ones.

Ohio was not a tall club with their center Paul Story standing 6-5, nor were they a high-scoring aggregation as they averaged almost 11 points per game less than Michigan. Despite their lack of size, they actually had a better rebound ratio against opponents than did the muscular Wolverines. The Bobcats' key was their acrobatic guard Jerry Jackson who had amazed the crowd and the Kentucky five the previous night with his contortions. But, of course, he hadn't had Bobby Cantrell to contend with either.

The effects of the opening night's action was apparent

in both teams' play over the first 10 minutes as neither crew could get its offense in motion. With Michigan leading by a 15-10 count, Buntin and Ohio's Don Hilt each had a seven-point splurge. Seeing his team struggling, Strack inserted Pomey, Myers, and Herner into the lineup and got some quick results. Pomey got a steal for a layup, Myers converted on a three-point play, and Herner captured a steal of his own leading to a Russell basket.

But the Mid-American champs continued to hang in and trailed by only five at intermission, 32-27. Hilt had been the big surprise for the Bobcats, pouring in 13 points, almost equalling his per game average on the season. Cazzie, who again was slowed to a walk at times by his injured foot, had 12 and Buntin nine. Neither team had approached their normal shooting accuracy, both hitting well under 40 percent from the floor. Jackson, who had tallied 25 against the Wildcats, managed only three against Cantrell but his club had proven they could hold their own on the boards against anybody — they had a 23-21 margin in that category. Myers, in limited duty, led Michigan with five.

The second half found the Wolverines again getting off to a snail's pace. They could muster only a pair of field goals in four minutes and found their lead cut to one. Strack went to his bench early as Myers replaced Buntin and Pomey took over for Tregoning. Trigger had been drained by his magnificent effort against Loyola while Buntin had picked up his third foul early in the half. But Pomey gave Michigan the ignition they needed.

With the score tied at 43, Pomey found Russell in the lane and fed him a pinpoint pass for the tie-breaker. Seconds later he forced the Bobcats into a traveling violation and Michigan quickly turned it into another bucket by Cazzie. Then came the play which everyone agreed later did the Cats in.

Pomey had come up with another steal but as he turned to bring the ball up the court he was tagged with a questionable travelling call.

While Pomey was arguing with Steve Honzo about the call, Ohio's Mike Haley came rocketing across the court to attempt to grab the ball from George and get the play underway. But instead of finding the basketball he found Pomey's nose with his elbow. Although a defensive demon, Pomey was normally a placid individual not prone to temper displays. Haley's wild swing changed all that.

After checking over to the bench to swab his offended nose, Pomey returned to the court with a vengeance. Stealing the ball from Hilt, he led the charge up the court for a bucket that put Michigan up by six. The next time up the floor he swished one himself. Seconds later, after Pomey batted the ball away from Jackson, a Darden layup plus a Russell free throw catapulted Michigan to a nine-point lead. Although nine minutes remained, it was all over for the Cinderella Bobcats. The eventual margin turned out to be a dozen as Michigan captured its first NCAA regional championship, 69-57.

After their Iowa and Loyola celebrations, this one was almost tame by comparison. When Strack went around the room slapping each of his players on the back, he gave special attention to Pomey.

"If I had to pick an MVP of this tourney, he would be it," said Dave.

Myers, who had gotten off to a sizzling start in the season only to suffer a mid-year slump, was also instrumental in the second-half push finishing with seven rebounds, tying for second place with Darden behind Buntin's

10. He was obviously a long way towards recovering the confidence he had lost a few weeks before.

The NCAA finals that year were notable for a number of reasons. It was the ninth time that Municipal Auditorium in Kansas City would be the site — tops for one location. And it would prove to be the last. In the earlier days of minimal media coverage, the auditorium was a perfect spot — a seating capacity of around 11,000; a central location for the four teams participating; a city with generous hotel space. Unfortunately, the old arena was not equipped to deal with the steady increase of radio, TV, and newspaper personnel. And that resulted in an embarrassing situation. Since the only accommodations for the media were courtside, it meant that broadcasters and writers had to be stacked in rows, all at the same level. This resulted in a great deal of bobbing and weaving during the games as we all attempted to peer around the people in front to follow the action. The outcry following the tourney convinced the NCAA that perhaps they should look elsewhere for host arenas.

The field also brought together the AP poll's number one, two, and three teams as UCLA, Michigan, and Duke had all survived regional competition to join Kansas State, the surprise of the quartet. It also featured semi-final matchups between teams who had earlier met. Michigan, of course, had defeated Duke, 83-67, in that landmark game in Ann Arbor while UCLA had nipped Kansas State, 78-75, also in December. Michigan also had that shellacking at the hands of the Bruins in Los Angeles which they very much hoped to avenge in the finals. Many Wolverine backers felt it was only a formality for Michigan to earn a slot against Johnny Wooden's crew for the championship. After all, their club had whupped the Blue Devils the first time out, hadn't they? But Duke coach Vic Bubas issued an ominous promise from Durham.

"I made a mistake the last time and tried to slow it down because of Michigan's power. I shouldn't have. We won't make that mistake again. Michigan had better watch out."

Dave Strack did not take the warning lightly; he was well aware of two factors that made this a different chapter. In the first meeting, Duke had an ailing Jay Buckley while Michigan had a healthy Cazzie Russell. In the Friday night battle, those roles would be reversed. It was also apparent that the Blue Devils were on a roll with eight straight victories including waltzes over Villanova and Connecticut in the Eastern Regional. So overconfidence was not going to be a problem for Strack.

For about five hours that Friday I was faced with the possibility of watching Michigan and Duke square off via my television set. My laryngitis had had now developed into a full-blown, rip-roaring chest cold by the time I returned to Ann Arbor. Thus I had delayed leaving for Kansas City until the day of the game to give myself a bit more time to recover. That decision almost proved to be the worst of my life come Friday morning.

At that time there were no direct flights to Kansas City—a detour through Chicago was needed. We were delayed for a half-hour on our first leg but finally got off the ground at Metro and on our way to O'Hare. We were about 30 minutes out and nearing the Chicago area when we started making lazy circles in the sky. After about 30 minutes of this, we were informed by the pilot that he had given up on O'Hare because of the thick fog there and was heading back to Detroit.

Back at Metro, it was a frustrated, milling group of

fans (plus one broadcaster) trying to find alternate routes to Kansas City. With time running out we got lucky. A United flight to Omaha (that city again) would be leaving in 20 minutes with a close connection to Kansas City. It would be a tight fit but it was our only shot at getting there. In a photo finish, we made it and went straight from the Kansas City airport to the arena. Taking our seats four rows deep, it appeared that calling the game from behind the packed-in press was going to be as difficult as getting there in the first place.

As soon as the ball was tossed up it was clear that Vic Bubas' warning was genuine—the Blue Devils intended to run the basketball at every opportunity. This tactic didn't work to Michigan's disadvantage that much, however, as the Wolverines also picked up a couple of buckets off the break to match Duke. The real surprise was Cantrell, who was more or less ignored by a Duke defense keying on Cazzie. So Bobby came up with four looping jumpers including three in a row midway through the half. Buntin was also off and rolling in his usual first-half pattern. In addition to piling up 13 points in 12 minutes, Bill came up with three blocked shots and two steals to confound the high-powered Duke offense. His 13th point came with 7:46 left and gave Michigan a 30-28 lead. It would prove to be a landmark for the Blue as slowly they began to drop behind.

The biggest culprits in the turnaround were rebounding and turnovers. Michigan, who had controlled the boards by a 61-35 margin in the first meeting, was hammered this time. The biggest discrepancy came on the offensive board where the Blue Devils grabbed 12. On more than one occasion Duke was getting three and four whacks at getting a shot down. The evidence that Buckley's recovery was indeed complete was that he picked off eight himself. Meanwhile Michigan turned the ball over 12 times to make things that much easier for Duke. Complicating things even further were Buntin's three fouls, all in the last six minutes of the half. So it was not with a great deal of optimism that Michigan fans prepared for the second half with the Blue Devils up by a 48-39 count.

By the midway point of the second half the Duke run-and-shoot game had propelled them to a 13-point lead. A flurry by the Wolverines cut it back to seven. But that was to be only a brief respite and the only question over the final eight minutes was the size of the winning margin for the Atlantic Coast Conference champs. When the final buzzer sounded, Buntin, Russell, and Darden were all on the bench with five fouls and Duke was in the championship game versus UCLA with a 91-80 victory.

A look at the final stat sheet established quickly the difference between December and March. Jay Buckley had simply been awesome—25 points, 14 rebounds, and three blocked shots while holding Buntin to 19 points. This compared to Buckley's first-game stats of seven points and two rebounds. Cazzie, meanwhile, had been magnificent in defeat with 31 points including 13-of-19 from the floor, plus grabbing 8 rebounds. All from a guy who probably should have been on crutches. So the dreams of the national crown had evaporated. Strack summed it up very well in the interview room following the game: "I can't complain about my boys. They've played well all year and they did their best tonight."

There was still the matter of the consolation game on Saturday evening with Kansas State. The difference between third and fourth place is not that big to collegiate basketball players and fans and with the pressure off, both teams came out in relaxed and offense-minded fashion. First of all, though, Michigan had to adjust to the absence of Cazzie. Dr. Tom Peterson had determined that Russell's injured foot and ankle shouldn't take any more punishment. So the Chicago Carver's All-American's season ended one game early. But what a season it had been!

While fully aware of their great teammate's contributions to their 1963-64 success, the rest of the Wolverines also felt they had a little something to prove of their own — that they were not a one-man ball club. And when Bobby Cantrell took a feed off the opening tip and drilled one home from just this side of the Missouri River, the gates were opened. Herner, taking over for Russell, played no favorites. His pinpoint passes set up Darden, Tregoning, and Buntin inside while Cantrell continued to pepper away from downtown. However, Kansas State was having their own picnic on offense to make it 52-47, Michigan, at halftime. Cantrell had already exceeded his season's average by eight points with 14 in the half.

The pace continued in the second half. With four minutes remaining, Michigan was up 88-86. Darden, who would cap his great sophomore season with 17 points and 14 rebounds, then found the mark from the circle and when Buntin followed with a three-point play, Michigan was home free.

Fittingly, the final points of the 100-90 win came on two free throws with a second to go by Cantrell, his 19th and 20th points of the contest. Buntin had been unstoppable although Tex Winter, the K-State coach, had tried everyone and everything to no avail. Billy wound up with 33 points including a 15-17 showing at the free throw line and a 14-rebound total that matched his buddy Ollie's for game high. Tregoning had almost equalled his great

Loyola performance with 16 points and eight boards while Herner finished with 10 assists, the best single-game total for a Wolverine that season.

At a post-game reception, a tired but smiling Dave Strack accepted the congratulations of Michigan fans who tagged their compliments with the line, "Just wait 'til next year."

"Let's just enjoy this one a bit first, okay?" was the standard reply of the Michigan coach.

His point was well taken—it was a season to savor and save. There would be more, but this was the first.

Back in Ann Arbor, I picked up a Sunday paper to read the game account and learn of Michigan's march to the NCAA hockey championship. Thumbing through the rest of the sports section I found an item buried on page 10:

"Michigan's football team will begin spring practice in 10 days according to athletic director Fritz Crisler. The Wolverines will be trying to improve on their fifth-place finish of a year ago. Bump Elliot, entering his sixth season as coach, is guarded in his evaluation of the 1964 squad. 'We're not among the contenders,' says Bump. 'I'm not sure we're even among the dark horses.' "

"Well," I thought, tucking the paper away. "Two championships in one year might be expecting a bit too much."

SIX

That Championship
Season
(Part II)

Bump Elliot was faced with a different situation at the start of his season than Dave Strack had been nine months before. For one thing, while the fans were expecting great things from Cazzie and company, there was doubt about the gridiron crew.

Bump himself sounded a bit skeptical prior to spring drills when he told reporters, "I don't know if we can be a good enough team to be a contender. We have some big question marks."

Taking his cue, one Detroit writer ripped off an article proclaiming the Wolverines to be a mediocre club with little talent coming back from a team that finished at the .500 mark in 1963. This didn't sit too well with most of the squad who felt that it overlooked the fact that a heavy dose of injuries and ineligibilities had turned the '63 season into a 2-3-2 disaster in the Big Ten.

Captain Jim Conley remembers coming out of spring drills with the definite feeling that this could be Michigan's year. Rough and rugged Bill Laskey called it "anxious optimism" while fullback Mel Anthony said he could hardly wait for the season to get underway. Obviously, none of this veteran trio was too impressed by newspaper articles. As it turned out, they weren't to be bothered by some of their strongest critics during the season since the Detroit papers went on strike in July and never got back on the stands until after the completion of the season.

Bump's coaching staff was the same one we looked at in 1962 with one notable exception. Gentleman Jack Fouts had moved on to Ohio Wesleyan as head coach and athletic director and in his place was a 250-lb pixie by the name of Tony Mason. The ebullient Pennsylvania native had blazed an unbelievable mark in Ohio high school circles where his Niles McKinley teams had posted a 47-0-2 record over the preceding five years, claiming the 1963 state championship. Several members of those teams, including Dick Rindfuss, Rich Sygar, Charlie Kines, and Dennis Flanagan had come north to play for Michigan. So Tony wasn't exactly unknown to Bump. A complete contrast to the reserved and soft-spoken Elliott, Tony would bounce around the sidelines, chomping on his wad of tobacco, waving his arms, all the while screaming encouragement to his linemen. His pre-game speeches would have done credit to a fire-and-brimstone revivalist. And the players loved it. Hard times would await Tony upon his departure from Ann Arbor which saddened all who had played for him.

Nineteen-sixty-three was a bit deceiving when considered on its record alone. The Wolverines had defeated the Big Ten champs, Illinois, before a stunned crowd in Champaign, while tying runnerup Michigan State. It also had rivaled 1962 in the injury department as Bump lost the highly touted Sygar in pre-season drills with a broken leg. However, in 1964, Sygar was hale and hearty along with Tom Cecchini, Bill Yearby, John Henderson, and Rindfuss—all of whom had been battered the year before. And, oh yes, Bob Timberlake.

After being shuffled between quarterback and halfback his sophomore season, Bob had been installed as the number one signal caller in his junior year. Unfortunately for Timbo and Michigan, he suffered a debilitating shoulder injury which reduced his effectiveness greatly. When the same problem popped up in pre-season drills in 1964, Bump could only cross his fingers and pray that a little good luck might drift his way for a change. His prayers were answered as the giant Presbyterian minister not only stayed healthy but gained All-American honors during his senior season.

His teammates kidded Timberlake unmercifully about his lack of speed. Dave Butler once suggested that in a foot race between Conley and Timberlake, neither one was fast enough to win. Timbo himself admitted he might not have been a world-class sprinter. He often joked about catching a pass against Iowa in his sophomore year while playing halfback. No Hawkeye was within 20 yards of Bob as he came down with the ball.

"My lead dissolved in seconds," recalled Bob, "and I was, as the euphemism has it, pulled down from behind."

He wasn't fast but he had the inborn quality of a leader. And being 6-4 didn't hurt either.

"Bump liked to turn me upfield on the option, because if I got pointed in the right direction, my fall alone guaranteed two yards. This accounts for my frequent two-yard sneaks for scores."

Actually, that was only a part of it as Bob had tremendous strength and judgement in picking the right hole on the short-yardage situations.

Bump called most of the plays from the sidelines that year, a practice that would become familiar five years later with another Michigan coach. The way Timberlake remembers it though, Bump left him on his own during the crucial Illinois game of that year when Dick Butkus was terrorizing everybody.

"I looked over to the sidelines in the third quarter when we had a fourth down and one on their 35. But Bump just turned his back on me and started chatting with someone. I guess he felt it would deepen my character if I had to do it alone."

By then, Timberlake's character didn't need a whole lot of strengthening. By his own admission, Bob was a something of a hell raiser in his younger days. By the time he had reached his senior year, however, he had made public his strong commitment to Christian living and was a driving force (along with Cazzie Russell) in the Michigan chapter of the Fellowship of Christian Athletes. The media made heavy use of this, much to the surprise and at times, chagrin of Bob.

"If I had known how much publicity I was going to get, I would have announced my conversion in my sophomore year," grinned Bob.

But it wasn't his evangelical leanings that had Michigan fans pounding each other to a pulp that year. It was simply one of the most versatile performances ever by a Michigan gridder.

The pre-season drills were only three days old when Bump must have wondered if he had slipped back to 1962. During a non-contact dummy scrimmage, Timberlake's backup, Rich Vidmer, stumbled over a teammate and fell clumsily to the ground. Jim Hunt raced to the scene and in one look correctly assessed the damage—a broken leg.

This projected senior Frosty Evashevski into the number two role. But also mentioned now was a young sophomore out of Wauseon, Ohio, who also happened to be the nephew of Michigan's legendary Bob Chappius. His name was Rick Volk, who would eventually cause almost as much of a stir as his famous uncle, but not at quarterback.

Another devastating blow came shortly thereafter— Bump learned he would be without his starting left halfback, Jack Clancy. A balky back had refused to mend and finally the fleet junior had to be scratched from the roster. He had entered Michigan as another quarterback but had been switched to halfback in his sophomore year. As every Michigan fan knows now, when Clancy returned in 1965 he would be switched again, this time to receiver, where he would team with Vidmer to smash every Michigan pass reception mark in the book at the time.

But all this was unknown to Bump in the second week of September in 1964. All he knew was that once again he was watching key personnel drop by the wayside. Within a week, the injury bug would be hard at work again. Clancy's replacement, John Rowser, suffered a knee ligament tear that would sideline him for 1964 also. Now Bump was down to his third-string left halfback and shuddering every time he walked by the training room. But that third string halfback just happened to be a big, handsome brute named Jim Detwiler, a Toledo sophomore who had expected to see only spot duty on the year. Three months later in Columbus, he had a date with destiny.

The arrival of Detwiler as the starting left halfback

assured Michigan of two other distinctions. A pair of rookie halfbacks and an all-Ohio backfield. Lining up at the right half was Cincinnati speedster Carl Ward, a 5-9 bundle of explosives, while manning the fullback slot was Anthony, another product of the Cincinnati high school football machine. A deeply sensitive youngster, Mel had come close to leaving school following the disastrous 1962 season. A severe ankle sprain had put him on the bench most of the year while in the classroom he had become increasingly unhappy with his academic major. To compound his problems, his father died suddenly from a heart attack.

"If it hadn't been for Bump, Hank Fonde and my family, 1962 would have been my last for Michigan," says Anthony. But luckily for the Wolverines, he did return. And he returned to lead the team in rushing in 1964 and to electrify a nationwide TV audience in the Rose Bowl on New Year's Day. His 84-yard touchdown scamper set a new bowl record as the longest run in history.

Actually, the Ohio connection didn't stop with the backfield; all but two members of Bump's starting offensive line were also Buckeye expatriots. Their acrobatic pass catcher, John Henderson, came out of Dayton as an all-stater in three sports—football, basketball, and track. Before Clancy started grabbing everything in sight, Henderson was regarded as Michigan's quintessential receiver, a 6-3 ballet dancer in pads. He would find a football laying on the ground at Ohio Stadium in November that would change the course of Michigan football history. His nagging shoulder injury, a carryover from 1963, lingered throughout fall drills, but if it ever bothered John during the 1964 season, it sure wasn't visible to the naked eye.

Manning the tackle posts were Tom Mack and Charley

Kines. Mack's chief claim to fame when he arrived in Ann Arbor was that he was the son of former Cleveland Indians second baseman Ray Mack. Tom had been converted from an end to tackle in spring drills, a move that would have some tremendous positive effects. First of all, it solidified the right side of the Michigan offensive line. Secondly, it triggered an All-American and All-Pro career for Mack, who upon graduation would be handed an unprecedented $80,000 bonus to sign with the Los Angeles Rams. No one ever gave an offensive lineman that kind of money up to that time, but the Rams weren't about to let this sure-fire great get away to the American Football League. Tom thus received more money before he ever played a game than his father did during his entire major league career.

Mack, at 6-3 and 220 pounds, could outrun half the backs on the Michigan team. One of the most famous pictures in Michigan football lore is the shot of Mack loping alongside Anthony during Mel's recordbreaking dash in the Rose Bowl. Timberlake tells one of the classics involving Mack which occurred during the 1964 Purdue game: "To my amazement I had broken through the line and found myself in the open. Our off-side linemen had leveled their defensive backs and I stretched out my long legs and huffed and puffed my way into the end zone after a 54-yard rumble. I felt pretty good about myself until the Monday movies when I watched Tom Mack, barely exerting himself, saunter alongside for the final 40 yards. Here I was going at full throttle while Mack was about at half-speed. It was embarrassing."

It was also pretty embarrassing for opponents, who found themselves staring up at the sky after being run over by a sprinter playing tackle.

Kines was one of Tony Mason's boys out of Niles, who

like Mack would be seeing his first extensive duty. His sophomore season had been tempered with injuries and while not in Mack's class (who was?) he was a rugged competitor at 230 pounds.

Center Brian Patchen, out of Steubenville, had logged the most minutes in 1963 of any of the offensive linemen returning. This had come about as a bit of a surprise since Patchen had taken over for Tom Cecchini after Cecchini had gone down with a knee injury. With the liberalized substitution rules coming into effect in 1964, Cecchini could be utilized mostly at linebacker with Patchen taking over the snapping duties.

Brian Marcum couldn't truly be called an all-out Buckeye although he had been born in Hamilton, Ohio. He had moved onto Michigan soil to play his high school ball at Monroe and, despite a knee blowout as a freshman, had returned to see lengthy duty as both a sophomore and junior.

His running mate at the other guard was another senior and easily the most singular character on the team, Dave Butler. Dave had seen very limited duty in his first two years but came out of the pack to seize the left guard spot. And he was the center of attention with his Friday night performances as coach Rudy Bazoote or a South American dictator recruiting players as mercenaries. His crowning achievement came on the Friday night prior to the climactic Ohio State game. As a tense group of coaches and players gathered for their traditional movie, Butler strode to the front of the room.

"Gentlemen, you have probably wondered why I called this meeting tonight. I have come to ask, why in the world our waxed animal crackers are not selling?"

The room exploded with laughter, the tension disappeared and the team's performance the next afternoon is now a part of Michigan tradition.

Joining Butler as the only other non-Ohio native on offense was the biggest starter, tight end Steve Smith. At 6-5 and 230 pounds, Smith had given basketball a brief whirl before deciding to concentrate on the gridiron. Ten years later, another Illinois native, C.J. Kupec, would reverse the cycle. The combination of Smith and Mack, or Smith and Kines blocking down on a poor unsuspecting linebacker could make for a miserable afternoon.

During the spring of '64, the NCAA Rules Committee had relaxed the substitution rules even further enroute to unlimited substitution. Fullscale switching could be made during any stoppage of the clock and two players could be inserted while the clock was running. While it meant that there still would be instances of players having to double up a bit on offense and defense, for the most part players now had pretty clearly defined roles. In Michigan's case, it was especially beneficial since some extremely talented individuals had come along who excelled in pinning the offense's ears back. As with the offense, a great deal of the credit for the defense's success would ultimately go to a tackle who would surpass everybody's expectations before the year was half over.

Bill Yearby had arrived in Ann Arbor three years earlier as one of Detroit Eastern's top athletes. Like Mack, he was first projected as an end, but one look at his 6-3, 222-pound frame convinced Bump that he was in the presence of another Wistert. Quick enough to play basketball, as we have seen, agile, fast, tremendously strong, he could have played about anywhere he wanted. Under today's conditions, he probably would have been a devastating outside linebacker with his speed and power, but he certainly wreaked enough damage from the tackle slot.

At the other tackle was senior Arnie Simkus, out of Germany via Detroit, who was even bigger than Yearby at 6-4, 230. Despite his bulk, Arnie was the top tennis player on the team.

At the defensive ends were the fun-loving pair of Captain Jim Conley and fellow senior Bill Laskey. "Crazy Jim," as Laskey called him, came out of Pennsylvania as an all-state fullback but as Conley was quick to point out, never threatened Mel Anthony. He was, however, a sure and punishing tackler who lived for the thrill of clobbering enemy ball carriers. To Jim, though, his crowning achievement came in his junior season and had nothing to do with defense. On third and long for Michigan, Bump decided to put his defensive ends in the game to prepare for the change of possession. (Remember, he was limited to two players a down in that season.) As the two romped onto the field, Laskey turned and yelled to his coach, "We're offensive ends, too!"

Timberlake called a deep pattern and retreated while under a big rush, throwing the ball as far as he could. Conley picks up the story: "The safety for Northwestern watched it go over his head, and he thought out of play. But there was this headwind of about 10 m.p.h. Since my "speed" was 12 m.p.h. I looked up and lo and behold, there was the ball. Even more amazingly, I caught it and routinely walked the chalk into the end zone! Joe O'Donnell, our stunned captain, carried me off the field."

It was Conley's only touchdown of his career. He delighted in arguing with Timberlake about who was the slowest. Jim maintains that one day when snow covered the practice field, Jocko Nelson announced that drills were suspended for the day because, "Without the stripes, we would never know if Conley was moving."

Laskey was even tougher as his glory years in the AFL would prove. As in Conley's case, Bill had been a standout runner at Milan High. But it didn't take Bump long to ascertain that Lask enjoyed loosening the football from other halfbacks as much as he enjoyed carrying it himself.

The middle wasn't any picnic for other teams either with Rich Hahn and John Yanz at the guards along with "Chick" Cecchini, Barry Dehlin, and Frank Nunley at linebackers. Chick would take his place among the great backers in Michigan folklore on the strength of his performances in 1964 and '65. Knocked out of the '63 season with a knee injury after four games, he had returned even stronger in his junior season. At an even six feet and an arguable 200 pounds, he was one of the smallest linebackers in recent memory but oh, could he hit! On top of this, he was a brilliant student of the game, a perfectionist who could smell a football a mile away. It was no surprise when his fellow Wolverines elected him captain in 1965.

Dehlin had come out of nowhere to take over the opposite linebacking spot as a sophomore a year earlier. His one-man wrecking crew performance against Illinois earned him the cover of *Sports Illustrated*. It also aided the Wolverines in that astounding upset of Dick Butkus and crew which gave Michigan the strong hint that they could stay with any team in the Big Ten.

Barry would get belted out of action during the '64 season, but that only opened up a spot for another eventual NFL linebacker, Frank Nunley. The Belleville towhead had made the transition from freshman fullback with amazing ease. He picked up the baton from Dehlin without missing a step and at age 18, played like a veteran.

If by chance, the defensive secondary was caught on the field (as sometimes occurred) they were not exactly helpless since all were recruited equally for offense and defense. Volk, as we have noted, was a good enough quarterback to be pushed up to number three when Vidmer crumbled. Once the coaching staff got an eyeful of his sledgehammer hits and his thievery at safety, his days on offense were over for the most part. Bump, of course, had been a partner of Chappius in that famed 1947 backfield that found both gaining All-American honors. This pretty well assured Volk's matriculation at Michigan since from his earliest days he had listened (at his uncle's knee) to tales of the Wolverines. Like so many others, he was in awe of Bump at first meeting him. And he continued that respect throughout his All-American career. Rick revered his coach to the degree that he even bought two-toned cordovan and black shoes because that was what Bump wore.

Up front of Volk at the defensive halfbacks were two more of Tony Mason's protégés, Rick Sygar and Dick Rindfuss. Sygar had already been awarded the hard luck trophy for the decade after suffering a broken leg prior to the 1963 season, and then slipping on the ice five months later to break it again. That meant he had missed a season plus spring drills and was a question mark coming into the 1964 campaign. He didn't waste much time erasing the doubts with his work in the secondary, returning punts, and as we will see, sneaking into East Lansing in an unfamiliar role.

Rindfuss hardly saw the sidelines in 1963, playing a staggering total of 425 minutes in nine games—more than 47 minutes a game. Against Ohio State, he was on the field over 57 minutes. No wonder that his 190 pounds melted down to about 175 by the end of the season. However, with the arrival of Detwiler and Ward, the quiet Rindfuss could concentrate on defense for his final year. But injuries whittled his playing time even further, so that he ended up with only about half the time he had accumulated the previous season.

The only remaining piece to the championship puzzle was at the punting spot. O'Donnell had taken his talented left foot to the pros and by doing so had opened a gaping hole. The man who filled it was so lightly regarded that he didn't even rate a mention in the press guide.

Stan Kemp had come to Michigan as an end candidate out of Greenville, where he had been a standout athlete. Much to Stan's chagrin, however, he put his end-playing days behind him once he started lofting punts downfield. His strength was not in distance — although he could boom with the best of them when needed. The two ingredients that captured the attention of everybody that season were his accuracy and consistency. He was a magician in placing the ball — that resulted in extremely meager punt returns.

His roommate Volk, whose twin sister Marsha ended up as Mrs. Stan Kemp, credited Kemp as being the difference in the Ohio State game that year. Three times the Wolverines were backed up to their end zone and three times Kemp blistered punts of nearly 50 yards into the teeth of a vicious November gale. Only once did Stan come up short in his career but even that was a thing of beauty. In 1965, before a national TV audience, Stan trotted out to do his thing. As was his practice, he began loosening his leg by swinging his foot high over his head while the team lined up in punt formation. Maybe the fact he was performing before millions caused a bit more vigorous rip because suddenly his other foot went out from under him and Stan lay flat on his back to the accompaniment of coast-to-coast chuckles. He would not hear the end of that throughout his stay in Ann Arbor.

September 26—Air Force at Michigan

Finally, newspapers or not, on September 26, a crowd of 70,000 gathered at Michigan Stadium to get their first look at the 1964 Wolverines.

It was a brilliant and warm afternoon in Ann Arbor, although a stiff breeze came straight up the field from south to north. Volk and Kemp stayed in the back of the pack as the team raced onto the field so they could take in the sight of the sunshine bouncing off the familiar helmets as the crowd rose across the field. The crowd looked like a million to the pair who were used to playing before three or four thousand.

Air Force, in their ninth year of existence, had already opened their season with a 3-2 victory over defending Pac 10 champion Washington. The defense, known as the "Hunters," was their strength as the Huskie score might indicate. Winning the toss, Bump decided to test his own defense while also taking advantage of the 30 m.p.h. wind by kicking off and defending the south end zone.

A pumped-up Timberlake almost booted the ball out onto Green Street—the season was officially underway. The Falcons ran two times for first down and then made

Bump look like a genius. Circling right end, Paul Wargo was met head on by Conley who loosened both the football and Wargo's senses. Simkus pounced on the ball and U-M was at the Air Force 35 — first and 10. The "Hunters" thus got a chance to demonstrate their skill in a hurry.

Four running plays moved the ball to the 25. Timberlake and Henderson then hooked up on a seven-yarder — a preview of things to come in '64. Detwiler's first career carry took it to the 13. Then it was vintage Timberlake, as the towering quarterback powered around the right side to the one and on the next play took it over on a sneak — the first of eight touchdowns he would tally that season. His conversion made it 7-0 with less than five minutes gone in the game.

Moving to the U-M 15, Air Force threatened to match the Michigan drive but the unfortunate Wargo again coughed up the football with Cecchini dropping on it this time.

A Henderson fumble returned the ball to the Cadets at the Michigan 22 but the turnover merry-go-round continued. Air Force quarterback Tim Murphy fired into the end zone on second down where end Bill Landes was waiting. Also waiting was Volk who stepped in front of the receiver and picked off his first interception. There would be many more before he was through.

Aided by a 34-yard scamper by Ward, Michigan marched to the five. Anthony took it the rest of the way to climax an 80-yard drive and give U-M a 14-0 lead just into the second quarter.

Midway through the quarter, Kemp was called upon for the first punt of his three years of duty. Kicking into the gale, he belted a 48-yarder — an indication of things to come.

Murphy quickly started peppering away to four different receivers and took the Falcons to the Michigan 7 where it was first and goal. This made it five times the Air Force had been in scoring range for the day. Would they find a way to botch it up again? Two running plays and an incompletion later they were only to the four and the hero of last week's game, Bart Holaday, came onto the field for a field goal attempt from 21 yards out. At least it appeared so as Murphy knelt at the 11 for the snap. Before Holaday could kick, however, Murphy snatched the ball away and headed around the right side where he stopped and fired a strike to bruising Detroit halfback Dick Czarnota in the end zone. Holaday stayed on to kick the conversion and the Air Force was back in the game, 14-7.

Only two minutes remained in the half when Michigan took over at its 35. After the long rest, Timberlake was raring to go. He peeled off 19 yards on a sweep and threw two quick sideline completions to Craig Kirby which pushed the ball to the 12 with a minute to go. Timbo cut the distance in half by plowing to the six but a personal foul call on the following play brought it back to the 18 with just 15 seconds to go. After an incompletion, Bump decided to wait no longer and instructed Timberlake to try a 35-yard field goal. The kick sailed wide but the Air Force was offsides which gave Bob another shot from five yards closer. Again the kick failed but again Air Force was hit with an offsides penalty.

On the far sidelines, Air Force coach Ben Martin wasn't sure if he wanted to strangle the officials or his players, but in any case was forced to watch another five-yard march by the referee. This time, there was no offsides, but it didn't make any difference as Timbo sent it through and on that bizarre note the first half came to an end with Michigan leading, 17-7.

Early in the third quarter, the Wolverines moved to the opposition's 28 before stalling. There a field goal attempt was blocked.

Murphy quickly went back to his first half bag of tricks on the ensuing series. He promptly passed the Falcons to the Michigan 16, with again completions to four different receivers. But again the Michigan defense got stingy and when a Bart Holaday three-point attempt sailed wide, the visitors were one-for-six inside the Michigan 20.

The Timberlake-Detwiler duo now stepped center stage as they combined on some dazzling power running to push the ball to the Air Force 15. The key play of the series came on a third-and-30 situation after Michigan had been pushed back by a holding penalty to their own 45. With 11 Falcons and 70,000 fans looking to see how far Bob could throw the ball, Timberlake simply tucked it away and rambled for 31 yards up the middle to get Michigan a first down by a foot. With the rain starting to fall, Anthony carried twice for a total of five and it was time for the bull from Toledo again. Crashing his way off the right side with two Falcons holding on for dear life, Detwiler bounced into the end zone for the touchdown. For the second time of the afternoon, Michigan had driven 80 yards for a touchdown, demonstrating a consistency that long had been lacking in Michigan offenses. Seconds later, following Timberlake's conversion, the quarter ended with Michigan in command, 24-7.

For all intents and purposes, that was the game as the slick ball gave Murphy all kinds of trouble in the passing department. Both coaches went to their benches midway through the final period and a fall shower had soaked everyone by the time of the final gun.

The 331 yards rushing by the Wolverines was a welcome sight for Bump and a shock to most since defense was supposedly the Falcons' strong suit. Not so soothing was Murphy's 23-for-40 passing afternoon which caused Bump to agree that the secondary needed more seasoning and the line more of a rush. But it was hard to find too much fault with a defense that six times was tested inside its own 20 and was nicked only on a fake field goal attempt. However, the next Saturday might prove even tougher — due in town was another service academy — and this one was led by Roger Staubach.

October 3—Navy at Michigan

The victory by the Wolverines over the Air Force had impressed the nation's writers enough to warrant an eighth-place rating in the weekly Associated Press poll. It also brought out the largest luncheon crowd in M-Club history — over 160 members packed their way into the North Commons Union to hear Bump.

The discussion, of course, began and ended with number 12, the marvelous Staubach. Many people had felt he had won his Heisman Trophy the year before at Michigan Stadium as he set a new total offense record in destroying the Wolverines, 26-13.

Navy had opened with victories over Penn State and

William & Mary but in the game against the Nittany Lions, Staubach suffered a leg injury. He played but four downs against the Indians and still was well under par when he trotted onto the field in Ann Arbor on another warm and sunny fall day.

Navy won the toss and elected to receive. Staubach wasted little time in testing the Michigan defense. Dropping back to throw, he found Yanz and Yearby bearing down on him. Unloading the ball in a hurry, he missed his intended receiver by five yards. Not a bit deterred, Roger went back again to throw and again he found himself ducking and dodging blue shirts. Just before Conley reached him, Staubach unloaded a pass intended for his great split end, Neil Henderson. However, Cecchini had drifted back into the middle to help on the coverage and made the interception at the Navy 37.

The crowd, again in the 70,000 range, exploded, and when on the second play Detwiler raced to the Navy 13, the din could be heard all the way to Annapolis. The roaring was quickly muffled, however; on second down, Navy linebacker Bruce Kenton leaped in front of Craig Kirby to match the interception of Cecchini's just moments before.

Staubach hit on one pass then faded back on third down and immediately set sail for the sidelines with Yearby and Yanz in hot pursuit. But this day was not 1963 and before Roger could get back to the line of scrimmage, Conley had nailed him for a loss. A jubilant Michigan defense, gaining confidence with every play, trotted off the field.

Navy's defense was every bit as tough on Timberlake but Kemp unleashed a 50-yard punt that pinned Navy at their four.

A running play lost two and the crowd sensed blood.

Staubach backpedaled into the end zone and finding no one open, raced up the right side for 25 yards to get Navy out of a mammoth hole. Soon it was third and five at the Michigan 39 and Staubach fired to Jim Ryan at the 34, enough for another first down. But the young third-string fullback was jolted by Hahn with the football bouncing away where it was quickly recovered by Hahn.

With four seconds left in the quarter, Ward squirted around left end for 25 yards and Michigan was at the Navy 17 as the teams switched end zones. Detwiler blasted to the two and then cleared the way for Ward as the little speedster shot into the end zone to give the Wolverines a 6-0 lead.

It was obvious on the ensuing drive that the Michigan touchdown hadn't taken a whole lot of spark out of the Navy attack. Steadily moving from their own 20, the Midshipmen advanced to inside the Michigan 20. Then Staubach hit Henderson with a pass at the six. Unfortunately, Sygar hit him also, drilling his helmet into Henderson's chest with such vehemence that the ball went flying halfway across the gridiron. This time it was Cecchini on the spot as he added a fumble recovery to his earlier interception.

Turnover followed turnover the rest of the first half. With time running out, Michigan had first and goal inside the Navy 10. But the giveaway continued as Timberlake's pass to Kirby in the end zone was picked off. It was the eighth turnover of the half.

The first half statistics were pretty indicative of the 6-0 score—only 20 yards and three first downs separated the two teams. But three fumbles and two interceptions had cost Navy dearly.

Early in the second half, the Michigan defense was

again put to the test. Mixing runs with his passing, Staubach moved his team to the 17. But the Michigan defense again stiffened, sacking Roger on fourth down. As the rollicking defensive platoon left the field, the uproarious crowd sensed that the Midshipmen had fired their last salvo.

Remembering a similar situation in the second quarter, Timberlake stuffed the ball off to Ward who dashed into the end zone from four yards away for his second touchdown of the afternoon. A two-point conversion attempt was good as Timberlake hit Ben Farabee and the Wolverines had taken a 14-0 lead.

On the subsequent series, Staubach was clobbered twice by Yanz with Roger retiring to the sidelines after the second sack.

On that note the third quarter ended and so really did the game. It took the Wolverines only three and a half minutes to drive 72 yards with Timberlake, Anthony, and Ward all ripping off 10 or more yards a crack. This set up a four-yard plunge by another Ohio soph, Dave Fisher, who at 5-10 and 215 pounds looked like a cannonball fired at close range. Timberlake's conversion upped the count to 21-0 and although 11 minutes were left on the clock, the suspense had vanished.

Timberlake had more than held his own with the Heisman winner, trailing by only 16 yards in total offense despite throwing only 11 times to Roger's 30. Michigan had come up only eight yards shy of the 400 mark again with Detwiler and Ward running neck and neck for the individual leadership. For young Craig Kirby, it would represent his finest hour as never again would he be so consistently utilized. His four receptions represented two-thirds of his season's output as only Navy's great receiver Ed Orr caught more that day.

The win nudged them into seventh place in the AP ratings but still left them shy of Illinois, voted number two and Ohio State, lodged in the fourth position. And just a bit behind at number nine were the Spartans of Michigan State. The Wolverines would receive an opportunity to see for themselves just how warranted State's ranking was as the following Saturday, Michigan would be making the trip north to face a team they hadn't beaten in nine years.

October 10—Michigan at Michigan State

To gauge just how deep the frustration was for Michigan fans, one only had to go back to the previous year when a heavily underdog Wolverine team played the Spartans to a 7-7 tie in Ann Arbor. The ensuing celebration by rooters of the Blue was worthy of a conference championship. Maybe Michigan hadn't beaten their East Lansing counterparts, but they hadn't lost either. That was enough to start the snake dancing down State Street.

MSU was fresh from a 17-7 victory over Southern Cal which had earned them a spot in the top 10. Although they had lost All-Americans Sherm Lewis and Earl Lattimer from the '63 squad, the Spartans had a good-looking quarterback in Steve Juday and a future All-Pro in wide receiver Gene Washington.

An unseasonably cold 40-degree day greeted the fans who wedged their way into Spartan Stadium. They didn't even have to wait for the kickoff to get a clue that this game would be played at a high intensity level. Michigan was warming up at the north end of the field as the Spartans came charging out of the tunnel. Two years earlier, the Wolverines had meekly stood aside and let the boisterous hosts bolt through. Not this time however. Rick Sygar took offense to a green-clad opponent who had bumped him while Rick was going through his calisthenics. Sygar proceeded to deck the Spartan offender and a full-scale but brief melee broke out.

Winning the coin toss, Michigan received. On the second play, Timberlake pitched outside to Mel Anthony but the fleet fullback failed to find the handle. With less than a minute gone in the game, State lineback Ed Macuga had recovered the fumble and MSU was at the Michigan 17. It was a familar story to Michigan's defense—backed in their own territory on a mistake by the offense.

With third and seven at the 14, Duffy Daugherty sent the Spartans into a spread formation for the first time of the season with third-string quarterback Dave McCormick split as a flanker. Cutting to the outside, he speared Juday's pass just before he fell out of bounds at the four. Two plays later, Juday sneaked over from the one. Lou Bobich's PAT added another point and with just over three minutes gone, Michigan State had a 7-0 lead.

The jitters continued for both teams. Detwiler fumbled the kickoff in the end zone but luckily Ward was there to cover up. A few minutes later, Detwiler wouldn't be so lucky. A Timberlake-to-Smith bomb and a 13-yard scamper by Ward had pushed the ball to the State 18. But on the next carry, Jim again got separated from the ball and Ron Goovert was there to recover for MSU and stifle Michigan's first deep threat of the game.

The Spartans got as far as the Michigan 15 when Juday fumbled the snap and Yearby fell on the ball to thwart any hopes of a MSU runaway.

On the subsequent series, the Wolverines got their first close look at the man later voted as the greatest State player in history, George Webster. Trying to pass on third and long, Timbo found himself in the grasp of Number 90 in green. Every bit as big as Bob, Webster simply flipped him to the ground as he would so many enemy ball carriers over the years.

With the first quarter drawing to a close, another Spartan All-American came into the picture. Taking a handoff from Juday, Clint Jones started back to the line of scrimmage. But the Wolverines had called a blitz and Cecchini drilled the great sophomore halfback immediately. Jones never had a chance as the ball sailed 10 yards upfield where Dehlin recovered for Michigan. It was already the sixth fumble of the day. It was evident that the tackles were a bit above the norm in ferocity, even for an MSU-Michigan game.

Midway through the second quarter the Blue moved to the Spartan 11. But the unlucky Detwiler was creamed as he dashed off the right side—again the ball was jarred loose. Jim was able to recover the ball but for a seven-yard loss. Two plays later, a 32-yard field goal attempt by Timberlake was wide and Michigan's second foray into Spartan territory had been shut down.

With only 45 seconds left in the first half, U-M got a big break as a personal foul penalty against the Spartans gave Michigan a first down at the MSU 35. A 22-yard completion to Henderson got Timberlake within field goal range again and this time he didn't fail—his 29-yarder was perfect and the half ended with State up, 7-3.

It was a down Wolverine squad that filed into the dressing room, according to Conley.

"We wanted to win so badly, but we were having doubts about how good we really were. Bump just sat us all down and calmly told us that we were the better team and had worked too hard to lose it all on a sunny afternoon in East Lansing."

Between halves it was announced that a new Spartan Stadium record had been set as 78,234 were officially on hand. It didn't take long for the record gathering to get caught up in the spirit of things again as the third quarter opened with a shocker.

State's kickoff drove Ward into the end zone where he had trouble fielding the ball. Getting a grasp on it he raced to the 18 where he was met by fellow Ohioan Phil Hoag. Again the ball popped loose but this time Bobich was on it and a highly excited MSU offense prepared to take over at the U-M 18.

A couple of running plays gained only two yards. Juday then tried to go to the acrobatic Washington but Rindfuss, who gave away five inches in height to Gene, got there first to bat it down. Dick Kenney, the barefoot Hawaiian who had set a school record the week before with a 49-yarder against USC, trotted out for what appeared to be a cinch three-pointer from 31 yards away. But Kenney pushed his kick to the right and Michigan had escaped with their life once more.

Neither team had any luck moving the ball for the next 10 minutes until the Spartans took over with only seconds remaining in the quarter. Duffy had decided to come in with McCormick at quarterback to give his team another running threat. And, on the final play of the period it paid off when the Chicago junior swept around end to the Michigan 20. The drive sputtered at the nine where Duffy elected to make another switch. Instead of Kenney, he brought in Larry Lukasik to attempt a field goal of 26 yards. The move was a wise one with the kick perfect and with two and a half minutes gone in the fourth quarter, State had improved its lead to 10-3.

The Michigan offense had been all but non-existent in the second half, having picked up but one first down and never getting across the 50-yard line. So the upcoming series was obviously the make or break point for the Wolverines. It didn't look too promising when four minutes later they faced a fourth and inches from their 48. So, Bump had a choice—go for the first down and risk giving the Spartans the ball in Michigan territory or punt and hope the defense could get it back quickly—a decided gamble either way. Bump opted for the first down and called Timberlake's number. As he would be time and again on the year, Bob was fully prepared, sliding off guard for the needed yardage and the Wolverines' attack was still alive.

With the exception of the next-to-last play of the second quarter, Henderson had been shut down completely by MSU. But on first down, Timbo caught the Spartans napping. Following a fake to Anthony, Bob drifted back and tossed a strike to Henderson that was good for 29 yards. And when Sygar took a pitch on the next play and dashed to the nine, Michigan had their deepest scoring threat of the afternoon. Two rushes by Anthony got them to the five. Then, for the fourth time in the drive, the Mutt and Jeff combination clicked as Timberlake ripped a spiral to Sygar in the end zone and Michigan had their first touchdown at Spartan Stadium in four years. That made it 10-9.

Now, play for the tie or the win? Bump never hesitated. He motioned for the two-point conversion attempt. Anthony got the ball but before Mel could crack the goal line little Charlie Migyanka pulled him down and the Spartans still held their one-point margin.

With over seven minutes to go, the plans of the MSU offense were clear — hold onto the football as long as possible. But three running plays gained only three yards and the Spartans had to surrender the ball. Rindfuss gathered in Bobich's punt at the Michigan 43 and tightroped down the sidelines to the MSU 41. The clock read 4:55.

Michigan needed about 20-25 yards to get Timberlake in field goal range, which was limited to around 35 yards. A slant off the left side by Ward picked up four. Timbo rambled around end for four more. The clock had ticked down to 3:24. On third and two, Anthony bulled his way just past the first down marker but less than three minutes were left.

From the sidelines, Sygar came racing onto the field to replace Ward. The Spartan defense warily watched the fiery little competitor line up at halfback, correctly figuring that he was involved in whatever play Bump had sent in with him. Sure enough, the pitchout went to Tony Mason's boy who began a sweep around the right side. The Green and White defenders quickly closed to the area to converge on the white-shirted number 18. But in doing so, they completely forgot about another Wolverine wearing those numbers in reverse. Galloping down the sideline, Henderson had just reached the goal line when Sygar put on the brakes and lofted a perfect pass into the end zone.

Not a State player was within five yards of tall John when he cradled the ball to his jersey, while complete pandemonium broke out among the Michigan players and fans. With the Spartans still in deep shock, Timberlake tossed to Smith for a successful two-point conversion and Michigan took a 17-10 lead with less than two and a half minutes to go.

Juday returned to quarterback in an attempt to pass the Spartans upfield but the Michigan defense was not about to let this one get away. A sack and three incompletions later the Wolverines had put the finishing touches on their first win over their bitter rivals to the north since 1955.

The only negative note for Michigan came when they learned that Conley's father had suffered a heart attack in the stands and had been rushed to a nearby hospital. However, the elder Conley proved to be just as tough as his son; a quick recovery put him back in the stands before the season was over.

While the seventh and ninth place teams were meeting in East Lansing, the nation's second and fourth place clubs were squaring off in Champaign. Unlike the civil war in Michigan, however, the other game was a dud—the Buckeyes walked all over the Illini, 28-0, to propel the Bucks into second place in the AP ranking with Michigan now fifth.

The fear of a letdown is voiced following every Michigan State game—1964 was no exception. Especially considering the emotional high of the victory and the physical pounding each player had taken.

"It was a tremendously bruising affair," admitted Bump, "and we'll need some time to recover. But I'm afraid Purdue isn't going to allow us much rest on Saturday."

October 17—Purdue at Michigan

The Boilermakers were a rather unknown quantity. They had opened with a win over Ohio U. but then were shelled by Notre Dame. They bounced back to easily defeat Wisconsin the following Saturday.

They had been forced to replace their three-year starter at quarterback, Ron DeGravio, with an untested sophomore whom the Purdue press guide described as not being in the same class with DeGravio, Lennie Dawson, or Bernie Allen. However, the coaching staff did express some confidence in the youngster. His name was Bob Griese.

With their untried commodity at quarterback, coach Jack Mollenkopf had thrust a great deal of his offense into the hands of his fine pair of running backs, Gordon Teter and Randy Minniear. Both averaged over four yards per carry while Teter ranked behind only All-American candidate Bob Hadrick (who was described as a loose end) in catching the ball.

Oddly, only 60,424 showed up in Ann Arbor on a glorious mid-October afternoon to watch the battle. Michigan fans were not yet convinced that Bump had a Big Ten contender.

For those fans who were a bit tardy in closing down their tailgate parties on the warm fall day, the crowd's roar told them they had already missed some early excitement. Following the kickoff, Michigan put the ball in play at their 29. Rindfuss had started at halfback in place of Ward which should have tipped Purdue that something was afoot. Taking the pitch, the versatile senior fired a perfect pass to Detwiler who hauled it in at the Boilermaker 40 and rambled to the 24 before safetyman Ken Eby could pull him down. One play — 47 yards and a foothold well into Purdue territory. Six plays later, U-M was at the four where a convoy of Detwiler, Mack, and Smith escorted Timberlake into the end zone untouched. Less than four minutes had expired and following Bob's successful conversion, Michigan had jumped to a 7-0 lead.

Things settled down after the quick start by the Wolverines until late in the period with Purdue in possession. Dropping back to throw, Griese found Hadrick bottled up by Rindfuss and Volk. Shifting targets in a flash, Griese floated a beautiful spiral to wingback Jim Morel who fought off both Sygar and Cecchini at the Michigan 18 and raced the rest of the way to complete a 66-yard scoring play. Griese, who like Timberlake doubled in the kicking department, booted through the extra point, and before a stunned crowd, Purdue had tied the score at seven with only 43 seconds left in the quarter.

The bomb may have shaken up the defense a bit, but not Timberlake who also came out throwing. Back-to-back completions to Smith and Henderson picked up 38 yards and three plays into the second quarter, Michigan was at the Purdue 29. The Blue stayed on the ground until they reached the 17 where it was third and nine. Cranking up his right arm again, Timberlake found his huge end Steve Smith all alone in the corner of the end zone and delivered a strike for the go-ahead touchdown. It was Steve's only TD grab of the season. Again Timbo was letter perfect with his PAT and just two minutes into the second period, Michigan again led by a touchdown.

On Michigan's next series it was a different story. Backpedaling to throw, Timberlake faced an all-out Boilermaker blitz and tried to unload the ball. Before he could do so, linebacker John Charles reached over Bob and knocked the ball away. With no Wolverine in the area, Charles was able to drop on the ball himself at the Michigan 16 and Purdue was staring at the Wolverine goal line.

Griese went to his main man, Hadrick, for six and then scooted to the two on an option play. The husky Minniear took it in from there and just like that it was again a tie game following Griese's conversion.

From there on out, things got a bit frantic with turnovers on both sides stalling promising drives and the half ended at 14-14.

The half-time stat sheet looked more like a pro game than a collegiate affair pitting two teams who supposedly relied on their rushing attacks. Purdue had gained twice as much through the air than on the ground while Michigan was just short of doubling its rushing total. This sheet also failed to justify a tie score with U-M outgaining the Boilermakers by almost 100 yards and holding almost a two to one edge in first downs. But all that did was serve notice to the Wolverines that they had failed to take full opportunity of their scoring chances while allowing Purdue to score on a bomb and a turnover—a frustrating situation but not a desperate one as the second half began.

Midway through the third quarter, Griese hit his favorite target Hadrick at midfield and when a personal foul call went against Michigan, the Boilermakers were at the U-M 36. Another reception by Hadrick, this one good for 19 yards, pushed the ball deeper. Shifting to the ground attack, five carries by Minniear enabled Purdue to reach the three. Here, Griese decided enough was enough as he faked to his hard-working fullback and then tossed him a little floater in the end zone where he had gone unnoticed by the Michigan defense. A Griese PAT and Michigan was down, 21-14.

Neither team was able to mount an attack after the Boilermaker drive until early in the fourth quarter when Michigan moved to the Purdue 39. Rolling to his right, Timberlake picked up a couple of blocks from Mack and Smith and churned for 25 yards. The next call was for Detwiler, getting only his third carry on the day. Finding an opening, he slipped through the line and headed for the goal line. But before he made it, he was met head-on by a pair of tacklers and the ball danced crazily into the end zone. For a moment, it looked as though a touchdown was still possible as Michigan's Marcum seemed to have the ball in his grasp. But John couldn't hold on and when it next appeared it was in the arms of defensive end Hal Wells, an Air Force veteran and at 26, the oldest player on the field.

The Boilermakers were stymied on offense and with still half of the period to go, Michigan took over at its 36. A first down scramble by Timberlake brought it to the U-M 46 and set the stage for another crowd pleaser. Noticing an overshift by the Purdue defense to their left, Bump signalled an option for Bob but instead of going to his right as he had all afternoon long, Timbo was to run the play to his left (Purdue's right). Rounding the corner, Timbo put a great fake on end Jim Long and cut into the middle. While Marcum, Mack, and Smith were leveling the secondary, Timberlake was on his way to the longest run of his career — a 54-yard rumble for the touchdown. This was the play that brought Bob the blushes on Monday when he watched the films.

Now came decision time for Bump. Should he play for the tie and hope Michigan would get another shot at scoring? Should he shoot for two, figuring the one-point margin might be enough? And if Michigan failed on the two-point try, would they be able to get the ball back? Bump chose to live and die with his brilliant quarterback. Again Bob rolled right. But this time the outside was sealed off and he was forced to cut back into the field. There, at the one-yard line, the entire left side of Purdue's defense swallowed him en masse. It was a move that Bump admitted he second-guessed himself on for days.

"I argued with myself on that until two in the morning. I still do at times."

Should he have run Anthony, who was normally good for at least three? Should Timbo have sneaked rather than trying to sweep? Could they have fooled Purdue with a short pass? Who knows? But with five minutes left, nobody at the time felt there wouldn't be another chance.

They were right—Purdue was stopped on three straight plays by a Michigan defense which had allowed only one first down the entire quarter.

So there were still three and half minutes to go when Michigan took over at their 42. Ward and Timberlake picked up nine between them and Anthony slashed for 10 more to the Purdue 39. Timbo gained four more and with two minutes left, a field goal attempt loomed as a distinct possibility. At that point, Bump inserted Dave Fisher in place of Anthony, a move that puzzled both Mel and his teammates. Later, Bump explained he wanted to give Mel a quick breather in preparation for the final push. He never got the opportunity. On the next play, Fisher couldn't negotiate the pitch from Timberlake with the ball spinning back upfield, right into the arms of the aged Hal Wells again. The final blow.

Michigan did get the ball one more time and when four desperation passes failed to click they had suffered their first loss of the season.

A distraught Dave Fisher raced from the field into the tunnel, his number 33 disappearing long before his dejected teammates or the joyous Boilermakers joined the trek to the locker rooms. But Fisher, for all of his self-recriminations, played a small part in the loss. It was obviously not Michigan's day.

Timberlake had been magnificent in defeat, accounting for an even 300 yards himself. But there was the matter of four turnovers, each killing a Michigan scoring threat. To make the defeat even harder to swallow, both Hahn and Dehlin had suffered knee injuries in the battle and would have to undergo surgery. For Hahn, it was the end of his career, but Dehlin would recover in time for the trip to Pasadena.

If it was bitter for Michigan, it indeed was sweet for Purdue. By virtue of a schedule that omitted Ohio State and gave them one more game than the Buckeyes, the Boilermakers could sniff their first Big Ten crown since 1929.

October 24—Minnesota at Michigan

The mood of the Wolverines, as they prepared for their Little Brown Jug battle, was not enhanced by the word that Ohio State had been voted the nation's number one team following their win over USC. But by mid-week, most of the attention had gotten back to the Gophers who had owned the jug since 1959.

A strong gale greeted the 62,000 who filed into the stadium. The breeze prompted Bump to go with the wind rather than the ball after winning the coin toss. True to Bump's expectations, the Gophers couldn't move the ball and a weak punt into the wind gave Michigan the ball at their 48 to begin their initial drive.

Not willing to risk putting the ball up in the breeze, Michigan stayed on the ground with Anthony working off some frustrations of the previous Saturday. Four off tackle smashes by Mel and an eight-yard pickup by Ward moved the ball to the Minnesota 27. Another dash by Carl gained 14 more and two more plunges by Anthony made it third and five at the eight. Ward swept the left side for the third time in the drive, for six where it took Anthony only two tries to bang it over to climax the drive of more than six minutes. The PAT was good and Michigan had an early 7-0 lead.

On the following series, U-M got as far as the Minnesota 17 but Evasheski missed Ward off a fake field goal attempt and the Gophers got the ball back at their 10.

Again the Gophers failed to move past midfield and Michigan put the ball in play at their 25. On the second play from scrimmage, Timberlake burst through a maze of would-be Minnesota tacklers and peeled off 24 yards before safety Andy Haines could run him down at the Michigan 49. But the attack eventually bogged down at the 15 and Evashevski came back onto the field as a holder. This time it was for real and Timbo belted it through from 29 yards out for a 10-0 lead which stood up for the remainder of the half.

The first half domination was pointed up by the fact

that Ward had outgained the entire Gopher running attack by better than a two to one margin with Anthony close to doing the same. And for the first time on the season, Michigan had gone through a half of errorless ball. The Purdue loss was starting to recede into memory as the second half began.

After failing to move, Minnesota was forced to punt from deep in its end zone but the punt never got away as the snap sailed well over the head of punter Bruce Van De Walker and out of the end zone. A safety for the Wolverines and a 12-0 lead.

The teams then began jockeying for position with neither offense able to gain a first down on the next two series as Michigan took over at the 50 with half the quarter expired.

Alternating the ball-carriers on each play, Ann Arbor reached the one where Timberlake crashed over for a commanding 19-0 lead with just four minutes left in the quarter.

Oddly enough, the Michigan march seemed to do more toward inspiring the Gophers than demoralizing them. Starting at their 20, the visitors roared down the field and as the gun ended the third quarter the Gophers were planted at the Wolverine 10. Quarterback John Hankinson took care of the rest when on the second play of the final quarter, he threaded a pass through three defenders to Kent Kramer and Minnesota was on the scoreboard. A two-point try was mandatory and it seemed successful for a brief moment. But the Gophers' other massive tight end, Tiny Brown, couldn't hold onto the pass in the corner of the end zone and the margin held at 13, 19-6.

In a reprise of their last possession, Michigan's ground attack was again relentless. Nine straight rushing plays put Michigan at the Minnesota 13. Bump decided now was the time to shake up everybody with a pass. It did, but not in the way that Bump had planned. Retreating to the 20, Timberlake spotted Henderson crossing to the middle. But Bob failed to note the Gophers' Kraig Lofquist also cutting to the center. Timing his move perfectly, the converted quarterback snared the ball just before it reached Henderson and set sail for the far sidelines. The momentum had carried everyone away from that side of the field and there was no one within 20 yards of Lofquist by the time he had left Henderson in his wake. Ninety-one yards later he was in the end zone—the longest interception return in Minnesota history and at the time the longest in Michigan Stadium records. But most important to Minnesota was the fact they suddenly found themselves back in a game that looked like a blowout a short time earlier. Again the two-point conversion was in order but again a pass misfired and the margin stood at 19-12.

Now the enthusiasm had shifted completely to the Gophers. The defense stopped Michigan on three downs and with half the quarter still be played they had the football at the 50.

Suddenly it was the Gopher ground attack which was eating up the yardage with six straight rushes pushing them to the Michigan 27. Passes to Ken Last and Brown gained 20 yards more and it was first and goal at the seven. The stage was set for a series of downs that could make or break Michigan's hopes for title contention.

Fullback Mike Reid, who earlier had picked up two yards on a fourth and one, tried a dive up the middle. Yearby and Cecchini were there to meet him and it was second and goal at the seven. Hankinson tried the outside next but Conley nailed him at the five. Now it was third and goal with time ticking away. Having tried the middle and right with no success, the Gophers used their other option to the left with again Hankinson carrying the ball. He gained two yards before Volk came up to bang him down. It was down to one play.

The hero of moments earlier, Lofquist checked into the backfield and Michigan guessed correctly he would be a key to whatever coach Murray Warmath had dreamed up. Sure enough, the handoff was given to Lofquist who started to the right on an option. But before he had a chance to explore his receivers, Volk, who had taken a gamble and blitzed, reached the ball carrier. In desperation, Lofquist lateraled to Brown, who was to have been the lead blocker in the sweep. But Brown fared no better with the steady John Yanz wrapping him up at the five and the goal line stand of the year was in the books. And so was Michigan's 19-12 victory.

An odd win in many respects. Michigan had put the ball in the air only nine times. Anthony and Ward had each outrushed the entire Minnesota team. An almost errorless game with the only turnover resulting in a record. But a win, nevertheless, at an all-important juncture for Bump and his boys.

October 31—Northwestern at Michigan

As they prepared for the Wildcats, no one had to tell the Wolverines that they had escaped by the skin of their teeth the previous Saturday. Northwestern had fallen into hard times following their 7-2 mark two years earlier but with Tommy Myers at quarterback, they were potentially dangerous.

Despite another sunny and mild afternoon, the stadium was only a little over half full as the Wolverines kicked off to open the game.

On their first series Michigan moved close enough for a field goal attempt by Timberlake which missed to the right. The second series was more successful. Detwiler peeled off 12 yards on a sweep and then hooked up on a pass from Timbo for 22 more. Henderson then made a great leaping catch at the two where long Bob stretched his frame over the goal stripe on the next play and Michigan was up, 7-0.

The next Michigan series proved even more exciting. On a third and 10, Ward exploded off the left side for 52 yards to the Northwestern 33. The Wildcats had hardly recovered when Volk came in to give Ward a breather. Whether Northwestern knew they were dealing with another quarterback isn't known, but when Volk took Timberlake's pitch the entire defense converged on him. Rick braked to a halt and threw a perfect spiral to Henderson who had gone down the field unmolested. Tall John was able to jog over for the touchdown with not a Wildcat in sight. Ironically, it was the only pass Volk threw in his collegiate career. Seven minutes were left in the second quarter but realistically the game was over.

Another stretched-out drive of 14 plays was climaxed with Timberlake's second touchdown of the day and the half ended with the Blue showing a 21-0 lead.

Midway through the third quarter, Anthony gathered in a pitch and sped down the sidelines for 30 yards and Michigan's fourth touchdown. Bump allowed Sygar to boot the extra point, his only attempt of the year.

Bump turned things over to his bench at that point with Anthony even seeing action at linebacker due to a slight head injury to Cecchini. The final scoring came on a three-yard plunge by Dave Fisher just into the final quarter. Final score: Michigan 35, Northwestern 0.

Sixty-one players saw action for Michigan, including another of Tony Mason's products, sophomore Jim Sieber, who on the final play of the game got to carry the ball for the only time in his career. Poor Jim never got the chance to see his effort officially inscribed since the following year's press guide omitted his one shining moment.

An easy win, allowing Michigan to get their second wind before facing tough Illinois the next Saturday. But it moved them no closer to the number one rated Buckeyes or Purdue. Both had posted victories also and were 4-0 in the Big Ten.

November 7—Illinois at Michigan

The Illini were a hard team to figure. They had a 4-2 mark but had been wiped out by both Ohio State and Purdue. Yet this was a team with five future NFL stars including the man himself, Dick Butkus. It was basically the same team that would have been unbeaten in 1963 but for the shocker at the hands of Michigan. They were out of the conference race but very much spoiling for revenge.

For Michigan, it climaxed an unprecedented fourth

straight Big Ten Saturday at home. And although this would be the final appearance of the superlative Timberlake, Anthony, Henderson and the other seniors, only 62,415 showed for the Michigan finale. It was always a matter of great curiosity why the two non-conference foes had outdrawn all Big Ten opponents.

One surprise was quickly forthcoming when after receiving the kickoff, Illinois trotted out Butkus at center. It seemed to pay quick dividends when future all-pro Jim Grabowski went up the middle for five yards on the first play. Another would-be NFL star, Bob Trumpy, paired with quarterback Fred Custardo for 12 additional yards and when Custardo tacked on 11 more on a rollout, the Illini looked like the team they were supposed to be. But there the drive stalled.

That was about all the offense either team could muster throughout the first quarter with Michigan unable to do anything against Butkus and company. But the combination of Kemp's booming punts and Tony Mason's defense kept the Illini bottled up also.

Finally, on the last play of the first period, Michigan got the break they were looking for. Frank Nunley stepped in front of Trumpy for an interception at the Illinois 35 and Michigan had their first look at the Illinois end of the field.

Timberlake and Anthony went back to their "your turn, my turn" formula and it worked. Alternating on each play, the two took Michigan to the 13, the last 11 yards on a rollout by Timbo.

But there things got sticky. Butkus leveled Mel for a two yard loss and a pass to Henderson was dropped. On third and 12 Michigan decided to introduce the Illini to Carl Ward. Gathering in a pitchout, the Cincinnati Comet snake-hipped his way through the defense until none were left and Ward was in for the first touchdown of the day. It had taken Michigan five plays to capitalize on Nunley's theft and go up, 7-0.

Stung by the score, Illinois quickly moved to midfield on their next possession. That set the stage for the 6-5 Trumpy. Flying down the field, the lanky sophomore receiver found himself in a footrace with Volk. But even the 6-3 Rick had to give away a couple of inches and when Custardo dropped a perfect throw into his arms at the 15, Trumpy was gone. A 50-yard strike and only the second time that the U-M secondary had been beaten deep for a touchdown. Still pumped up over his throw, Custardo pushed his PAT attempt to the right and Michigan still led, 7-6.

Getting the ball back quickly, Illinois started looking like the Keystone Kops. Fumbling twice in succession, they were able to recover both. The third time they weren't so lucky. Trumpy fielded a pass at the 40 and promptly coughed up the football where Jerry Mader dropped on it for the Wolverines.

As before, Timberlake didn't waste time. He first nailed Henderson with an 11-yarder, ran for five more himself and then found Detwiler on a crossing pattern over the middle. The Toledo strongboy gathered in the pass at the one and stepped into the end zone to re-establish some breathing room for Michigan. Timberlake's PAT made it 14-6 and ended the scoring for the half.

One disturbing note was sounded in the locker room at the break. John Yanz had suffered knee damage and would have to undergo surgery. Thus the unsung Chicago senior would have to join the evergrowing hospital list that now included six key members of the roster. For Bump, it was beginning to be a war of attrition and he wasn't sure if he could win it.

Early in the second half, following a mammoth Illinois punt, Michigan was backed in a corner at their six. This triggered a Michigan drive that would be the longest of the season and take over seven minutes to complete. Except for a 23-yard burst by Ward, it was accomplished in five and six-yard increments. A one-yard plunge by Timberlake on the 19th play of the series finally brought the march to its end. And when number 28 belted through the conversion attempt to make it 21-6, the scoring was done for the afternoon.

Michigan threatened to add to its total midway through the fourth quarter when they drove to the Illinois four. But Evashevski, who had replaced Timberlake at quarterback, fumbled the snap with the ball rolling free to the one where George Donnelly recovered for the Illini. It also prompted a wild, fist-swinging brawl with two players ejected and Michigan tagged with a 15-yard personal foul call.

One other fact was noted in tribute to the Michigan defense. With 45 seconds to go, Illinois penetrated Michigan territory for the only time on the afternoon, with the exception of the Custardo-to-Trumpy bomb.

The second half did have a disconcerting note for the winners when Rindfuss had to be helped from the field after twisting an ankle. By Monday it had been placed in a cast and another Wolverine was sidelined.

But the news wasn't all bad. Purdue had been upset by Michigan State, 21-7, at West Lafayette, while the Buckeyes were being thrashed by Penn State to remove OSU from national title consideration. So the standings now showed Ohio State on top at 4-0, followed by Michigan and Purdue at 4-1. The Wolverines had a chance to deal with the Bucks themselves but a tie with Purdue would send the Black and Gold to Pasadena on New Year's Day. And there was the little matter of facing the Big Ten's top quarterback the following Saturday at a place they hadn't tasted victory since 1956.

November 14—Michigan at Iowa

Gary Snook had already set new Hawkeye records in both passing and total offense and was close to becoming the Big Ten's all-time leader in both categories. His fellow junior, Flint's Karl Noonan, was breaking school records on the other end of Snook's aerials. The two had scared the life out the Buckeyes, losing by a narrow 21-19 count. To combat this potent air attack, Bump and Bob Hollway juggled their secondary with different looks on every play. They even went so far as to use Henderson as an extra defender in certain situations.

A cold, rainy afternoon would have aided Bump's efforts to bottle up Snook but it wasn't to be. A balmy, sunny day, with temperatures well into the 70s bathed the packed house at Kinnick Stadium.

Both teams looked shaky in the early going. A Snook fumble gave Michigan the ball after Iowa had driven to the Wolverine 16. But the Blue gave it back on the next play when Ward's bobble was recovered by Bob Mitchell, the second of four Flint starters for the Hawks. Two of them, Craig Nourse and Dalton Kimble, manned the halfback spots and on the next play Nourse skirted the right side and streaked 15 yards for the touchdown. Gary Simpson added the extra point to make it 7-0 and for the first time in five games, Michigan found themselves trailing in a ball game.

Iowa made a bid to increase the lead on their next series before Mike Bass came up with a key interception for Michigan at their five. It was his only theft of the season, but couldn't have come at a better spot for his team.

Michigan's offense couldn't get untracked and Iowa prepared to move again. But before they could get a drive underway, Nourse was jarred by Cecchini on a sweep with the football popping out and Mader pouncing on it for Michigan at the Iowa 20.

In five plays, Timberlake and Anthony took turns advancing the Wolverines to the six. With the Hawkeyes creeping in on defense, Timberlake lobbed a pass to the double-duty Henderson who caught it well into the end zone. Timbo's conversion made it 7-7.

On the next Iowa series, Bump's defensive scheme began to pay dividends. Finding his deep receivers covered, Snook tried to go short to Kimble in the flat. But Laskey got there first and Michigan had the ball back at the Iowa 10; the fourth turnover of the game for Iowa. Anthony ended any suspense in a hurry as he shook off several potential Iowa tacklers, lugging the final two with him, and legged it over the goal stripe for a 13-7 lead. A bad pass from center cost Timberlake a chance to retain his perfect PAT record for the season.

The Hawkeyes quickly motored out to midfield on their next possession. Then came a variation of one of the oldest plays in the book. Coming around on a flanker reverse, Noonan snatched the ball out of Snook's hand as he stood poised to pass. The Wolverines moved up quickly to stop the ancient Statue of Liberty play which prompted Noonan to screech to a stop and fire a bullet to Rich O'Hara who was caught on a desperation tackle by Volk.

The Hawks went back to the more conventional pattern on the next play with Snook throwing to O'Hara over the middle. Nunley got a hand on the ball but couldn't stop it from deflecting into the arms of O'Hara for Iowa's second touchdown of the day. Going for two, Snook couldn't connect with Noonan and the 13-13 count stood.

Only minutes were left in the half when Michigan began their next series at the 20. That proved to be more than enough time. On the second play, Anthony got a wide pitch, steamed around the corner and rambled 62 yards down the sidelines before being pulled down at the Iowa 14. Timberlake felt Mel had contributed his share for the drive and did the rest on his own, tucking the ball away and dashing the remaining 14 yards himself. Three plays and 50 seconds had added up to 80 yards and a go-ahead touchdown. There was no confusion on the snap this time and Michigan owned a 20-13 halftime lead.

The halftime statistics showed the devastation Michigan's quarterback-fullback combination had wreaked. Between them, the two had gained all but 12 of Michigan's 147 yards. And the Michigan defense was up to their old tricks—two fumble recoveries and two interceptions.

The Wolverines added to that total quickly as on the first play of the third quarter Snook mishandled the snap and Simkus was there to gobble it up. Forty-two seconds into the period Michigan was at the Iowa 25. Three plays later found them at the one after a Henderson reception and an 11-yard carry by Detwiler. Again, it was Marvelous Mel's turn with the great fullback banging over to make it 27-13. The air was fast escaping from the Iowa upset balloon.

Michigan continued to put the pressure on Snook who was suffering through his worst day. A Volk interception on the next series put U-M at the Iowa 12. But a holding call pushed them back and Timberlake couldn't connect on a field goal try.

Two plays later Snook fumbled away the ball for the fourth time with Bill Keating coming up with it this time for Michigan. But the fumbleitis was becoming contagious with Detwiler giving it back at the six.

Late in the quarter, Michigan had taken over at their 44. Slowly grinding it out to the 30, Timberlake suddenly speeded up things with a 20-yarder to Henderson. It was now time for the Bob-and-Mel show again and four plays later Anthony banged over for his third touchdown of the game. That put Michigan ahead 34-13 with three and a half minutes left in the third quarter and the Wolverines were starting to entertain thoughts of Columbus.

Iowa was able to mount an early fourth quarter attack that culminated in Snook's 20-yard touchdown scamper. Simpson's kick cut the score to 34-20 and with 10 minutes to go, the loyal Iowa fans could still hope for a comeback.

But the Wolverines dashed these hopes with a patented, methodical drive that saw 22 plays run off and by the time Iowa got the ball back at their 10 the clock read only 0:46. The victory was intact.

Snook did have the consolation of becoming the all-time conference leader in completions while Noonan moved into the school's record book with 40 receptions for the season.

Over four hundred fans were on hand at Willow Run

to greet the winners who learned they had gotten a hand from Minnesota in their championship quest. The Gophers had upset Purdue, 14-7, which left the Wolverine's fate directly in their own hands. That fate would be decided the succeeding weekend in another rather unfriendly locale, Ohio Stadium.

November 21—Michigan at Ohio State

To understand the hysteria that we all got caught up in that week, you have to keep in mind that Michigan had not been involved in a title showdown since 1955. Most of the students weren't yet in kindergarten when the last Big Ten Championship had been gained back in 1950.

The excitement for both the team and the fans began building Monday. By the time over two thousand assembled on the diag Friday night to hear Conley, "Doc" Losh, Wally Weber, Bump and the rest, the fever was out of control. Cecchini called it unlike any week he had ever experienced, before or later. Laskey said the enthusiasm and electricity was overwhelming.

"I don't think any of us spent a quiet night and I know that few of us made many classes."

During the week-long study of films, the coaching staff had noticed a quirk on the part of Ohio halfback Bo Rein. When he moved into his stance, he would put his right hand down if the play was to go left. Conversely, the left hand would be down if the action was to go right. It would play a major factor in the game with Cecchini using the information to call defensive signals throughout the afternoon.

Friday night, after getting settled down by Dave Butler's speech, the team retired to their motel only to be serenaded by Buckeye fans throughout the evening. Situated at the old Deshler Hotel downtown, my crew and I had the same problem—through the night, up and down High Street, the pre-game wildness surged.

The first thing that hit us when we strolled into the mid-morning Columbus gloom was the 20 m.p.h. wind and a 15-degree temperature (Wind chill factors hadn't been invented yet which was a blessing or we might have felt even colder.) As the team hustled out of the locker room, to the taunts of the wild-eyed Buckeye fans, they got their first taste of the Arctic conditions in which they would be playing.

"I can still feel the wind hitting me for the first time," Cecchini recalls. "My first concern was for my hands since I was responsible for snapping the ball on all punts. How could numb fingers snap a football 15 yards?"

Cecchini never faltered all day.

Mel Anthony had to take the brunt of the Ohio insults during the warmup sessions: he was a close-by native son who had gotten away from Woody. But that only provided a little more fire for the bruising fullback coming off a three-touchdown performance.

"Heck, I didn't have any doubts we would win, it was just a matter of how much," said Mel. "After all, the best players from Ohio went to U-M that year."

Anthony later added that he was happy to see the game get underway knowing he would only have to face 11 men at a time.

Woody's offense was almost a mirror image of Michigan's. The Buckeye offensive line was anchored by future NFL star Doug Van Horn, a counterpart to Mack. Quarterback Don Unverferth was a clone of Timberlake in size and had been allowed to throw an unheard-of 170 passes for Woody that season. His arm was on par with Bob's, but like most everybody else this season, he couldn't compare to the preacherman as a runner. The fullback comparison was even closer. The Bucks' Willard Sander and Anthony were not only neck and neck in yardage and size, but both had also played their high school football in Cincinnati.

Rein, at right half and a sophomore like Ward, had been a high school teammate of Sygar, Rindfuss, Kines (and don't forget Sieber) at Niles. Not quite as fast as the lightning-like Carl, he still was a breakaway threat on the team. On the other side, Tom Barrington at left half was a 210-pounder as was Detwiler and could block almost as well as his Michigan opposite number.

But, of course, it was defense that had shoved OSU to their 5-0 conference mark—the grudging Bucks had allowed Big Ten opponents only 31 points, best in the pack. They may not have had a Yearby or Cecchini, but they were a rugged bunch from end to end.

Winning the toss, Woody took advantage of the icy conditions and gave Michigan the first crack at handling the frozen football. The Wolverines moved to mid-field before stalling and that gave the Buckeyes a taste of what was to come. In came Stan Kemp to slide a punt out at the 23 and Bob Hollway and Tony Mason's defense shucked off their heavy parkas for their first crack at Ohio State.

Although this was the year that Woody had supposedly opened up, he stayed on the ground for six straight rushes which picked up a pair of first downs to the Ohio 47 where big plays by Conley and Nunley brought the drive to a halt.

Punting with the wind, Steve Dreffer still managed only a 31-yard punt and when Timberlake peeled off 15 yards on the first play, the Wolverines were back close to midfield. But the Bucks defense closed down again with Kemp back in to punt. The kick sailed high and deep to Rein who let the rock-like ball slip through his fingers. Instead of bouncing away, however, it caromed right back into his hands.

When Michigan's defense had trotted off the field after the first series, Nunley and Laskey had been met by Hollway, Nelson, and Bump.

"Nunley, what the hell is going on out there?" asked Hollway.

"We're just feeling them out," was the blond bomber's reply.

Nunley later laughed about the exchange.

"How should I have known what was going on?" he chuckled. "I was only 18 years old."

On the third play from scrimmage, Sander broke through the line into the secondary. Racing over from his linebacking slot, Nunley slammed into the Bucks' bull with such velocity that the runner's facemask shattered into pieces. But, for the third time in the quarter, luck was with Ohio as end Bob Stock corralled the fumbled ball up at the 46 — a near-disaster became a 14-yard gain.

Two plays later, the first quarter ended with the locals having inched into Michigan territory for the first time. But the 49 was as far as they could manage. A punting contest ensued with neither team able to move and with half the second quarter gone, Michigan began at its 20. Two Detwiler carries made it third and short. But Timberlake fumbled when blitzed by Bill Ridder with both Ridder and Tom Kiehfuss dropping on the loose ball. The Buckeyes were at the Michigan 29 and the stadium was rocking.

But the Scarlet and Gray couldn't move and brought kicker Bob Funk in for a 44-yard try. A year later, Funk would boot three field goals in Ann Arbor to give a 9-7 victory—but today his kick was well short.

To most of us, the ball appeared to go into the end zone for a touchback, giving the Wolverines a first down at their 20. However, referee Ross Dean ruled that the ball had rolled dead at the one. Michigan crept out to the six before Kemp, standing in the end zone, punted to the 50. But a good runback by Rein brought Ohio back to the 33.

But this was the day of defense—especially a Michigan defense that remembered the humiliation of three years earlier. Unverferth got only two on first down and Rein, tipping the play, ran into a swarm of tacklers off the left side for a two-yard loss. Then Unverferth put up a 15-yarder intended for Barrington, only his second pass of the day. But getting there first to bat it away was a guy who wasn't even supposed to be in Columbus—Dick Rindfuss. The gutty secondary ace hadn't made the trip to Iowa City and by mid-week was still hobbling on his immobilized ankle. I had already crossed him off the spotting chart and had penciled in Dick Wells in his place.

But as Sygar said about his high school companion and roommate, "There's no way Ryn is going to miss this game."

Barrington had found that out. So with the drive stalled, Funk was back on another field goal attempt. At least that's what Ohio wanted Michigan to believe. Taking the snap, holder Arnie Chonko yanked the ball away from the tee and fired to Barrington in the flat. But Cecchini and Sygar weren't fooled a bit as they pulled down big Tom at the 25 and killed the second deep Ohio threat of the game.

Timberlake took quick advantage of the boost in spirits with a 14-yard pass to Ben Farabee on the first play from scrimmage to get Michigan out of the shadow of its goal posts for the first time in the quarter. But again the Buckeye defense shut down the Wolverines and again Kemp was forced to make an appearance. Standing on the sidelines, preparing to return for the snap, Cecchini remembered a remark Bump had made that week.

"This game may well be settled on a break," forecast Bump.

It wasn't a unique prophecy, most coaches make the same statement before games expected to be close. But it stayed with Tom as he hurried onto the field to center the ball back to Kemp.

"I just hope the break isn't a bad snap," he mumbled to himself while trying to blow some warmth back into his numb fingers. He needn't have fussed since the snap was again perfect and so was Kemp's kick—another 50 yarder. Bo Rein, who would die in a tragic plane crash 15 years later, again had trouble fielding a Kemp punt. The ball slid through his fingers and bounced squarely off his chest. But this time there were no Buckeyes to save him—instead there was a white jersey wearing a blue 81 belonging to John Henderson. Cecchini proved to be clairvoyant after all, his crystal ball was just a little foggy as to which way the break would go.

Michigan had the football but they didn't have a lot of time to play with—only 1:15 showed on the clock, which glowed like a beacon through the gloom. Timberlake explored the left side on the first play and gained three yards to the 17. He immediately asked for a timeout and with 0:44 on the board, trotted to the sidelines to confer with Bump.

"Let's try double swing special," said Bump. "But be sure of it before you throw. We're in field goal range if we can't move it in."

It was a play Bump and his staff had cooked up that week for such an occasion. Farabee would run a down-and-in pattern, 20 yards deep. Detwiler would trail, running the same route only 10 yards shorter. A brand new play that the Ohio defense had never watched on film.

The two ran their patterns concisely, with the secondary concentrating on Farabee. Adjusting quickly, cornerback Don Harkins shoved Jim offstride as he shot by. By then, the ball was on its way to the five where Detwiler reached out and gathered it in. At the same instant, he was hit by a tremendous shot from linebacker Dwight Kelley that sent the sturdy sophomore catapulting into the end zone. But the ball was safely secured by the future dentist who was swarmed upon by his ecstatic teammates. Timberlake connected on the extra point and the half came to a close with the scoreboard reading MICHIGAN 7 OHIO STATE 0—a beautiful sight to a small, chilled group of fans wrapped in maize and blue blankets.

Except for the score, the halftime stats couldn't have

been much closer. Each team had managed just five first downs. OSU had outgained U-M by two yards, had run one more play, and hit one less pass. But the difference was what each team had done with the turnover given them.

Woody took the wraps off a new fullback, Paul Hudson, as the second half again found the Buckeyes receiving the kickoff. It didn't help much as they could advance only to their 40 before having to punt. Michigan had no better luck but they did have Stan Kemp who knocked one dead at the Ohio 15. Rein stayed completely away from all second-half punts either on Woody's orders or of his own choosing. With the temperature dropping by the minute, the ball became even more of an ice cake.

After Barrington bobbled the ball for a loss on Ohio's third play, it was Steve Dreffer's turn to punt. It also was Michigan's turn for a miscue as Sygar failed to come up with the ball and for the second time, Van Horn was on it for the Bucks. They kept it only for two downs. Ohio's second pass of the day was completed to Stock at the Bucks' 44 but attempting to turn upfield, Stock dropped the ball and Nunley found it. On the sidelines, Woody looked to be in the final stages of apoplexy as he watched his club fumble for the sixth time.

Runs by Detwiler and Anthony set up a 33-yard field goal try but Timberlake was wide of the mark. Minutes later, though, a 26-yard punt return by Volk put the Wolverines at the Ohio 24. Again, the Bucks stopped Michigan short of a first down and it was Timberlake's turn for another three-point effort. The attempt from 27 yards was a bull's-eye and the Bucks, staring at a 10-0 deficit, realized they would need more than a touchdown to reach Pasadena.

However, with all but eight seconds left of the fourth quarter, no one was ready to celebrate yet in Ann Arbor, especially when Unverferth threw to Rein on first down for 28 yards and followed up with another toss to Bo for seven more. This put OSU at the U-M 32 and when Sander broke off the left side for an additional 11, the Scarlet and Gray had their deepest penetration of the day. But Unverferth went to the well once too often. Rein again was the target but Rick Volk shot in front of the intended receiver at the eight to wrestle away the ball. The Michigan defense was still pitching a shutout.

Kemp's only short punt of the day put Ohio back at the Michigan 43 but the Bucks had made their lone long thrust. On a fourth down pass attempt, Yearby climaxed his great afternoon by batting down the ball as it left Unverferth's hand. Michigan ran down the clock until Kemp punted dead at the Ohio 10 with six minutes left. On the third play from scrimmage for the Bucks, Volk pilfered his second pass of the quarter.

Ohio got the ball one more time and managed to gain their second first down of the quarter before Volk was there again with a big play— batting down a fourth-and-10 pass. And with a minute to go the celebration was on.

In the victorious locker room, the coaches went into the showers one by one, Jocko Nelson with his cigar still blazing. Sygar led the most stirring rendition of "The Victors" yet that year. Roses were tossed from player to player as they started to realize that for the first time in 14 years, a Michigan team would be in Pasadena on New Year's Day.

Things were just as crazy back in Ann Arbor as fans spilled out of homes, bars, dorms, and apartments to dance with strangers. By the time the team plane touched down at Willow Run, 7,000 exuberant fans lined the taxi-strip to cheer the conquering heroes. To avoid danger to the fans on the main taxiway, the pilot detoured to a distant hangar. There the team buses picked them up and brought them back to the milling crowd.

Some fans had given up after seeing the plane disappear to the other side of the field but thousands who stayed greeted each player with ear-splitting screams and roses.

Slumping behind the wheel of my car, I watched the buses pull away with the fans close behind. As I watched, I reflected that in a space of nine months I had seen two U-M teams capture their first conference crowns in a generation. First the mania at Yost, now the hysteria of Columbus and Willow Run. Cazzie and Timbo . . . Yearby and Buntin . . . Cantrell and Sygar . . . Tregoning and Conley . . . Darden and Anthony . . . they seemed to meld into an uproarious scene. The final curtain had fallen for 1964. No more encores.

"Wait a minute," I thought, "in a week, they'll start bouncing the ball at Yost again."

But I knew as good as the future might be, it would have to go some to be better than this championship year— my first.

SEVEN

The Good, The Bad, and The Ugly

I'm convinced it's nigh impossible to delve into one's past and resist the urge to categorize people, places, and events. The great thing about this, of course, is that it gives others a chance to disagree — as I love to do when reading another's idea of best and worst. But as long as we know that such lists are purely subjective, they're harmless and fun. So here we go with Hemingway's strictly biased and unscientific book of U-M sports lists.

GAMES I WOULD LOVE TO BROADCAST AGAIN

February 15, 1965
Michigan 96—Indiana 95
(2 overtimes)

If I ever get a chance to do a more exciting basketball game than the one that night in Bloomington, I may not

265

come out alive. Two great teams battling through 50 minutes of non-stop thrills with the Wolverines' pair of comebacks bordering on the impossible. When I introduced myself to Tom VanArsdale upon his arrival with the Pistons, his reply was, "Oh, then you must have broadcast THE GAME." That's what most people who were there still call it—THE GAME.

November 22, 1969

Michigan 24—OSU 12

It is doubtful if Michigan will ever take the field as such a heavy underdog as on that afternoon in Ann Arbor. Nor will they ever come up with such an unexpected victory. ("Unexpected to you maybe, but not to us," Bo would probably say.) Objectivity went out the window that day as Bo's boys did their number on the reputedly invincible Buckeyes.

October 27, 1979

Michigan 27—Indiana 21

Okay, this could easily go to the top of the list but remember, we're talking about games and not individual plays. And until Wangler and Anthony got together in that last frantic moment, the game itself was rather bizarre. It was, however, the most exciting single play I'll ever be fortunate to call.

June 1, 1980

Michigan 9—California 8

(11 innings)

If the 1969 game established Bo in Ann Arbor as a resident genius, this did the same for Bud Middaugh. Bud pulled more rabbits out of the hat that day in Omaha than

Doug Henning will do in a lifetime. Oldtimers call it one
of the College World Series best. I won't disagree—it was
a beauty.

March 13, 1964
Michigan 84—Loyola 80

Michigan's first NCAA basketball tournament victory and
my first tourney broadcast. I'll always have a soft spot
for old Williams Arena because of this masterpiece which
put Michigan on the roundball map to stay.

November 20, 1971
Michigan 10—Ohio State 7

It seems odd that one of the few games in recent history
that had nothing riding on the outcome should rank as
the second best in this series. It also provided me with
the rare opportunity of doing a play-by-play of sideline
markers being torn apart.

December 30, 1964
Michigan 80—Princeton 78

Just being in America's most-revered indoor arena would
have been enough for me to put this one in the top 10.
But then along comes the Wolverine's incredible 18-point
comeback, Bill Bradley's superman performance, and Cazzie's shot at the buzzer. (I might have this gem at Madison
Square Garden rated too low also.)

November 24, 1973
Michigan 10—Ohio State 10

Generally tie games are not very memorable. And this
one preceded one of the greatest injustices in Big Ten Rose
Bowl balloting. But these were two of the best teams you

will ever see matched. It was a game no one wanted to
see end.

March 5, 1966
Michigan 105—Northwestern 96
Cazzie's final game at Yost. Even the pigeons were over-
emotional that day. Michigan's third straight Big Ten title
was almost overlooked in the farewell to number 33.

November 30, 1962
MSU 2—Michigan 1
The first of over 800 broadcasts I have done at the Michigan microphone. I can't remember a whole lot about the
hockey game at the old Coliseum but I can vividly recall
the exact location of each of the 234 butterflies that ran
their post patterns in my stomach that night. (Maybe this
one should go to the top.)

BROADCASTS I WISHED
SOMEONE ELSE HAD DONE

November 30, 1963
Ohio State 14—U-M 10
One week earlier, John Kennedy had been slain in Dallas
causing the only postponement in Michigan Stadium
history. We were all too numb to focus on a meaningless
game in a quarter-filled stadium. Absolutely the worst
broadcast I have ever done and I'm sure other announcers
felt the same about their work that day.

March 15, 1975
UCLA 103—U-M 91
(overtime)

This would probably be leading off the other list if C.J. Kupec's shot had gone in at the end of regulation time. Michigan was that close to pulling off one of the biggest upsets in NCAA basketball tourney action. I can still see the ball bouncing away to give the lordly Bruins their reprieve.

January 2, 1984
Auburn 9—Michigan 7

A great game, I just wish I could have seen it. A broadcaster's nightmare come true with a booth tucked away in the extreme corner of the Superdome. Once the action moved across the 50, I was helpless. My partner, Tom Slade, rescued me enough times that night to qualify for a Red Cross lifesaving medal. The irony was that prior to the game, nobody had ever taken better care of the media than the Sugar Bowl people. They just haven't figured out where to put their radio broadcasters.

November 18, 1967
Michigan 27—Wisconsin 14

Nothing wrong with the game, in fact I think it was rather exciting. That's the trouble though, I don't remember it very well. You see, I had helped an ex-colleague celebrate his move to Madison the night before and somehow the housewarming got out of hand. I do recall my engineer, Jim McEachern, taking one look at me the next morning and calling a local priest for last rites. Our booth that day at Camp Randall Stadium was located next to WWJ's

Don Kremer and Bennie Oosterbaan. As I collapsed in my chair, Bennie stuck his head around the corner.

"You know, Tom, you can't run with the rabbits at night if you want to fly with the eagles in the morning," he smiled. It was my last race with the rabbits before a broadcast. To complicate matters, I had to travel to Chicago that evening to do a Pistons' game, But, then again, sometimes in those years, that was the best condition to be in for a Piston game.

February 7, 1976
Indiana 72—Michigan 67

No announcer worth his salt should ever allow his anger to reach a point where it eliminates the actual reporting of the game. But it almost happened here in one of the most outrageous examples of shoddy officiating in history. Even Bobby Knight was embarrassed over the hometown calls.

December 31, 1981
Michigan 33—UCLA 14

Nothing wrong with either the game or the booth location. In fact, both were great. However, during the second half, a sideline photographer was decked during a pileup causing a delay of almost 30 minutes. Slade and I found ourselves reviewing the entire history of football in order to fill the dead air. We were all certain the poor fellow would be listed in critical condition in the Houston papers the following morning. Wandering into the hotel watering hole that night, whom should we come upon but the very same shutter-snapper regaling the crowd. That delay, along with a 30-minute halftime show, made it probably the longest Bluebonnet Bowl game in history.

April 14, 1984
U-M 16-0—Indiana 10-16
Now, I love baseball but not when sitting in the stands
in 38-degree temperatures with a 25 m.p.h. wind for five
and a half hours at the microphone. I don't think I thawed
out until two months later in Omaha where it hit 85. I
will say, though, it is probably the only chance I will ever
get to describe 42 runs in an afternoon.

October 24, 1981
Michigan 38—Northwestern 0
A lifeless game made even more so by the knowledge that
our buddy, Bob Ufer, lay near death at a Detroit hospital.
One of the most cheerless days at Michigan Stadium.

March 11, 1966
Kentucky 84—U-M 77
It was bad enough to bow out of the NCAA tournament
but knowing it was the last of the Cazzie era made it even
more discouraging. Had we known it would be eight years
before Michigan would be back, it would have been even
more dismal.

March 20, 1977
UNCC 75—Michigan 68
I truly thought this would be the year that I would sit
in on my first Michigan NCAA championship. But Corn-
bread Maxwell and the U. of North Carolina-Charlotte
had other plans that day in Lexington. It's a game that
Johnny Orr has probably played over in his mind a million
times.

PLACES I MOST PREFER
TO TAKE MY MICROPHONE

Rose Bowl
Pasadena, California

This has to head the list for the view alone. No stadium that I know of has such a breathtaking backdrop as provided by the San Gabriel mountains which are always bathed in a late afternoon sun. Our rooftop radio locations have been a bit on the austere side at times, but it's still the best spot in the house for watching the cyclorama of changing colors. The temptation to twist around and enjoy the California sunset can be hard to resist. And unless you're very hard to please, you can find something in the Los Angeles area to tickle your fancy. (Just steer clear of the Cactus Arms.)

Husky Stadium
Seattle, Washington

The sight of the yachts on Lake Washington, moored almost in the end zone, pushes this stadium into a close second for best setting. Seattle gets some hard knocks for its climate, but it's truly a picturesque city with some of the best seafood palaces in the world. The ferry ride up to Deception Pass is chilly but gorgeous. When Michigan played in Seattle in 1970, everyone warned me that Nantucket rain gear would be appropriate at all times. Whereupon, the sun shone for three days with temperatures in the 80s. Mt. Rainer looked as though someone had painted it on my hotel window.

Camp Randall Stadium
Madison, Wisconsin

Despite my one fall from grace here, it still ranks among the best in the country in scenic splendor. We have been fortunate in visiting Madison early in the season when the weather is still summerlike, and that leads to some rather fetching costumes by the Badger coeds, whom my more knowledgeable friends tell me are also the most fetching in the Big Ten. But even during the Wisconsin winter, Madison is a pretty place.

California and Stanford Stadiums
Berkeley and Palo Alto

Both are old-time, ivy-covered arenas that are a joy to walk into. The Stanford band alone is worth the price of admission. Since victories tend to be scarce here for the home teams, the crowds are unspoiled and free-wheeling. They are just happy to see their team score. Consequently, they have a better time than any crowd I have come across. And, of course, each of these stadiums is nearby everybody's favorite city, San Francisco. I've often wondered where you go to visit if you happen to be one of the chosen few who live here. Everything else must seem like faded canvas.

Convention and Sports Arena
Las Vegas

This Disneyland for grownups is truly Poe's "Eldorado". I'm not sure how I squeezed a pair of basketball games in here.

Mackey Arena
West Lafayette
Rates a spot strictly because of its radio broadcast locations. High enough to see but close enough to hear the grunts and groans. No fans seated in front to block the action and no gravel-voiced public address announcer trying to drown out the crowd. All run by one of my favorite people, Jim Vruggink.

Spartan Stadium
East Lansing
No one does it better than Nick Vista and his crew when it comes to taking care of the football media. From the dining room to the dressing room, Nick has it under control. The only think Nick doesn't seem to have the knack of yet is controlling the weather. It always rains in East Lansing for a MSU-UM game.

Notre Dame Stadium
South Bend
The minute you step onto campus, the tradition starts oozing up your pantleg. Any broadcaster would hope that someday he be given the chance to call a game from the home of the Gipper.

Coliseum
Los Angeles
Ditto of #8. The only problem was when I finally got my first opportunity to see the legendary site, they had torn down the famous old round clock and replaced it with a run-of-the-mill scoreboard.

Carver-Hawkeye Arena
Iowa City

The newest and potentially best of the Big Ten basketball playgrounds. A scoreboard that gives you running stats, tremendous sight lines for broadcasters, and a press room that offers honest-to-goodness food. Bump can be proud of this one.

DON'T TAKE
YOUR MICROPHONE HERE

Madison Square Garden
New York

A perfect example of progress in fullscale retreat. Other than more room for the obnoxious New York fans, the new place doesn't measure up in any respect to the classy old joint. Radio broadcasters are tucked away into hidden and obscure nooks. If anything works properly at your location the first time, you have just been blessed with a miracle. The vileness of the crowd is exceeded only by the surliness of the arena officials. A place to avoid at all costs.

Dyche Stadium
Evanston

It's not the fault of Northwestern that when Michigan visits town it's always 24 degrees with a breeze straight off Lake Michigan. However, some heat in the radio booths might save a few cases of frostbite. It's also the only football stadium I know of where the booths are so low that fans can stand up and block the view.

Wisconsin Fieldhouse
Madison

When I tell you that this is one of only two basketball arenas in the Big Ten that is older than I am, you get the idea. Counter space is minimal at broadcast row with the fans occupying the space immediately behind. By the time the game is over you get a great massage of your backbone by some exuberant fan's kneecap. But the Badger rooters are a well-controlled group, maybe because they've had little to lose control over.

Kenan Stadium
Chapel Hill

Nestled among the towering pines, the stadium does a great job of holding the heat and humidity of a North Carolina afternoon. The concrete broadcast booths feel like the original towering inferno. This is the spot where Michigan almost ended the 1966 season on opening day.

Memorial Stadium
Minneapolis

If it had come down to it, I'm sure the Big Ten football broadcasters would have taken up a collection to ensure the move of the Gophers to the Metrodome. The main press box for the old stadium was fine, except few of the stations were allowed to use it. Instead, most of us were situated across the way in what was called the auxiliary box, but was more affectionally known as the corn cribs. To reach them, you inched up narrow rungs set in the side of the stadium. The booths were about big enough to hold a full-grown calf and looked as though that is what they were designed for. By the second half, the sun was squarely in your eyes, making an already incomprehensible scoreboard even more so. Thank you, Twins and Vikings, you are included in our prayers every night.

Williams Arena
Minneapolis

I don't like to pick on the Twin Cities because really they are a delightful place to visit. And I do have the fond memory of the Wolverine's victory over Loyola here in 1964. However, by the time you trudge to the top of the arena, you seldom have enough energy to broadcast a game. Tom Greenhoe does his best to keep you up-to-date on the stats but the floor is so far away that it is sometimes days before word gets through to the broadcasters. Next to Jenison Fieldhouse in East Lansing, it's also probably the noisiest. Maybe we can convince them to move to the Metrodome.

Assembly Hall
Bloomington

I don't care where you do a game from in this town—and this is the third facility I've done games from—you can't avoid the famed Hoosier fan. As if this weren't bad enough, the broadcasters are crammed into a small platformed area at courtside. It gives you a spectacular view of the Indiana cheerleaders, who stand along the sidelines for most of the game, but not a very clear shot at what's happening on the floor. But, not to worry, Bob Knight is usually clearly visible, just a chair's throw away.

Meadowlands Arena
East Rutherford

Taking a cue from their cousins in Manhattan, broadcast facilities at this new spa in New Jersey were an afterthought by the designers. So, the same low and outside areas are accorded the wretched mikemen. And the arena attendants have learned to snarl almost as well as their New York brethren.

Rosenblatt Stadium
Omaha

A truly magnificent minor league stadium that has been a home for years to the College World Series. The NCAA does a great job of wining, dining, and informing the media from the day we hit town. So, what's the problem? Well, when the stadium was redesigned for the press, no one bothered to check with a broadcaster. As a result, radio announcers must peer out of half-windows that reduce their vision of the field by 50 percent. Believe me, there's a whole lot of guessing going on there folks.

Fisher Stadium
Ann Arbor

Sorry guys, but ever since the rooftop press box was torn down, the broadcast facilities have gone from best to worst. Seated in among the fans and writers, cut off from some spots on the diamond by girders, it's just not a very good spot to call a ball game. I yearn for the return of the top side press box — it would even be fun ducking foul balls again.

MY FAVORITE HUMAN BEINGS

Bennie Oosterbaan

Big surprise huh? I've already detailed his efforts in making me feel at home in Ann Arbor but I have a hunch I would have him at the top of the list even if I had met him once a year. His warmth and sincerity can melt the most cantankerous individual in seconds. Probably Michigan's greatest athlete, without a doubt the finest person I have had the pleasure of knowing.

Jimmy Dutcher

Possessor of one of the greatest and most subtle senses of humor in the coaching profession. But unlike many of the so-called jokesters of the business, Dutch is a genuinely nice person. His good-natured banter doesn't end as soon as the pads and microphones are put away. Lou Holtz may get all the attention as Minnesota's good humor man but Dutch is every bit as pleasant to be around.

Johnny Orr

The Jekyll and Hyde for the media. Sure, he had some memorable battles with some members of the press — but he went out of his way to smooth my path. In addition to his yarn-spinning talents, John is just as interested in your side of the conversation as his. Even during his rockiest years, Tall John was someone I always looked forward to seeing.

Newt Loken

I hope nobody ever tells Newt that he is supposed to slow down. This guy has enough energy to light a city the size of Tokyo for a year. I assume he retired because he was reaching the age that causes most of us to pause for a second breath. In Newt's case, he probably is just looking for a second career to embark on. Whatever he chooses, it will never be the same again. A perfectly delightful person.

Rudy Tomjanovich

I've never seen anyone blossom more than this shy young man out of Hamtramck. Not one to waste words, Rudy was still one of the most popular players in Michigan history and one I always sought out when my travels took me to Houston. One of the classiest super stars you will ever meet.

Bud Middaugh

A relative newcomer to the Michigan scene but a friendlier soul I have never met. Following Bud around for a baseball season spoils you because he'll do everything but bat you cleanup to make you comfortable — and he'd probably do that if asked. Greatly respected among his peers and deservedly so.

Lenny Paddock

He could make anyone's spirits rise within five minutes. For years he dispensed advice, medication, and an invaluable personal touch to Michigan athletes. I used to dream up excuses to visit the Wolverine training room just to listen to Lenny.

Bill Frieder

It's no mean feat to get to know Bill. First you have to slow him down enough to chat. This is one of the most intense but at the same time affable people you will meet. Bill's special brand of humor saw him through some prickly times in his early years as Michigan's head coach. No one was more pleased than I when it all came together for the little guy in 1985.

Dorothy Johnson

Without Dorothy, Bump's secretary when I moved onto the scene in 1962, I would have been lost. Maybe it was because things didn't move as fast back then but she always made you feel as though you were the most important matter of her day. Just a beautiful person and one whose early death saddened all who knew her.

Jim Betts

If anyone had a right to be bitter, it was this gifted athlete who Bo moved from quarterback to safety where he became all-Big Ten. Then a freak injury that cost him the sight of an eye nipped a promising pro career in the bud. But it never cost him his great wit and happy countenance. You always felt better after being around Jimmy.

PLAYERS I WOULD HAVE PAID TO WATCH

Cazzie Russell

Caz would have to get the nod over AC simply because

he handled the ball almost every play while Anthony was lucky to touch it 15 times a game. Time sometimes tends to erode rather than substantiate memories when it comes to athletic exploits. This may be true in Cazzie's case. But one only has to consider the fact that this great All-American could probably have played any of three positions for Michigan to remember just how tremendously talented he was. Trying to do justice to Cazzie's exploits was an impossible task but it sure was fun to try.

Anthony Carter

One of the things I quickly learned with AC was, as long as he was in the vicinity, not to call a pass incomplete until it had bounced on the ground. I don't think Bo or AC himself knew how he wriggled free for half of his receptions. But when number 1 was on the field, every eye was focused on him—and that's the supreme compliment to any player in any sport. Carter and Cazzie couldn't have been further apart in personality, size, and temperament, but Michigan's two most exciting players were twins when it came to electrifying an audience.

Ron Johnson

His rushing marks have been surpassed a number of times now but nobody has surpassed his ability to manufacture yardage out of thin air. His record five-touchdown performance in the sleet and mud against Wisconsin in 1968 remains the most amazing one-man show I have ever seen. Articulate, intelligent, and outgoing, he has become one of Michigan's greatest advertisements.

Victor Amaya

This huge, 6-7 lefthander from Holland, Michigan didn't defeat Big Ten tennis opponents, he devoured them. He seemed to cover half of his side of the net with his wing-span while his screaming serve sent players and spectators ducking for cover. It's truly a shame more people didn't take the chance to watch this great player during his stay in Ann Arbor.

Rickey Green

Lute Olsen once described Rickey challenging the other team at half court: "A one-on-five is a mismatch in favor of Green." For sheer speed, I can't recall any player close to Rickey. It took his teammates half of his first season to readjust their timing to where he would be rather than where an ordinary human being would end up. Quick-silver in sneakers.

Rick Leach

For sheer competitiveness, I don't know if I can think of an equal. Despite the brutal pounding he took running Bo's option attack, he was indestructible. Absolutely fearless, he had a superb sixth sense of when to throw and when to run. And he was also something to see in a U-M baseball uniform.

Gordie Bell

I don't know if it was because of his size (5-7 at the most), his instant acceleration, or his ability to change directions in mid-air, but this little tailback may have been the most elusive of them all. How many times I recall saying, ". . . and Bell is hit and dropped at the . . . wait a min-ute . . . he's still on his feet and now in the open."

Bill Frauman

This is going to bring a few puzzled looks. You have to be a pretty heavy basketball fan to remember Bill who graced the Michigan courts in the early '70s. His teammates called him "The Unguided Missile" since it was never too certain where Bill would wind up. Sometimes it was in the stands, sometimes draped over the scorer's table, sometimes taking out four players at once in a scramble for a loose ball. (Whether they were wearing a Michigan uniform didn't make much difference.) But nobody ever hustled more on the court and was such a genial person away from it.

Rick Volk

The greatest enigma in the world of U-M sports. No more friendly or humble individual ever donned a Michigan football uniform and no Wolverine was ever more proficient at slicing people in two on the gridiron. His bone-rattling tackles were simply awesome—and we are talking about a very tall, 210-pounder delivering those hits. His ability to snare interceptions was sometimes overlooked because of his one-man demolition derby in the secondary but he rates with the best in that department also.

Steve Grote

An all-state linebacker in high school, the Cincinnati Kid played the same style of roundball for Johnny Orr. He wasn't a great shooter, he certainly didn't win any foot races, and his ball handling didn't make you forget Cazzie. However, after going 40 minutes with Grote, opponents would probably have taken their chances with

Volk the next time. They didn't name the annual defensive player of the year award after him because it had a nice ring to it.

THE ENVY OF THE SPORTSCASTER
(AT LEAST THIS ONE)

Dick Enberg

The epitome of class behind the mike. The vocabulary of an English professor (which he once was), a delightful wit, a complete lack of self-importance, and a thorough knowledge of whatever event he is broadcasting. There is no question why he has risen to the top of our profession.

Al Michaels

Not that far behind Dick but he hasn't been blessed with the talent at his side at ABC that Dick has enjoyed at NBC. Al's work at the 1980 Olympic hockey championships was a high point of television sportscasting. When you consider the fact that hockey was almost foreign to Al prior to the Olympics, you can judge just how competent this young man is.

Harry Heilmann

If you cut your teeth on the Detroit Tigers in the late forties and early fifties, Harry was a god. To an impressionable young boy who would have rather missed a roast turkey dinner than a Tiger broadcast, this great Hall of

Famer was among the closest of friends. That's just how he broadcast a baseball game, as though you were sitting together over a beer and he was telling you what he had seen at the ballpark. I felt as though I had lost my granddad when he died.

Red Barber

Probably the greatest baseball announcer of them all. Unfortunately, those of us in the Midwest never got a chance to hear the old redhead except at World Series time when the Dodgers always seem to be playing the Yankees. What a joy it must have been to grow up with the Boys of Summer as your team, Ebbetts Field as your park, and Red as your voice.

Don Kremer

I know, I know, he's not an announcer anymore. But once there was none better. His voice alone would have been enough to capture you but Don had all the other ingredients to go with it. It was a loss to our profession when Don joined the Lions' front office.

Bruce Martyn

Hockey is not an easy sport to broadcast. In fact, I think it's the toughest. But this guy sits high above the ice night after night making it sound like a piece of cake. With everyone wearing helmets now, I don't know how Bruce even identifies the skaters, let alone keeps pace with a smooth rapid-fire commentary as he does.

Bob Costas

Nobody should be this good, this young.

Skip Caray

Unless you're privileged to be on the cable or happen to live in Atlanta, you don't get a chance to hear this whimsical Braves baseball man do his thing. Takes neither himself or the game too seriously, an element all too often missing among some of the brethren.

Bill King

For years he was the voice of the Golden State Warriors and no one, I mean *no one*, could do a basketball game like this gentleman. He made the rest of us want to pack up and seek a new occupation.

George Kell and Ernie Harwell

They are a tandem to me since that's the way I remember them in the earlier days. Two nicer people never sat at a microphone and I'm sure the listeners have no trouble picking up that fact.

MY ALL-TIME
MAIZE AND BLUE TEAMS

FOOTBALL

Offense	G-Stefan Humpheries
WR-Anthony Carter	C-Walt Downing
WR-Jack Clancy	QB-Rick Leach
T-Dan Dierdorf	FB-Russell Davis
T-Bubba Paris	RB-Ron Johnson
G-Reggie McKenzie	RB-Rob Lytle

Defense
E-John Anderson
E-Dan Jilek
T-Curtis Greer
T-Bill Yearby
MG-Henry Hill
LB-Mike Taylor

LB-Tom Cecchini
DB-Rick Volk
DB-Dave Brown
DB-Randy Logan
DB-Tom Curtis

BASKETBALL

F	Rudy Tomjanovich
F	Campy Russell
C	Bill Buntin
G	Cazzie Russell
G	Rickey Green

BASEBALL

1b	Ken Hayward
2b	Jeff Jacobson
SS	Barry Larkin
3b	Chris Sabo
Of	Rick Leach
Of	Jim Paciorek
Of	Mike Watters
C	Gerry Hool
DH	George Foussianes
RHP	Rich Stoll
LHP	Steve Howe

EIGHT

Thanks for the Memory

Delving into the past 22 years, I was stunned at how many people have been a part of my life at Michigan and how many broadcasts there have been over that period. Trotting them back onto center stage for another look has been one of the most enjoyable and interesting experiences I have had. In some cases I was startled at what the record proved in contrast to my memories of the event. Instances completely forgotten came flooding out of my mind's recesses—triggered by a film, or play-by-play sheet or game story. For that I will always be grateful to my good friend Bill Haney for having the needed confidence in me to get this project underway. Except for Bill, I never would have undertaken such a task on my own, and what a lot of fun I would have missed. I hope I have been able to share that fun with you.

GO BLUE!